Space and Time in German Innovative Activity

Imke Rhoden

Space and Time in German Innovative Activity

Regional Allocation Patterns, Determinants and Geo-Econometric Models

Springer Gabler

Imke Rhoden
Faculty of Management and Economics
Ruhr-Universität Bochum
Bochum, Germany

Dissertation, Ruhr-Universität Bochum, 2019

ISBN 978-3-658-28599-9 ISBN 978-3-658-28600-2 (eBook)
https://doi.org/10.1007/978-3-658-28600-2

Springer Gabler

This Springer Gabler imprint is published by the registered company Springer Fachmedien Wiesbaden GmbH part of Springer Nature.
The registered company address is: Abraham-Lincoln-Str. 46, 65189 Wiesbaden, Germany

Contents

I Regional Allocations of Innovative Activity – The Case of 3D Printing

II Regional Determinants of Innovative Activity – Geoadditive Modeling of Diverging Allocations

List of Figures

List of Tables

List of Variables

A	Technological Progress
$adminid$	Spatial Index: Administrative Districts
β	Coefficients
C	Covariates
$clus$	High-tech Clusters
$district$	Placeholder for Administrative Districts
$dummies$	Placeholder for Dummy Variables
ϵ	Error Term
f	Function
$fund$	Research and Development Funding
$\boldsymbol{g}_i$	Geographical Location Vector
$gdpem$	Productivity
grw	Policy
h	Bandwidth parameter
H	Human Capital
i	Individual's Index
ind	Industry
$innov$	Innovative Activity
$inst$	Research and Development Institutes
inv	Investment
j	Individual's Index
K	Capital
κ	Knots of (Penalized) Spline Function
KER	Kernel function
$know$	Knowledge Intensity

L	Labor
$linear\ covariates$	Placeholder for Linear Covariates
n	Number of observations
$nonlinear\ covariates$	Placeholder for Nonlinear Covariates
ν	Additive Predictor, Varying over Space and Time
$open$	Openness
p	Index for Penalized Coefficient
P	Maximum Number of Penalized Coefficents
$popd$	Population Density
$ppot$	Market Potential
s	Maximum Number of j Indices
S	Zero-Mean Stationary Stochastic Process
$Sigma$	Scale Estimate of Variance
sme	Share of Small and Middle Enterprises
$spatial\ effect$	Placeholder for Spatial Effect
sx	Spatial Effect Coefficient
t	Time Index
$turn$	Firm's Turnover
u_p	Penalized Coefficients
X	Random Variable
x	Value of Random Variable / Predictor
y	Dependent Variable
Y	Output
$yearid$	Temporal Index: Years

List of Abbreviations

AIC	Akaike Information Criterion
AM	Additive Manufacturing
Avg.	Average
BBSR	Bundesinstitut für Bau-, Stadt- und Raumforschung (Federal Institute for Research on Building, Urban Affairs and Spatial Development)
BIC	Bayesian Information Criterion
BMBF	Bundesministerium für Bildung und Forschung (Federal Ministry of Education and Research)
BMWi	Bundesministerium für Wirtschaft und Energie (Federal Ministry for Economic Affairs and Energy)
df	Degrees of Freedom
EIS	European Innovation Scoreboard
GAM	Generalized Additive Model
GAMM	Generalized Additive Mixed Model
GDP	Gross Domestic Product
GLM	Generalized Linear Model

GRW	Gemeinschaftsaufgabe "Verbesserung der regionalen Wirtschaftsstruktur" (Joint Federal / Länder Task for the Improvement of Regional Economic Structures)
IPC	International Patent Classification
KDE	Kernel Density Estimation
MCMC	Markov Chain Monte Carlo
MISE	Mean Integrated Square Error
ML	Maximum Likelihood
NUTS	Nomenclature des Unités Territoriales Statistiques
OLS	Ordinary Least Squares
R+D	Research and Development
REML	Restricted Maximum Likelihood
RIS	Regional Innovation Scoreboard
SME	Small and Middle Enterprises
STAR	Structured Additive Regression
Std. Dev.	Standard deviation

1 Introduction to the Thesis

This dissertation consists of three papers concerning the regional allocation of innovative activity and its determinants in Germany. The analyses focus on revealing the structure of innovation activity among German administrative districts on Nomenclature des Unités Territoriales Statistiques (NUTS)-3 level (meaning *Landkreise* and *kreisfreie Städte*) in the timeframe of 2000-2016.

Throughout this thesis, the term *region* characterizes regions in the sense of German administrative districts on NUTS-3 level. The overall matter investigated is *innovative activity*, which will also be referred to as innovation, innovation activity, and is explicitly measured by the count of applicants of published patents.

First, innovative activity is generally characterized. Location of hotspots and cold spots of innovation are illustrated, and it is examined if and how high-tech innovations in the field of 3D printing locate differently. Furthermore, socio-economic determinants theoretically connected to the spatial distribution of innovations are introduced for several model specifications. Their effects on innovation are then investigated closely. It is also proposed where on NUTS-3 level innovation promoting economic policies can be applied. This is based on the estimated effects which are geographically referenced to the exact region where innovation allocates.

Each paper uses a separate approach but the methods build upon another. The first paper lays down the base, and the following papers

I. Rhoden, *Space and Time in German Innovative Activity*,
https://doi.org/10.1007/978-3-658-28600-2_1

add more information and dimensions regarding socio-economic data, space, and time.

The dataset used throughout the dissertation is the same. It is obtained by the German Patent and Trade Mark Office and processed to filter for the geographic location (address) of the patent applicant (or, respectively, the inventor) and, if there are more than one, the number of the other applicants and their locations. The date of application and publication of the patent, as well as the classification of the patent (via the International Patent Classification (IPC) code) are also extracted.

These data are then further augmented by data of publicly available official socio-economic indicators accessible on NUTS-3 level, which is, with exception of the first paper, the geographic unit used in the thesis.

Covariates operated (in some or the other combination) in this dissertation are knowledge intensity, funding by the German policy Gemeinschaftsaufgabe "Verbesserung der regionalen Wirtschaftsstruktur" (Joint Federal / Länder Task for the Improvement of Regional Economic Structures) (GRW) and Research and Development (R+D) funding mainly by the Bundesministerium für Bildung und Forschung (Federal Ministry of Education and Research) (BMBF), investment, productivity, market potential, industry share, openness, population density, proxies for firm size and dummies for high-tech clusters and R+D institutions.

1.1 First Part

Regional Allocations of Innovative Activity – The Case of 3D Printing

The research question of this paper is the illustration of regional innovative activity in general and high-tech innovation in particular. Furthermore, it is aimed at investigating whether there exists a different spatial distribution pattern for high-tech innovation. Such a different allocation from unspecified innovations can then lead to better understanding of innovation processes and to more precise policies targeting growth in innovation (and ultimately growth of the economy).

Questions

Does innovative activity concentrate elsewhere than innovation in general? If so, then where are hotspots and cold spots? Where are the differences? What are implications of the results?

As a case study, the paper presents and analyzes innovative activity in the technology field of Additive Manufacturing (AM) (industrial 3D printing). This technology branch can represent high-tech innovation and is, in the course of the paper, furthermore, contrasted to all innovation activity irrespective of technology type.

The paper starts by illustrating the general innovation landscape of Germany by mapping patent data to zipcode areas. Hotspots of activity appear, and first connections to underlying socio-economic factors like economic productivity or population density are made. A Kernel Density Estimation (KDE) approach then allows the investigation of hotspots and cold spots of innovative activity and of the differences between all innovations and high-tech innovations in particular.

1.2 Second Part

Regional Determinants of Innovative Activity – Geoadditive Modeling of Diverging Allocations

Concerning the second paper, the research question focuses on the explanation of innovative activity by several theoretically grounded socio-economic determinants. Moreover, the spatial allocation of innovation is explicitly accounted for.

Questions

Which factors can explain the spatial pattern of innovative activity in Germany, and to what extent?

The paper enlarges the analysis of the regional distribution of patents and incorporates a theoretically founded model to explain the effects of socio-economic covariates on innovation activity. The goal is to explain spatial variation in innovative activities among German NUTS-3 level regions, with the help of factors relevant to innovation theory.

First, a general non-spatial estimation by means of Ordinary Least Squares (OLS) is executed. Then, a spatial dimension is introduced by setting up a geoadditive model based on a Generalized Additive Mixed Model (GAMM) approach. It supports not only parametric next to nonparametric regressors, but also incorporates a spatial effect to account for geographical variation in innovative activity. The analysis is executed for the year 2016 over all German administrative districts in a Restricted Maximum Likelihood (REML) estimation. A time-lag in innovation generation (as patents are published on average two years later than they are applied for) is also accounted for.

Considering the spatial dimension explicitly is important, as the creation of innovation has a distinct locational effect. Thus, accounting for spatial autocorrelation helps in generating more precise information about innovation, its determinants, and consequently, where it locates and why.

1.3 Third Part

Innovative Activity over Space and Time – Spatiotemporal Modeling of Innovation Promoting Factors

The research question for the third paper aims for adding relevance to the model explaining innovative activity by considering not only space but also a time dimension. Theoretically relevant factors are corrected for spatial and temporal autocorrelation. The allocation of innovation in Germany can be traced back to socio-economic factors. Innovation promoting policies can be targeted according to the results.

Questions

Where can innovative activity be explained by which determinants, and to what extent? Where should policy promoting innovation best be applied, based on the model's results?

In this paper, the preceding geoadditive model is augmented by a time dimension that is added as a further regressor. This is possible because of the characteristics of the model specification allowing flexible incorporation of random and fixed effects. The aim is to increase explanatory content and reduce bias. This is done by a dynamic approach in contrast to a static geoadditive model without time effect.

For the geoadditive model the data are compiled into a longitudinal dataset, where each covariate can adopt another value for each year of the timeframe. The timeframe ranges from 2009-2016, already incorporating a time-lag accounting for the duration of a patent application until the innovation is being published. Innovation activity can now be explained by theoretically relevant covariates, a space, and a time dimension.

The estimation method is Markov Chain Monte Carlo (MCMC) simulation, which follows Bayesian statistical reasoning. This allows to incorporate specific prior information into the calculation which seems reasonable as the generation of innovation already features the time-lag (between application and publication of the patent); and the activity is a result of efforts having been raised prior to an innovation of market maturity (which is expressed by a published patent). This knowledge about the innovation efforts is therefore available and adds to the explanation of the allocation of innovation.

2 State of the Art

2.1 Position Towards Other Research

The literature on the broad topic of regional innovation dispersion has many facets and several strands of theory stand out. Among them, there exist the (regional) innovation systems theory, considerations about related variety, innovation geography, growth theories and cluster approaches, as well as concentration indices and research about regional spillovers and externalities. Furthermore, the strands of literature containing urban economics or the technology regime approach also add thoughts about innovation generation and behavior. (McCann and Ortega-Argiles 2016, p. 22)

In this chapter the papers of this thesis are enqueued with other research and work on innovation activities. Although each paper of the thesis has a theoretic introduction of its own, a comprehensive positioning in the literature on the topic is made here. This allows a better understanding of the papers, the relevance of the methods applied, and findings discovered.

The procedure is the following: Selected work by other researchers, who also investigate the spatial behavior of innovation in the widest sense, is briefly presented. Their methods and analyses, as well as their results and findings are then contrasted to the approaches applied and results gained in this thesis.

The so-called common denominator linking this thesis and the following works by other researchers is the matter at hand: an investigation of regional innovation activity, its determinants and allocation.

I. Rhoden, *Space and Time in German Innovative Activity*,
https://doi.org/10.1007/978-3-658-28600-2_2

The researches are subdivided by their prevailing theoretical framework and thus comprised accordingly. All of the works presented in the following have concerned themselves with the dispersion, respectively distribution, of innovation activity and determinants of it in one way or the other and in different magnitudes of profoundness. The methods used to generate insights about innovation are also as manifold, ranging from theoretic considerations to complex econometric models. All in all, the approaches used in this scientific field are very diverse.

2.1.1 Growth Theories and Innovation Geography

Innovation (or rather: technological progress) is a major part of various approaches in many growth theories. In earlier works, innovation is considered as technological progress that is exogenous (compare Solow (1956) and Swan (1956)) or endogenous (compare Romer (1986) and Lucas (1988)) to the models of economic growth.

In these models the regional dimension is lacking, but it is commonly to be found unquestionably relevant and scope of many books on innovation and geography (e.g. Shearmur, Carrincazeaux, and Doloreux (2016) and Polenske (2007)). The geographical dimension is stressed explicitly by Krugman's (1991) contributions building the new economic geography, although the importance of innovation is missing there. Nevertheless, the concept of agglomeration economics opened to innovation researchers, not only because innovation depends on resources which are differently mobile (Breschi and Malerba 2001, p. 817).

Guerrero and Sero (1997) for example investigate the distribution of innovation by analyzing the dispersion of patent applications. The latter is explained in a regression by determinants such as government support to technology and business and agglomeration characteristics of firms. The authors find that especially financial governmental aid helps regions which are already innovative, but they also hint that because of the eligibility criteria for aid, this might reinforce territorial imbalances.

Benos, Karagiannis, and Karkalakos (2015) examine regional growth by combining technological, economic and geographical factors to test for spillovers and their respective importance for regional growth. They specify growth functions based on endogenous growth theory and weigh regressors by e.g. geographical proximity. The data encompasses EU regions on NUTS-3 level. For explaining the relation towards labor productivity, physical and human capital and patents are included as well. The authors find that spillovers are important for regional growth, showing that regions in an innovative environment thrive and suggest policy should focus on increasing capital to boost growth further.

Also showing that knowledge and innovation are important for economic growth, but not substitutable, are Capello and Lenzi (2013). Here, regions can benefit from innovation without owning accumulated knowledge themselves. They measure several economic and innovative indicators to estimate a regional growth model and combine several R+D and innovation variables. Human capital, R+D expenditures and firms introducing new products are among the variables used for classifying knowledge/innovation; space is not explicitly considered, as it is only the unit of observation. Results of their regressions propose that innovation diffuses more widely than knowledge, and impacts on growth happen on different locational scales.

Relevance

The works of this subsection all follow the endogenous growth theory and execute simple regressions on growth or on innovation measured via patents. Several determinants are considered and spillovers examined and found relevant in the growth process. Policies occupy a large role in increasing growth.

This thesis is also based on endogenous growth models using a production function. Also, it incorporates similar determinants, but in geoadditive regressions on innovation (patents). In addition, it considers space as explicit factor, with models which are more complex and can account for more specific data.

2.1.2 Spillovers and Knowledge Externalities

Directly ensuing is the whole theoretical context of knowledge spillovers and externalities to innovative activities. Marshall (1890) being one of the first to suggest knowledge spills over, Krugman (1991) also supports this theory.

Brought on by several works by Jaffe (e.g. Jaffe, Trajtenberg, and Henderson (1993)), the suggestion is that knowledge can spill over to neighboring regions. The authors concentrate on R+D spillovers and use patents and their respective citations to prove that patents get cited rather locally. They investigate the time and spatial dimension of these innovation indicators and use regression to make out spillovers that do not need to be extremely regionally confined. (Jaffe, Trajtenberg, and Henderson 1993)

Audretsch (1998) shapes the understanding of knowledge spillovers and agglomeration further by showing that geography matters for innovation. With the help of a knowledge production function innovative output is explained, among others, by university research expenditure and a geographical interaction factor with corporate research on city level. This way the author stresses the shift of focus to the regional level when dealing with innovation promoting policies. In another work, Audretsch (2003) relates knowledge externalities to spillovers and illustrates the spatial dimension as the map on which innovation is created and commercialized. Knowledge spillovers are localized and tend to decay with distance and can thus lead to networks and systems of innovation.

A link to the special characteristics of peripheral regions is made by Grillitsch and Nilsson (2015), who check for knowledge spillovers in those regions. Collaborative patterns of innovating firms are analyzed in a regression via a geographical distance decay function. Space is explicitly considered in the model and so are several determinants of knowledge influencing factors, e.g. firm size, foreign sales and high-skilled labor. The authors find that firms which are located in the periphery collaborate more, while the extent of that depends on firm size and internal knowledge availability. Firms which do not have large capacities of internal knowledge have to rely more onto spillovers to be able to innovate.

Caragliu and Nijkamp (2015) consider knowledge spillovers not just on the geographical scale but also on further dimensions as on social or technological conditions. Proximity here has a richer component, as it encompasses several possibilities of knowledge and innovation being transferable. They use a knowledge production function in an OLS regression and measure spatial autocorrelation via Moran's I. Factors for explaining the spillovers are, among others, human capital and accessibility. The results indicate that clusters form where all types of proximity can maximize the returns to R+D investment.

Another work about spatial dispersion of innovation is by Coccia (2015). The author investigates regional patterns of technology transfers via OLS and relates R+D institutions to firms which request technological contact to that institution. The number of contacts is measured on a geographical distance scale. Results show that contacts decrease with distance and that a high density of institutions benefits technological transfer. The work therefore stresses the institutional side of technology transfer.

Relevance

This subsection contains works that all view the geographical dimension as the base layer on which innovation exists and prospers. Innovation and knowledge (leading ultimately to innovation) are not locally confined phenomena, but are dispersing over space. Methods used to measure spillovers are production functions and regression models, including functions for distances and autocorrelation over space. Several determinants can explain the extent of these spillovers. Innovation is not only represented by patents but also by R+D investment or institutes.

This thesis does not investigate spillovers explicitly, but it does not deny their existence. The geoadditive model contains space as explicit factor, measuring the neighborhood structure of the regions in the sample. It therefore relies on the importance of the model being able to explain the geographical pattern of innovation with the help of several determinants.

2.1.3 Regional Innovation Systems

The concept that innovation happens in a systemic environment is also widely renowned. It goes back to Lundvall (1992) and Nelson (1993) and is explained as a network of factors in the economy, including institutions, that impact learning and research in the broadest sense (Lundvall 1992, pp. 12-13). Innovation in that sense does not only include technological innovation, but also other forms which generate progress of production (Schumpeter 1939, pp. 87-88). The way from national innovation systems towards regional innovation systems is also a short leap and stresses again the importance of the spatial dimension of innovation (Fujita, Krugman, and Venables 1999).

Asheim and Isaksen (1997) cover the innovation systems concept via an application for Norway. Here, the local dimension is the major factor in the analysis, as it is most often in the innovation systems theory. They use survey data and apply a theoretical reasoning model by investigating the structure and extent of innovation activity in regions with different agglomeration rates. A shift-share analysis allows discovering the regional component in the allocation of innovation. The authors also cover the size and the costs of innovation and networking of the firms. The findings point to different extents of regionality in innovation.

In this tradition Binz, Truffer, and Coenen (2014) analyze technological innovation systems by using social network analysis and constructing a nationalization index to account for the regional dimension of innovation. This approach includes the spatial dimension as a main factor and shows where innovation develops and diffuses.

Gilbert and Campbell (2015) choose an approach to discover the factors influencing the emergence of radical technological paradigms. They use a comparative qualitative analysis to find that intellectual, industry, social and political factors influence the geographic origins of such paradigms. Those are, according to Schumpeter (1934), core types of innovation. The authors show the localized dimension of innovation and point out that the spatial dimension is essential in this context. Policy implications can be made accordingly, as the exact regional characteristics needed for innovation to thrive allow drawing on those conclusions explicitly.

Another different approach is by Hajek, Henriques, and Hajkova (2014), who use self-organizing maps to uncover the structure of regional innovation systems in Europe. The patterns of regional innovation systems are made visible with those maps, which can include linear as well as nonlinear relations of the components making up the systems. The authors find that the systems investigated are similar in their diversity. Knowledge intensity (which enhances innovation through education and government R+D investment) seems to benefit regions which are close but just catching up in their development. A distinction between lagging regions and prospering regions is recurred onto the positive effect of the European integration and onto knowledge intensity.

Relevance

The works presented in this subsection all understand innovation as a process happening in a system, influenced by several different factors on a regional level. Methods used are mostly relying on network analyses, special networking modeling techniques, shift-share analyses or other comparative means. Determinants for innovation (regarded as technological paradigms, knowledge intensity or innovation clusters) are manifold, and often incorporate social factors. The spatial dimension is elementary for the approach, as innovation is understood as geographical phenomenon.

This also corresponds to this thesis, although the theoretical background is not based on the concept of innovation as existing in a system, but rather on the notion of the endogenous production function. The analyses made here are based on econometric approaches including mostly economic determinants and do not incorporate network relations. Nevertheless, a spatial reference and neighboring structure are explicitly considered.

2.1.4 Cluster Approaches and Concentration Indices

Several large areas of research concern the emergence of clusters and measuring various magnitudes of concentration of industries and innovation, sometimes via a set of indices.

An example is the study of Fornahl and Brenner (2009), which sets up a whole range of concentration measures as e.g. Herfindahl indices, the Ellison-Glaeser index, or Moran's I. Applied to patent data and distinguished by technological fields, they find that some technologies cluster spatially while others do not. The authors also include local interactions, the role of dominant firms or the concentration of industries. Different causes for clustering of innovation can therefore be made out. Most significant for clustering of innovation is the presence of R+D institutes in highly agglomerated regions. The fact that different technologies also cluster differently is also an important finding.

Isaksen and Karlsen (2012) investigate regional advantages in innovation as part of territorial innovation models. They check for the role of regional factors in the innovation process by analyzing a large innovation cluster with the help of a specific theoretical case study in the oil and gas sector. They find that in exploiting a regional advantage, the cluster should focus on collaboration with cluster-external R+D partners and education. Overall, the work stresses the importance of local factors to innovation.

Geographical concentration is also considered with Castaldi and Los (2017), who compare patent publications and citations for especially influential patents in the US. They find a regional relocation of innovative activity by analyzing the data in a shift-share analysis, comparing shares and concentration measures. They do not explain why these shifts happen, but rather uncover trends in activity which may matter in several economic scenarios.

Alecke et al. (2006) analyze determinants of the localized concentration of manufacturing industries and contrast those to the efforts of promoting high-tech clusters. Employment data on plant level for manufacturing industries in Germany is used for the analysis. Agglomeration is measured mainly with the Ellison-Glaeser index. Further control variables like natural advantages, industry size and transport costs are included in an OLS regression. They find that there is no real link between theoretical agglomeration forces and the formation of high-tech clusters, as the latter do not seem to be benefiting significantly positively by those forces.

Relevance

Works of this subsection consider concentration measures and indices measuring clustering as the main issue. The assumption that innovation clusters is the basis, and reasons for these innovation agglomerations are investigated by various methods. Either indices are compared among technologies or regions or the indices are used in regressions or shift-share analyses. Innovation is indicated via patents or used to explain clustering of industries (and employment therein). Findings of these researches mostly point to non-negligible forces driving innovation towards spatial concentration.

This thesis investigates the regional allocation of innovation on the basis of a production function and does not rely on concentration measures. Via heat maps and geoadditive models hotspots of innovation are illustrated and explained. Several determinants are included to explain spatial variation in innovation and it is controlled for high-tech clusters, which seem to explain some part of the spatial variation as they indicate a positive relation towards innovative activity.

2.1.5 Technology Regime Approaches

The theory of technological regimes is based on the idea that the distribution of innovation is connected to the type of the most economically important technology in a region (Nelson and Winter 1982;

Malerba and Orsenigo 1993; Malerba and Orsenigo 1997). This is useful, as this thesis investigates the differences between all innovations and high-tech innovation in particular.

In their work, Almeida and Kogut (1997) use this approach, applying patent (and patent citation) data to check upon the innovativeness of small firms in the semiconductor industry in the US. The fields of technology and subsequent diversity of technologies these firms operate in play an important role here. They statistically test the geographical location of patent and patent citation and connect these to find that the main innovators are small firms in dense networks.

Breschi (2000) investigates geographies of innovation by showing that the spatial distribution varies considerably with the sector innovation happens in. He ascribes this to a large extent on the different characteristics of technologies. Patent data from the European Patent Office is used and the method of analysis is a comparison of different (concentration) indices. A similar approach is executed in Malerba and Orsenigo (1997), where technological characteristics explain innovation patterns. Additionally, a panel regression is analyzed and sectoral patterns are explained by technological types. Clustering of innovation can therefore be reasoned geographically.

Relevance

The works of this subsection focus mainly on the theoretical idea that innovation has to be considered not generally, but specifically. Depending on the type of technology, it is distributed differently. The methods used are comparisons of concentration measures and allocation of innovation. Innovation is approximated by patent data and patent citations. All results stress the geographical importance of innovation.

This thesis makes use of the idea behind these theories mostly in the first paper, where high-tech innovations are contrasted to innovation in general. The results suggest a slightly different allocation depending on the type of technology. The methods used are density estimation and, successively, comparisons of heat maps on innovative activity, separately for high-tech and general innovations.

2.1.6 Evolutionary Economics and Related Variety

The field of evolutionary economic geography includes the historical pathway in the theoretical considerations on technological progress. Roots lie with Nelson and Winter (1982) and others as for example Hodgson (1993). Research on innovation in the field of related variety draws on that, as e.g. Boschma (2016) points out, and the regional diversity which is understood as evolutionary concept is reason for geographical innovative activities. Boschma (2016, p. 357) shows that relatedness is a driver of regional diversification. The concept analyzed illustrates that knowledge clusters at the firm level and growth is the result of a diversified region (Boschma 2009).

Cantner, Graf, and Hinzmann (2015) show that the type of knowledge influences the manifestation of spatial proximity. They use a dataset of surveys among recipients of cluster funding and execute a regression on relevance of geographic proximity. Funded projects are therefore evaluated for the impact of geography on successful innovative collaborations. The spatial dimension here is also the major factor influencing innovation.

Relevance

The works following the evolutionary theoretical view on innovation focus mostly on the different regional endowment determining the allocation of innovation. In the research presented here it is worked with survey data and clusters are examined. A regression on the geographical relevance of innovation is executed. The spatial dimension is the major factor in this line of theory.

This thesis also stresses the spatial dimension as indispensable and it is implicitly assumed that innovation determining factors differ among regions and are thus responsible for diverging allocations of innovation. The methods used in the papers of this thesis are, however, on a more aggregated level, as not firms are the matter of investigation, but regions as a whole. Also, the geoadditive modeling provides no explicit focus on the evolution of regions and takes the data as they are, without scrutinizing them.

2.1.7 Other Applied Works

Several other researches focus mostly on applied innovation economics. The theoretical dimension is only used as a background against which analyses are carried out. As innovation is a major growth factor, several works aim for demasking innovation dispersion and determinants to identify leverage points in increasing innovation at last. Not few of the research that is made in this field goes back to governmental incentives and programs, where studies are mandated to uncover innovative behavior and to show leverage points for policy application.

The work by Berger et al. (2017) focuses on the innovative power of German economic regions and conducts a comparison between them. They use several indicators such as R+D costs and patents and rank the regions concerning their intensity in innovative activity. They find a strong regional downshift from north to south and east to west. Moreover, peripheral regions are also lacking activity. This applies mostly to the indicator patents, but the other indicators do not suggest a significantly different situation. The authors explain this mostly by a lack in R+D intensity and suggest specific support for the lacking regions.

Keller, Niebuhr, and Stiller (2004) find strong regional disparities in German innovative activity. They investigate R+D expenditure and intensity, employment in knowledge intensive industries, and patents and rank the federal states (*Bundesländer*) accordingly. They find potential for growth in innovative activity especially in the north and east of Germany, as these regions seem to be lagging compared to the large, agglomerated regions in the south and west. Policy recommendations are to be made accordingly.

Innovative activity in Germany is also the matter of several other studies which cover the factor innovation as part of a larger analysis of potentials for economic growth or even with innovation as the main matter. For instance, in the innovation report by Fertig et al. (2008) also a considerable importance of the regional dispersion of innovative activity throughout Germany is suggested. The authors analyze several innovation indicators, among them measures for patent intensity, with the help of OLS regression.

A focus on regional disparities is made in the study of Untiedt et al. (2016), as a new conception for a policy supporting structurally (economically) weak regions is the matter of that report. However, innovative activity is also a concern, as this factor is a key growth influence which is often absent, especially in structurally weak regions.

Other studies (Beise et al. (2002), Polt et al. (2010)) also consider several channels of innovation through indicators, among them patents. For the most part, these reports have in common that because of the richness of indicators to cover and the manifold facets of innovation, the analyses stay rather basic and lack the possibility of an explicit inclusion of space into the model. Regional distinctions are rather made on the base of comparisons, as the option to account for spatial autocorrelation is often lacking.

2.2 Subsumption

The preceding subsections list several different researches in the field of innovation economics and address the relation of innovation towards the geographical dimension, as well as determinants of innovation are covered extensively. What all researches presented precedingly have in common is this thematic focus, whereas the theories produced, the methods used and the exact combinations of contents in the various models and approaches are highly diverse. Some of the works presented do incorporate a spatial relation in the investigation of innovation, others do not. Different determinants are used in different combinations, and different models are calculated (if it is relied on a quantitative approach at all), and diverging results are found.

The approaches made in the three papers of this thesis rely on the theoretical framework of endogenous growth theory. Furthermore, an explicit spatial and temporal dimension are included, together with a broad set of theoretically based determinants of innovation. Also, a KDE is calculated, and not only OLS models are estimated, but moreover a (spatiotemporal) geoadditive model, which – in this thematic field of innovation economics – has not been executed to this concrete extent before. The results obtained by the models of this thesis generate insights in the reasons for spatial dispersion of innovative activity and suggest potential for exact selection of regions for innovation policy funding, based on estimated effects for impact factors.

Part I

Regional Allocations of Innovative Activity – The Case of 3D Printing

3 Introduction

A comparison between the regional allocation of innovation activity in general and the subset of activities in the technology field of AM in Germany shall be the matter of this paper.

It shall be examined where innovative activity locates in Germany, and if it seems to cluster in some locations. Hotspots of activity are contrasted to cold spots. The distinction of high-tech innovation, measured as AM technology innovation, from innovation irrespective of technology type can furthermore show if there exists a need to consider high-tech innovation individually. This can be relevant for innovation promoting policy, as innovation is a major driver of economic growth. Different spatial allocations of innovations according to technology type can therefore point to more differentiated policies.

The data are derived from patent publications in the timeframe of 2000-2016. The main methodology follows the process of KDE, which allows to illustrate the dispersion of innovation activities over Germany. It is shown that the type of innovative activity matters when analyzing allocations, which can in turn lead to better policy conceptions when supporting innovation.

The paper is structured as follows: The fourth chapter explains the way innovation exerts its spatial dimension. Reasons why innovation is important for economic growth and how space is involved in these considerations are analyzed. Further, the map presented in this paper is described more closely, presenting Germany and its sub-spatial administrative regions. This includes the distinct geographic distribution of economic and general innovative activity observable. The fifth chapter declares the tools used in the analyses, especially the

I. Rhoden, *Space and Time in German Innovative Activity*,
https://doi.org/10.1007/978-3-658-28600-2_3

scope of the variable *innovation activity* and its spatial relations. As the variable is based on patent publication data, patents and their relation to innovation are examined as well. Moreover, AM (often also called 3D printing or rapid manufacturing (e.g. Conner et al. 2014, p. 64; Hagl 2015, pp. 11-13)) as a continually aspiring technology field is presented. The sixth part will set up the methodology for investigating the changing dispersion of innovative activity in general, contrasting activity in AM innovations. The seventh chapter concludes with an interpretation and discussion of KDE, with respect to possible fundamentals underlying the distribution. Implied is the need for adapted regional policy conceptions.

To set up some concepts used throughout this paper first, the geographical units used for a *region* are, for the analysis of innovation, German zipcode areas (five-digit level, reference year 2017). For considerations of factors important for innovation and economic growth, the level is that of the German *Landkreise* and *kreisfreie Städte*, NUTS-3. The matter of the paper, *innovative activity*, will also be referred to as innovation or innovation activity and is measured as the count of published patents' applicants. The technology field *additive manufacturing* considers only the industrial branch of 3D printing.

4 Innovation and Space

4.1 Theoretical Considerations

Innovation and all its implied effects and processes are unquestionably related to the potential of increasing growth. It is seen as the key to a nation's and region's productivity, employment and welfare. Its role in regional economic development is unquestioned (Acs, Anselin, and Varga 2002, p. 1069), albeit it is clear that working in the field of innovation is operating under uncertainty in a rapidly changing, globalized world. To date, still not all underlying processes are completely understood, and this opens many possibilities for interesting analyses and explains the need to uncover the topic farther. (OECD 2005, p. 10)

As Cooke et al. (2013, p. 3) state, the intention of innovation is growth. As growth is inherent in the principle of defining a market, the analysis of the impact of innovation on growth has to consider not only regions, but markets (Cooke et al. 2013, p. 3). The process of innovation in all its complexity uses various sorts of knowledge and by combining these into new products, generates technological improvements which can increase economic growth. Additionally, knowledge is newly generated, distributed and altered over different dimensions in time and space. (Wolfe and Vatne 2011, p. 45)

The OECD in its Oslo Manual (OECD 2005) recommends – based on the existing research concerning innovation and ongoing policy discourse – to approach innovation in theory in a broad way. The origins of innovation, namely, why firms innovate, are relevant as well. Mainly, firms generate new ideas from knowledge to improve perfor-

I. Rhoden, *Space and Time in German Innovative Activity*,
https://doi.org/10.1007/978-3-658-28600-2_4

mance, for example because of increasing demand or for realizing a cost advantage respective to competitors. The overall motive however is to operate successfully in the market. (OECD 2005, pp. 28-29)

The need for long term sustainable growth to ensure welfare can be seen as major economic aim for government. Interference in the growth process can be targeted, for instance, at correcting for situations of market failure. Additionally, normative issues can be covered as growth may happen unbalanced and regions are to be compensated. Policy can adjust to additional societal needs and compensate for locational disadvantages or support disadvantaged or peripheral regions. In this, regional policies focus on increasing welfare. (Eckey 2008, p. 169)

Slowing or stagnating growth can therefore often be an argument to counterbalance negative effects by fostering innovation. For a country or region to postulate growth, focusing on innovation often presents itself as an acclaimed and future-proof way of reaching the growth goal quickly. This is because innovation and knowledge-focused regional policy can directly influence technological progress. The theoretical result is an increase in output and marginal productivity of input factors. (Eckey 2008, p. 220)

Another issue is that innovation possesses characteristics of public goods, which are defined by being nonrival and non-excludable. Technological progress, knowledge, and thus innovation are mainly understood to be nonrival, as they are per se independent of a physical object. They can furthermore be designed to exclude others from use, for instance if a patent is registered, making them at least partially excludable. Nevertheless, for filing a patent it is necessary to disclose all information and make it public, which presents the opportunity for others to build upon that knowledge (although commercialized use of the patented technology is permitted) (Arundel 2001, p. 612). The degree of excludability is designed by the type of policy regulating this by constituting property rights. (Romer 1990, pp. 74-76; Arrow 1969, p. 615)

4.2 Innovation in Space

Digital Space In the light of the established theories of knowledge, innovation and space, recent point of views claim a lessened importance of geography for the economy. This is due to digitalization and globalization, where all information is always available anywhere, so that innovation and at last production could happen anywhere. That way, time is seen to replace space because of the immense progress in information and communication technologies (Morgan 2004, p. 4). However, because of the many forms of innovation or knowledge, one cannot entirely dismiss the spatial dimension of certain phenomena. Whereas information can travel a long way in short time, understanding does not. Especially tacit knowledge, which has a major impact in innovation creation, is not substitutable over great distances. (Morgan 2004, pp. 3-7)

As Morgan (2004, p. 17) further states, the numerous studies on this topic lead to ambiguous results, however, the interest in the geographic dimension of industry, innovation and growth still increases. All in all, the influence and importance of geography depends on localization and diffusion, not only on dispersion (Storper 1997). The notion of tacit knowledge that it is inherently local is also responsible for the development of clusters, which are knowledge-intensive hubs of innovation. Clustering of economic activity via exchange of local knowledge is also an important process for the allocation of innovative activity. (Storper 1997; Maskell et al. 1997; Gertler 2003)

The basis for the investigation of innovation activities are patent data, and a major point is to reflect upon the spatial nature of a patent. Here, a long history exists (compare Acs, Anselin, and Varga (2002, p. 1070)); as there are as many analyses for spatial considerations of patents as there are for the acceptability of patents as innovation indicator itself.

Generally, the spatial nature of innovation is not questioned, as the innovation geography is an accepted term for many of theories on this matter (for an overview see for example Ratanawaraha and Polenske (2007)). The potential for knowledge – which is a requirement for innovation – to spill over, is examined by many. The main finding, as stated by Acs, Anselin, and Varga (2002, p. 1070) is that innovation is not distributed spatially evenly across an area. It moreover tends to cluster at certain points in space. Furthermore, knowledge spillovers are locally distinctive and there exist substantial differences between urban and peripheral areas. Economic activity differs as well, so that innovation behaves accordingly to the place where it occurs (Feldman and Kogler 2010, p. 384). These topics are all based on the work of Krugman (1990), Lucas (1988), and Romer (1990) as well as on Porter (1990) and Nelson (1993). The importance of space and time in the distribution of innovation is, despite the advantages of globalization and digitalization, unquestioned, although it may seem like a paradox (Feldman and Kogler 2010, p. 393). Following Marshall (1890), geographic concentration is based on an infrastructure of related industries in which firms support each other, on extremely specialized local labor, and on non-monetary externalities which result from local exchanges of knowledge. Innovation is best facilitated by its presence in space, as a major reason for it to thrive is regional tacit knowledge (Maskell and Malmberg 1999, p. 171). Important local factors in the development of an innovation are knowledge and skills, institutions and markets, which cannot be excluded from analysis as they contribute to knowledge creation, and therefore to innovation (Feldman and Kogler 2010, p. 387). Moreover, the fact that tacit knowledge is best transferred over short distance via face-to-face communication also stresses locality, albeit in some cases even tacit knowledge can be obtained via video-chat or technologies alike (Gertler 2003).

Nevertheless, local connections are not the sole environment on which innovative activity is based, as global networks also play a relevant role (Feldman and Kogler 2010, p. 401). Networks are inherently not exclusively spatially defined (Boschma 2005, p. 69). Therefore, one can argue that further factors have to be included, as not only spatial proximity is sufficient for knowledge to spill over, but social and cognitive distance matter as well. Only if the cognitive distance, which implies more than just kilometers of distance, is taken into consideration, external knowledge can be used beneficially, leading to technological change and ultimately, to innovation (Cohen and Levinthal 1990). This is also mentioned by Boschma (2005, pp. 62 & 71), who states that geographical proximity has to be considered together with other relevant locational factors when analyzing the spatial component of innovation. In this article, the concept of proximity is an all-encompassing one, so that it not only features geographical distance, but also social and economic implications as well as political, natural and historical factors. The reason for that is simply that geographical closeness can be proxied by other forms of closeness; social proximity for instance can substitute geographical closeness to a certain extent, as modern communication facilitates knowledge exchange (Boschma 2005, p. 71).

Generally, it is acknowledged that innovation concentrates where at least minimal essential knowledge inputs are located and that knowledge spillovers happen locally, decrease, and spread out with time (Feldman and Audretsch 1996; Jaffe, Trajtenberg, and Henderson 1993). Considering the type of the industry, its position in the life cycle and the importance of tacit knowledge, the degree of spatial clustering depends. This is especially relevant for emerging high-technologies as i.e. AM. The latter consists of a variety of technologies and these are prone to exhibit higher innovative activity (Feldman and Audretsch 1999, p. 427). Moreover, following the notion by Vernon (1966, p. 192), if a technology is relatively new, the tacitness of knowledge occupies a large part of the production of innovation in general and the amount of contribution to economic growth. AM, presented as a case study in this paper, is such a set of technologies that will reach full commercializability in short time (Lachmayer, Lippert, and Fahlbusch 2016, p. 4).

4.3 Space

Different spatial patterns of innovative activity are, following the new economic geography (Krugman 1990, p. 484), mostly the result of agglomeration and dispersion. Agglomeration fosters the creation of regional clustering of economic activity (Marshall 1890), when positive scale economies in production of goods or services develop. The emerging effects can either be considered as localized spillover effects or as urbanization spillover effects. Localized effects happen when companies search the spatial proximity of competitors to decrease average production costs via mass production effects. This centralization can benefit the general productivity of the cluster and the economy. (Fujita, Krugman, and Venables 1999, p. 4)

Urbanization effects ensue when a diversified field of suppliers is able to compensate consumers in case of the breakdown of a competitor. Neighboring regions can benefit from these effects as well, as they can spill over. These benefits of diversity go back to Hoover (1948) and Jacobs (1969), and are also restated by Harrison, Kelly, and Gant (1996), who explain that with a broad set of skills and industry connections, knowledge prospers especially in a diversified economy. (Feldman and Audretsch 1999, p. 427)

The creation of a cluster can thus not only prove promising for the region in which the cluster grows, but for other regions as well. A cluster itself is formed by several companies linked by supplier-buyer-relations, similar technologies or joint markets for their products or their labor (Enright 1996, p. 191).

4.4 Regional Localization

The German Case Comparing 2016 to 2015 in general, the growth of Gross Domestic Product (GDP) in Germany is 1.9%. For three years preceding 2016, GDP growth is relatively stagnating, whereas the process over earlier years looks much more volatile, with some peaks (e.g. 2010: 4.1% or 2006: 3.7%) and lows (e.g. 1993: -1% or 2009: -5.6%). Labor productivity decreased in the last years, now being 0.6% compared to 2015 with an absolute value of (2 932.5 Billion Euro/42,672' employees) 68,72 Euro. (Statistisches Bundesamt 2018a)

The European Innovation Scoreboard (EIS) and Regional Innovation Scoreboard (RIS) of 2016 illustrate Germany as one of the innovation leaders, among Scandinavian countries or the United Kingdom (EC 2016b, p. 17). Here, up until 2012, Germany's performance improved, only to decline in the follow-up. Nevertheless, in the fields of *firm investments* or *innovators*, it still shows above European Union-average performance by 21%. (EC 2016a, p. 51)

When breaking this down to regions on a subnational level, the south of Germany is especially high performing (EC 2016b, p. 16). This is also confirmed in the *Innovation Atlas 2017* (Berger et al. 2017, p. 10). These regions, so-called innovation leaders or strong innovators, reveal a high number of patent applications, especially in key enabling technologies like advanced manufacturing technologies. The increase in patent applications with relevance to the world market (registration at the European Patent Office or World Intellectual Property Organization) per million inhabitants amounts to 9% (2000-2013). This corresponds to 372 patents per million inhabitants, which is far above the European average (154) and even above the United States of America (216) (BMBF 2017, p. 14). The RIS's revealed technology advantage-index for the innovation leaders is significantly above 1, which indicates a positive specialization in the respective technology. This index exhibits positive specialization not only in southern Germany, but also in other parts of Germany, like selected areas in North Rhine-Westphalia for example. (EC 2016b, pp. 23-25)

The German High-Tech Strategy published by the German Federal Ministry of Education and Research recognizes the importance of innovation and its contribution to growth in Germany (BMBF 2017, p. 44). In 2015, R+D investment accounted for 3% of the GDP for the first time. This value resembles an increase in company investments of 10% compared to 2014 and stands for an increase of 60% compared to 2005. In the future, these investments shall always be at least 3% of GDP, as the newly proclaimed goal by the German government promises. Moreover, this goal also integrates into the European *Strategy 2020*. Correspondingly, the intensity of R+D spending resides well over the European average (BMBF 2017, pp. 12-13). As a set of measures for attaining this goal and improving the German position in the world market, the Federal Ministry of Education and Research proposed five key principles. They all consider important aspects of generating a new innovation policy fit for digitalization. For instance, the digital economy shall be fostered as well as the digital society. Companies shall be supported in managing their business models as digitalization changes processes and demand. (BMBF 2017, pp. 18-39)

In the Innovation Atlas, the motivation of the government is confirmed. For the authors, the main challenge is the increasing competition among the world's innovation leaders. To be competitive Germany has to support not only prospering regions, but foster innovation in currently still lacking regions. The latter will be crucial, if Germany wants to keep its position as innovation leader. This is elementary not only for Germany as a country, but also for the regional economies of its administrative districts and Bundesländer. (Berger et al. 2017, p. 56)

The Länder's Case The German federal states show a diversified development. Breaking down the key figures, the federal states with the highest increase in GDP growth are Berlin and Saxony (2.7%). The lowest value is found in the Saarland (0.0%) and in Saxony-Anhalt (0.1%). As an example, especially in the case of North Rhine-Westphalia the results presented by the task force regional accounts ("Volkswirtschaftliche Gesamtrechnung der Länder") in 2016 shocked most political decision makers and initiated several new concepts for increasing growth. Productivity growth took a turn for the worse, as it stagnated with 0.0% while the German economy as a whole grew with 1.7% in 2015 (VGrdL 2016). The federal state of North Rhine-Westphalia had to face the last position in the ranking of all German federal states (Breidenbach et al. 2016, p. 4). This led to a renewed focus on boosting the state's performance and not only the country but the federal states as well initiated innovation strategies with clearly delineated goals for sustainable growth through innovation. (NRW 2014, p. 19). Contrariwise, Baden-Württemberg is the example par excellence, as it successfully mastered its structural change decades ago. Now, the federal state is effectively the leader in innovative activity in Germany.

Overall, the positive development in innovation activity in Germany proclaimed by the government covers the diversifying evolution going on in the federal states. As Berger et al. (2017) frame it, there exists a downward slope from south to north, west to east, and from cities to rural areas; meaning the most innovative regions are cities in the south west of Germany. Here, as the main innovations are the result of few (mostly automotive) clusters, Germany has been able to achieve the 3%/GDP. To repeat this accomplishment and succeed among the accelerating competition of the most innovative nations, the lacking regions in Germany have to be supported as well. As the authors put it, three quarters of the regions are not or very sparsely exhibiting innovations. (Berger et al. 2017)

A similar view is presented by the *Future Atlas* (Prognos AG 2016), where Germany's most future-proof regions are identified in a locational ranking. An index consisting of several macro- and socioeconomic criteria determines the position of the administrative districts and appoints the regions with the best chances for being economically successful in the future. The authors also confirm a south to north direction in which chances decrease. Regions in southern Germany face the least future risks, and these regions moreover improved compared to 2004 (Prognos AG 2016, pp. 3-6). Furthermore, wealth in Germany increased slightly, but the gap between high and low income increased as well. The number of regions with balanced chances and risks decreased, so that either more regions with good chances or more regions with higher risks emerged. All in all, mainly regions in the south prosper. A few exceptions are areas around Cologne, Düsseldorf, Frankfurt (Main), Hamburg, and Berlin.

While evaluating several promising and widespread concepts, the underlying conditions of regions with high innovative activity are to be discovered under the premise that innovative activity does in fact differ regionally. Are some regions more active with respect to innovation than others? Are these regions productive regions where

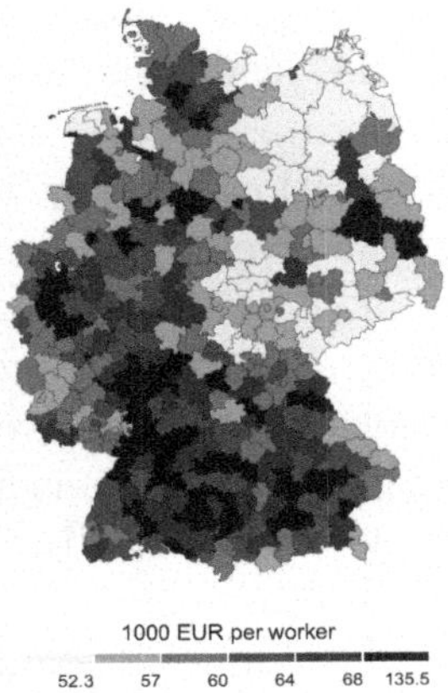

(a) Productivity.

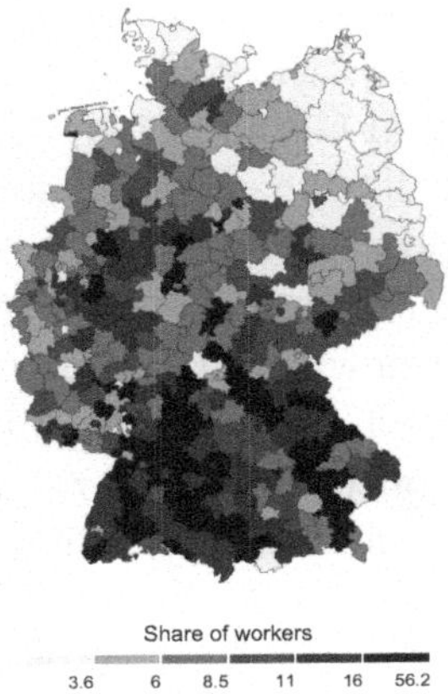

(b) Knowledge intensity.

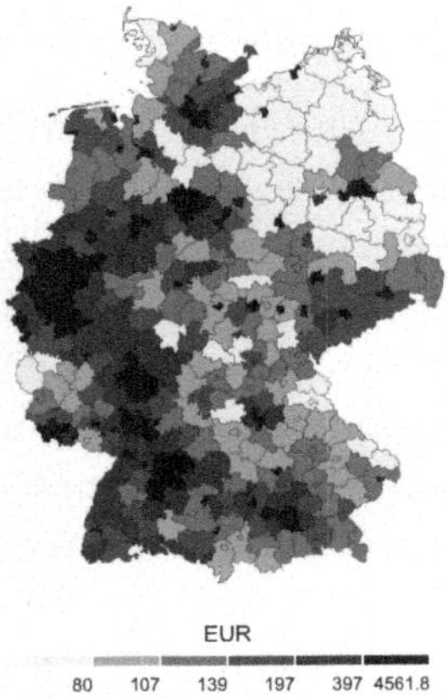

(c) Population density.

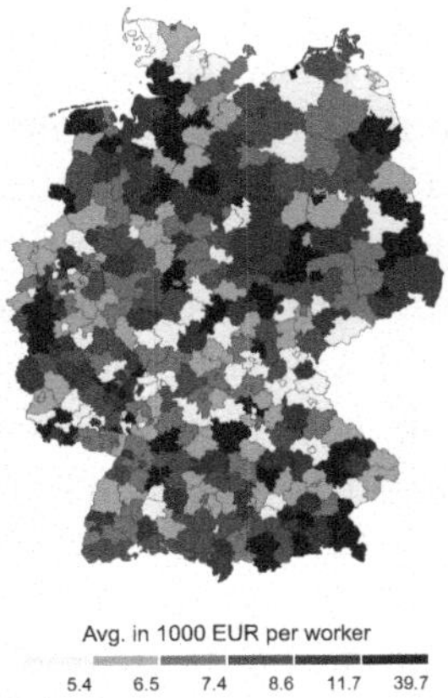

(d) Investment.

Figure 4.1: Exemplary determinants for 2014. The distribution and level of the indicators show the different regional situation on NUTS-3 level. Darker colors depict higher values, lighter colors illustrate lower values.

economic growth is emitted? Which conclusions can be drawn for regions that do not display innovative activity? Are policy implications possible?

As figure 4.1 shows, the highest values among the administrative districts in Germany are very differently dispersed with respect to differing indicators. Although the distribution of investment and the values for effective labor are not illustrating a clear-cut picture and are allocated scattered over Germany, the economic indicator GDP reveals that the east of Germany still lacks the strength of the western federal states of the country. Therefore, the underlying base for the development of innovation is equally distinct.

5 Technology Parameters

5.1 Innovation Activity and Patents

The history of patents as an indicator for innovative activities is a long one, as a patent is the quintessential symbol of innovative spirit (Griliches 1998, p. 287). It enables a company or an inventor to protect their invention from not being able to compensate initial R+D costs for developing the creation by excluding others from taking and using the invention without having to face costs for its R+D (W. M. Cohen 2010, p. 182). This way, a market for the innovated product is created, because the patent as an intellectual property right excludes others from usage (Arundel 2001, pp. 611-613). By definition, the invention which is patented has to be new, depend on inventive activity, and imply a commercial use (PatG 1936, §1). The patent persists for a maximum of 20 years (DPMA 2018). Based on the definition alone, a patent can be seen as a relevant indicator of innovation, because the implied commercial use is what characterizes it as innovation (e.g. Kürtössy 2004; Smith 1992, p. 386).

In general, the technological progress preceding the innovation is a major factor contributing to productivity and therefore to growth. Measurement of this technological progress is difficult, so that an indicator which indirectly contains these mechanisms is necessary (OECD 2009, pp. 26-29). It is possible to measure input, for example by listing R+D expenditures, or to measure revenue gained from the innovation. A proxy is using patents as measure of output of technological progress, as the implied commercial use is what qualifies the invention for a patent (e.g. Trajtenberg 1990; Hall, Griliches,

I. Rhoden, *Space and Time in German Innovative Activity*,
https://doi.org/10.1007/978-3-658-28600-2_5

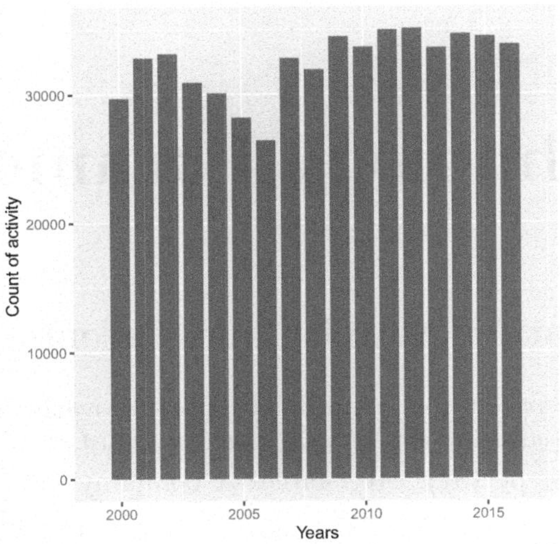

Figure 5.1: General innovation activity per year. Germany, timeframe 2000-2016, counts of activity manifest as one patent applicant of a published patent.

and Hausman 1984; Freeman 1982). Another view is that patents are incremental forms of innovation, as the success of a patented product is not determinable at the time of the patent application or granting of the patent (Acs, Anselin, and Varga 2002, p. 1069). The use of patents to indicate innovation is, although promising, also often criticized (see for example Smith (1992, p. 383); but Smith also states that patents count as a major indicator of innovation analysis (Smith 2005, p. 152)). Although it has to be considered that patents reflect inventions which result in innovations only at last, their interpretation as innovations is not axiomatic (Griliches 1998; Scherer 1986). Griliches (1998, p. 292) states a major reason that accompanies the difficile use of patents in the context of measuring innovativeness. The problem is that it is not clear what exactly patents measure, and how economically relevant the patented product will become. Also, not every technological activity leads to a patent. (Pakes and Griliches 1980, p. 378)

Furthermore, innovation seems to be geographically more concentrated than inventions (meaning patents) itself and more concentrated than production as well (Acs, Audretsch, and Feldman 1994). This is due to inventions being understood as concentrated R+D effort, and innovation as an already realized economic advantage resulting from invention. Nevertheless, as Feldman (2013) reports, there exists a correlation of 0.8 between innovation – measured by new products – and patents. This is sufficiently high, so that a significant influence cannot be disregarded, despite them not being fully substitutable in the strictest sense. (Feldman and Kogler 2010, p. 385)

However, the measurement capabilities of patents as innovations shall not be the concern of this paper, as the widely accepted opinion is that patents are data that are readily available and an extremely detailed measure to be employed in the analysis of innovation and technological progress. (Griliches 1998, p. 336)

5.2 Additive Manufacturing

Scientific progress via innovation and the resulting economic growth chances are nowadays mostly based on digitalization and its new concepts. The digital progress induces a structural change in the economy, which can lead to economic growth and increased welfare. New technologies within the scope of digitalization are developed in various fields of the economy, such as biology and genetics, climate research or industrial machinery. Without new innovations based on potentiated computational power these innovations would not be possible. On the one hand, there are innovations with digital components, on the other hand, there are spillover effects by digitalized processes that increase efficiency in existing technologies. (Prognos AG 2015, p. 3)

As digitalization is a collective term, many domains fall into this process. Via patent analysis, one can identify new technologies eas-

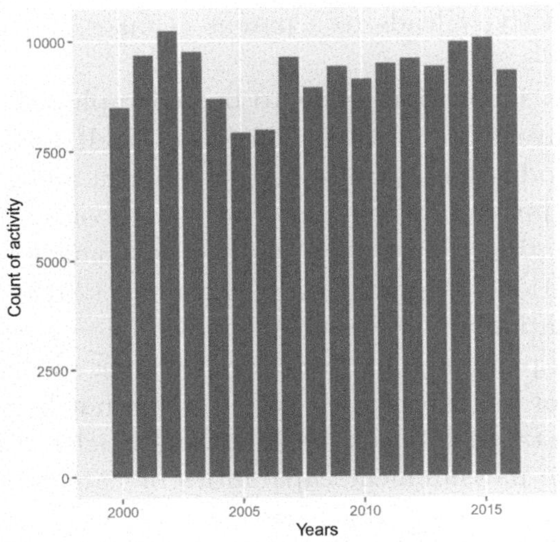

Figure 5.2: Innovation activity per year: additive manufacturing. Germany, timeframe 2000-2016, counts of activity manifest as one patent applicant of a published patent in additive manufacturing technologies.

ily, as every patent has to be classified according to the technological field it belongs to. Digital technologies most often consider semiconductors, digital communication, information technologies for management and computer technologies. One can see that in these areas the number of patents increased through several growth phases, with patent applications reaching a peak in these fields in 2012/2013 (Prognos AG 2015, p. 6). The report by Prognos cites a massive rise in digital technology patents. As mentioned before, digitalization happens not only via direct innovations, but also through increased efficiency by digital spillovers. 3D printing in this case is often consulted as major example, as the procedure involves technologies from several different fields of high-tech innovation. The process itself and its wide-ranging applicability for a myriad of other technologies allow massive gains in efficiency. 3D printed airplane parts can for instance reduce the weight of an aircraft, and 3D printed prosthetics enable more precise results of surgical operations. (Prognos AG 2015, p. 7)

In General, 3D printing, rapid prototyping and AM all concern similar technologies where material is additively applied to build a certain structure. Normally, material is added layer by layer, based on 3D model-data. Several technologies are part of AM, mainly Vat photopolymerization, material and binder jetting, material extrusion, powder bed fusion, sheet lamination, and directed energy deposition (ASTM International 2012, p. 2). One can summarize the processes of AM as liquid-based, powder-based, or solid-based (Kruth 1991). Discernible are a customer-centered technology field, where people can print their parts via do-it-yourself, and an industrial application (Lachmayer, Lippert, and Fahlbusch 2016, pp. 1-2).

AM is further characterized as the new industrial revolution and its ability to revolutionize manufacturing is strongly emphasized (Anderson 2013, p. 27). It is expected that AM will further offer extensive gains and promote entrepreneurship and innovation, so that several national and supra-national funds devote large sums into research and application of AM technologies (Harms et al. 2009; Ratinho, Harms, and Walsh 2015). For example, part of the Horizon 2020 framework is assigning AM to the key manufacturing technologies promising the creation of high-quality jobs and therefore increases in economic growth (EFFRA 2013, p. 113). Based on the hype cycle concept by US company Gartner, AM is partly (rapid prototyping) on the productivity plateau and seems to be fully marketable in less than 2 years, and partly (direct manufacturing) on the peak of expectations (Lachmayer, Lippert, and Fahlbusch 2016, p. 4). In their article, Gartner, Maresch, and Fink (2015, p. 586) show the distinct history of AM as an extremely heterogeneous field, which is already 30 years old. While it harbors certain advantages, mostly because of its flexibility to produce nearly anything, there are several drawbacks to consider as well. The structure and handling of intellectual property rights is unclear (Weinberg 2010), and a standard containing a consistent set of regulations is missing (SRA 2017; Gartner, Maresch, and Fink 2015, p. 587).

Moreover, AM has the indisputable quality of being a classical disruptive innovation in the sense of Schumpeterian theory (Schumpeter 1934), as it impacts traditional production technologies strongly. Average unit costs of production will equal those of mass production, warehousing will be obsolete, and therefore mass production will be individualized as customers are able to produce according to their own needs in single batch production. Furthermore, a decentralization of production infrastructure is expected. (Rehfeld 2015, p. 5)

Additional features that impact the economy when regarding AM are lowered barriers to market entry, fostering of local production while cost advantages of low-wage countries could decrease, or an acceleration of innovation as well as a reduction of assembly work. Possible risks are high marginal costs, missing scale economies because of individual production, and the need of highly skilled workers and technological knowledge. (Weller, Kleer, and Piller 2015, p. 46)

Considering the spatial implications of AM, Gress and Kalafsky (2015, pp. 46-47) stress the importance of this technology in influencing innovation geography to a large extent. This is due to AM being a complex set of different technologies operated on different organizational scales – by firms and individuals – which could lead to a re-conception of knowledge and information flows.

When comparing the counts of innovation activity from all technologies (compare figure 5.1) with those of industrial AM (compare figure 5.2), it is important to consider that data before 2000 is possibly not representative of the actual activity. This is due to changes in the development of the German zipcodes and their consistency and extractability throughout and of the raw data. Nevertheless, when comparing the counts of all technologies and AM technologies one can see that the increase in the years 1995-2001 is steeper for AM patent publications. The peak is more defined; for all technologies there seems to be a slightly shallower peak. Moreover, as the peak of the innovative activity happens to be in 2001 for both datasets, the valley of the activity in 2006 is, too. There is another lower peak in 2011, before activity decreases until 2016. Furthermore, the number of innovations in 2016 decreases even below the level of 1994.

6 Methodology

The main data source of this paper is the German Patent and Trademark Office's bibliographical patent publication's count data (DPMA 2017). For this paper's purpose, the data in a timeframe from 2000-2016 is investigated. The dataset includes data on the applicant of the patent and its inventor, both of which are almost always listed with an address with zipcode. In some cases, no address with zipcode is available. These observations are therefore removed as they cannot be located properly. Furthermore, the IPC is also given, as well as application and publication date of the patent. The data is then loaded into R (R Core Team 2019) and zipcodes are extracted. In a next step, the zipcodes are geo-referenced via the Google Maps Geocoding API (Google LLC 2019). The restructuring of the original data and tidying of the dataset lead to 550247 observations in total (2000-2016). Each observation stands for one innovation activity (in the data this corresponds to one patent applicant). A patent can consist of multiple such innovation activities (because of having multiple applicants). In this analysis, each applicant of a patent contributes the same, equal amount of innovation (namely, =1), irrespective of the patent being the result of multiple, differently located inventors (or applicants) or of a single inventor (applicant). Consequently, the approach of splitting a multiple-applicant-patent into fractions which are then assigned to the respective site of the applicant is not necessary. The 550247 innovation activities correspond to 525087 actual patents. 95.4% of the patents are registered by a single applicant. (DPMA 2018)

I. Rhoden, *Space and Time in German Innovative Activity*,
https://doi.org/10.1007/978-3-658-28600-2_6

As the innovation activity data relies on patent publications, the distribution of the data is highly skewed to the left. Checking the quantiles, 95% of the values in all years of the timeframe lie below 30 or even below 20. When regarding histograms of the patent data (compare figure 6.1), the extreme distribution is further illustrated. On the one side, many regions only display very few patent applications. On the other side, some particular regions exhibit a very high amount of patent applications. A region in the context used here corresponds to one zipcode area. This scheme applies for each year of the data. Consequently, the median lies considerably lower than the mean of the data, as is typical for patent data (Fahrmeir, Kneib, and S. Lang 2009, p. 33). The data is integer, and the highest density with over 0.7 is achieved for regions in which only a single innovation activity occurs. The histogram for AM technologies (compare again figure 6.1) looks similar, although it exhibits smaller values. The respective density function peaks higher, which is due to many regions not having published patents in these technologies. All in all, the distributions look relatively alike.

Regarding the innovation activity classified as associated with AM, the distribution of this subset of the data matches the distribution of general innovation activity in Germany, as the data is again highly skewed. The innovation activities in 3D printing related technologies make up roughly one fourth of all innovation activities. Considered as relevant for AM are 73 classes of the IPC on four-digit level (compare table A.1 in the Appendix), mostly belonging to the IPC main class B, *Performing Operations; Transporting*. But also classes A (*Human Necessities*), C (*Chemistry; Metallurgy*), and H (*Electricity*) are involved.

Observing the distribution of innovation activity in all technologies throughout Germany (compare figure 6.2), the localization does not seem to change substantially from 2000-2016. Each colored dot resembles an innovation activity, which is mapped according to German zipcode areas on their centroid coordinate. Regions where more innovative activity happens are therefore more colored. Comparing 2000 and 2016, one can observe an increase in activity, as the coloring

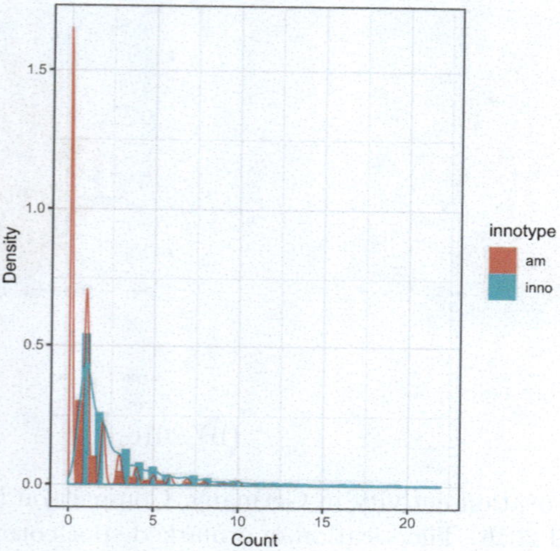

Figure 6.1: Histogram of innovation activity in Germany in 2016. With additional smoothed density curve. Comparison of all activity (inno) to additive manufacturing related activity (am).

of the map gets denser. In general, activity concentrates in the Ruhr area, on the Frankfurt (Main)-Stuttgart-Mannheim axis as well as in metropolises like Hamburg, Berlin, and Munich. Further activity happens in Dresden or Regensburg (compare figure 6.2). The general picture of innovation activities also does not seem to depend on the number of involved patent applicants, as their number fluctuates, but not massively so. For example, in 2012 171442 observations (patent applicants) count, in 2016 only 33795. The resulting distribution of innovation does not change sizably. What can be seen on all maps is a focus of the activity on western regions in Germany. The patents are allocated more evenly among the zipcode areas. Nevertheless, regions of major importance are still standing out. In the east of Germany, the allocation is much sparser, and Berlin is a center of activity, whereas other eastern zipcode areas do not exude extensive activity.

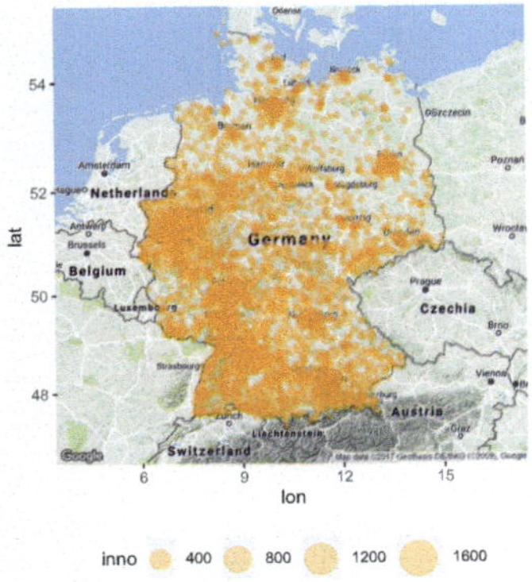

(a) 2000.

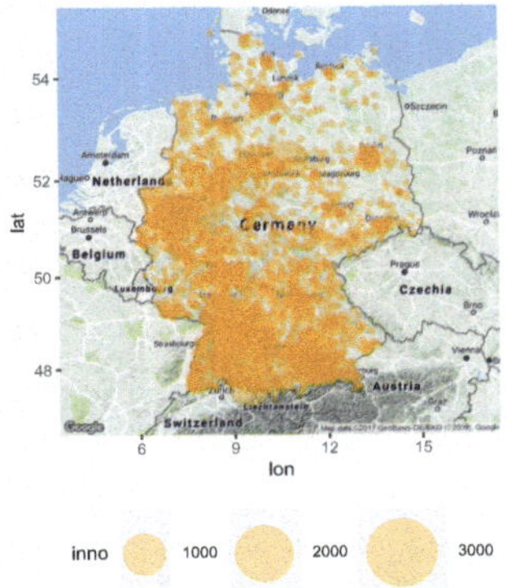

(b) 2016.

Figure 6.2: Innovation activity in Germany. Comparison between 2000 and 2016. The location of a marked spot corresponds to a zipcode area where a patent is published, the size of the circle illustrates the number of patents published in such an area.

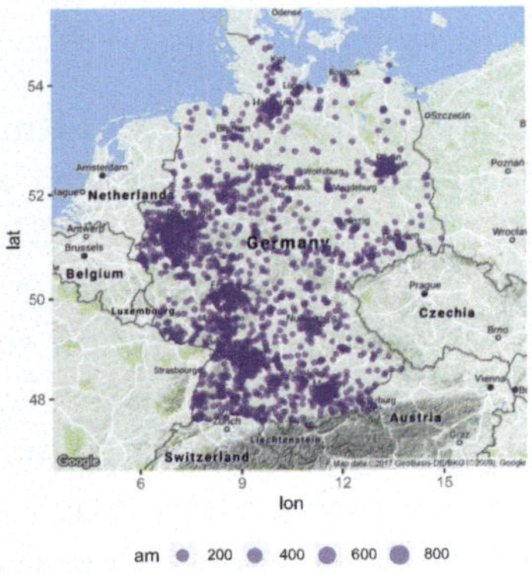

(a) 2000.

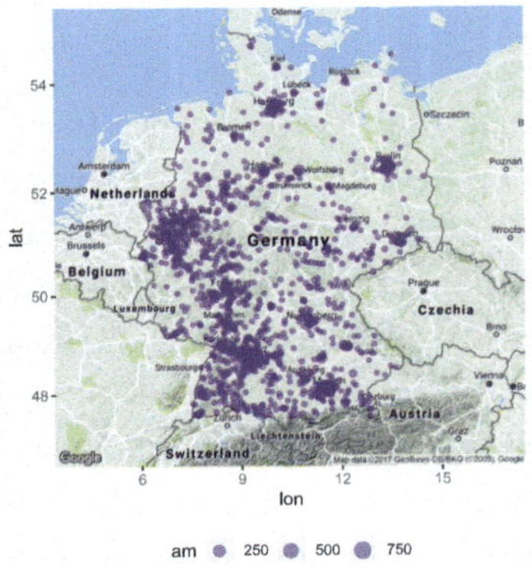

(b) 2016.

Figure 6.3: Innovation activity in Germany: additive manufacturing technologies. The location of a marked spot corresponds to a zipcode area where a patent is published, the size of the circle illustrates the number of patents published in such an area.

Switching to innovations belonging to AM technologies in figure 6.3, the distribution of activity does not change immensely from 2000 until 2016. One major difference is the reduced number of participating applicants. The allocation of the activity is similar to the location of all patent publications, no major differences are observable. The hotspots of activity are the Ruhr area, Stuttgart-Mannheim, Frankfurt (Main), Berlin, Munich, and Regensburg. Another similarity to all patents is the concentration in western German regions, although the allocation is less densely distributed.

For this paper, the definition of which technologies belonging to AM is held rather generous. This may be one of the reasons for the distribution of innovative activity in figure 6.3 resembling the localization of all innovation activity irrespective of technology (compare figure 6.2). The number of innovations per year in AM (figure 5.2) also shows a similar behavior of innovative activity per year in general, although the magnitude is only a fraction of all technologies' innovation.

6.1 Kernel Density Estimation

For a more detailed analysis, a KDE for the univariate case considering innovation activity is executed. KDE is a well-established and widely applied method, and the statistical analysis is easier than for histograms (Silverman 1986, p. 34). It can give relevant information about patterns or characteristics of the data which can be useful for further analyses (Ospina, Larangeiras, and Frery 2014, p. 401). To estimate the density of an unknown distribution, the nonparametric KDE can be understood as the more revealing tool compared to the histogram. KDE requires no assumption concerning the true density function, it is able to estimate it from the data presented to it (Chen 2017, p. 2). This flexibility is its great strength. The goodness of fit can be measured by the Mean Integrated Square Error (MISE), which describes the accuracy of the estimated density (Silverman 1986, p. 35). The kernel estimator is, referring to the histogram, the arithmetic mean of n i.i.d. distributed random variables X (Scott 2015, p. 142):

$$KER_h(x, X_i) = \frac{1}{h} KER\left(\frac{(x - X_i)}{h}\right), \tag{6.1}$$

where KER is the kernel function, and h is the bandwidth parameter. Both have to be chosen to fit the purpose. As Silverman (1986, p. 37) states, the estimated density consists of a smoothed form of the true density plus a random error. As for the smoothing, it depends on the chosen parameters, not so much on the sample size. Considering the selection of a fitting kernel, the ideal bandwidth will very slowly converge towards zero with increasing sample size. If one uses this bandwidth to find the optimal kernel function KER, the MISE should be also very small in the optimal case. The kernel resulting as the most efficient kernel, solving the afore mentioned case, is the Epanechnikov kernel (Epanechnikov 1969). Compared to other kernels, no kernels diverge substantially with respect to efficiency, as therefore the emphasis is not so much upon the choice of KER, but more importantly of h. (Silverman 1986, pp. 37-43)

A suggestion, again by Silverman (1986, p. 44) is to choose h with the aim of the analysis in mind, and compare the amount of smoothing done by smaller or larger values of h. It is recommended to start by slightly under-smoothing the density, as to not miss possible important features which vanish with a too large bandwidth. This approach is also promoted by Bivand, Pebesma and Gomez-Rubio (2013, p. 185). Choosing the bandwidth is very intricate though, as by smoothing bias and variance of the estimator are affected peculiarly. Nevertheless, the aim is to keep the MISE as small as possible (Van der Veeken 2010, pp. 55-56). Furthermore, this is difficult as the usual KDE applies a fixed value for h. It is possible to use a varying bandwidth, for example if in denser regions a smaller bandwidth is necessary than in less dense regions. In most cases, it is difficult to achieve a significant improvement by using a floating bandwidth, so

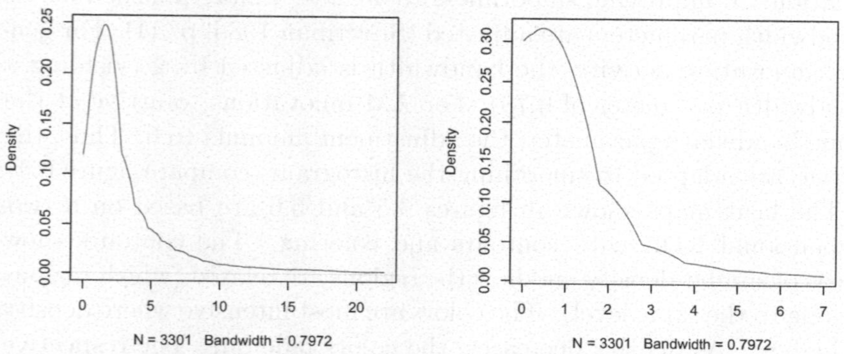

(a) Innovation activity in general. **(b)** Innovation activity in additive manufacturing technologies.

Figure 6.4: Density estimation of innovation activity 2016. Comparison of all activity to additive manufacturing activity, with Epanechnikov kernels used. Cut-off at the 95% quantile.

this can be omitted in favor of a fixed h (Terrell and Scott 1992, p. 1237).

To account for all possibilities, several kernels are compared, and various bandwidths are tested accordingly. There exist several methods for computing kernel density estimates, which differ mostly in dealing with different computational values for the bandwidth. This analysis is executed via the command `density` in `R`, which is relatively fast in computation and yields accurate estimates. (Deng and Wickham 2011, pp. 4-12)

6.2 Innovation Heat Maps

The first estimations with Epanechnikov kernels and automatic choice of bandwidth parameter for innovation in general all lead to bandwidths around 0.4. For AM technologies, a smaller bandwidth of 0.13 is calculated automatically, as less observations complicate the calculation. In improving smoothness to achieve a more polished curve, bandwidth parameters are adjusted (Silverman 1986, p. 44). For general innovation activity, the bandwidth is adjusted by 2 (yielding a bandwidth parameter of 0.79). For AM innovations to arrive at the same bandwidth parameter, the adjustment amounts to 6. Thus, the curves are adapted to smoothing the histogram (compare figure 6.4).

The heat maps shown in figures 6.5 and 6.6 are based on a two-dimensional KDE with contours and coloring. The contours show areas of similar density and how the regions are related (which regions belong to the same level). The colors are most intensive where density is highest. As density decreases, the colors fade out. The respective density levels are depicted next to the heat maps. The calculation is based on the same dataset as figure 6.4. The advantage here is that the density values can vary depending on the geographic location of the innovation activity, so that a more detailed interpretation over space is possible.

First, it is apparent that the density estimated for both groups of technologies is diverging, but not substantially so. Nevertheless, the density of AM technologies is higher than that for all technologies combined, which points to a higher concentration of AM innovation. Furthermore, one can clearly see differences, compared to the frequency maps of figures 6.2 and 6.3, which is possible because of the KDE method.

In Germany there exist main areas of innovation activity which locate strongly around the Ruhr area and south towards Cologne and the Bergisches Land. Around Frankfurt (Main) with an offset south to Stuttgart lies another focus. An additional center of gravity lies in Munich. Less dense areas are in Wolfsburg, and to the east of Stuttgart in the direction of Augsburg. A smaller area of interest is in Berlin and Hamburg, and one in Nuremberg (compare figure 6.5a). Only the connecting areas between the big cities exhibit less density. Other than in those regions, there seems to be no activity high enough to appear on the heat map. Beginning with the year 2000, selected maps are pictured in figures 6.5 and 6.6.

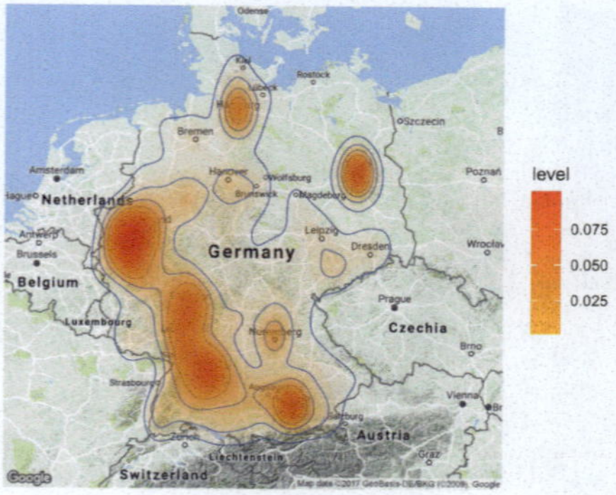

(a) All technologies in 2000.

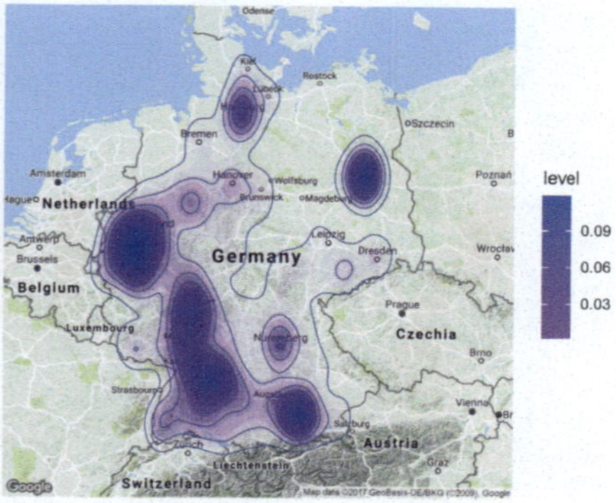

(b) AM technologies in 2000.

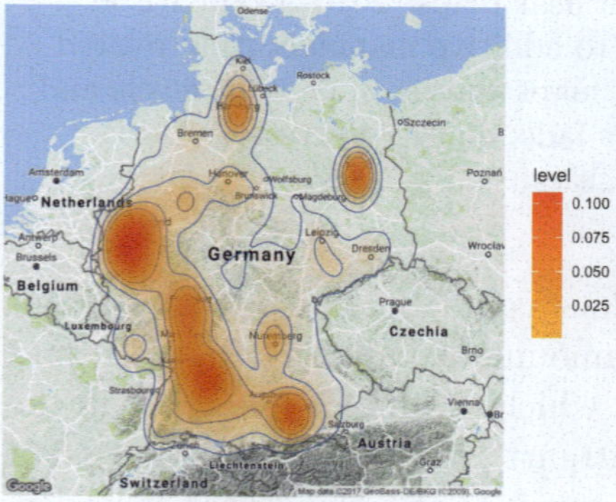

(c) All technologies in 2005.

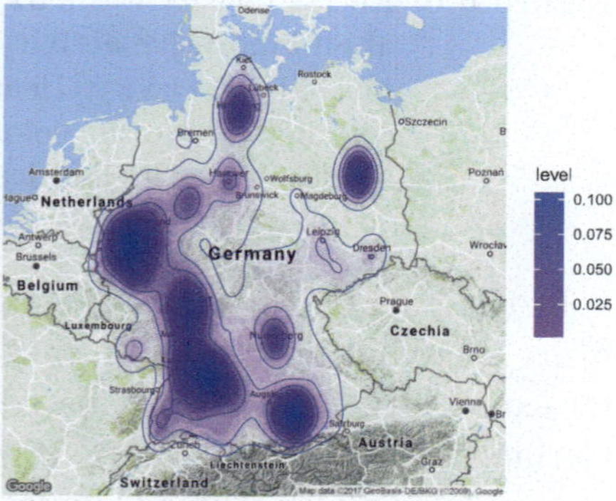

(d) AM technologies in 2005.

Figure 6.5: Kernel density estimation heat maps: 2000, 2005. Comparison of all innovative activity to additive manufacturing related innovative activity. Heat maps consist of contour levels and coloring, where the colors fade, density decreases. Darker shades depict higher densities.

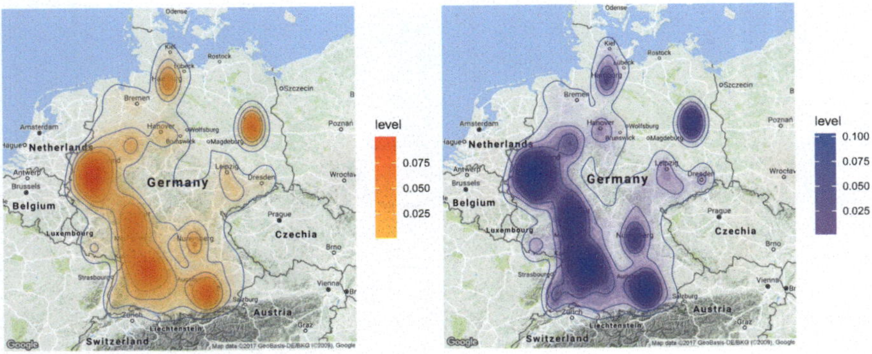

(a) All technologies in 2010.

(b) AM technologies in 2010.

Figure 6.6: Kernel density estimation heat maps: 2010. Comparison of all innovative activity to additive manufacturing related innovative activity. Heat maps consist of contour levels and coloring, where the colors fade, density decreases. Darker shades depict higher densities.

In general, the high density values could be explained by major firms contributing to the overall amount of patents. In Wolfsburg for example Volkswagen is located, which is a major innovator in the German automotive industry. Stuttgart is headquarter not only of automobile manufacturer Daimler, but it is also the center of Baden-Württemberg, which is one of the most innovative federal states of Germany. Munich is also another center of the prospering innovative south. These dense regions close to another can explain this axis of innovation activity in Germany residing in the western areas of the south. Also, the hotspots seem to locate in areas of high population density, mainly in major cities. Apart from the metropolis regions not much activity is recorded. The Ruhr area seems to be the major hotspot of innovation activity in Germany, which could be explained by its unique agglomeration structure, not only because of the region being one of the most densely populated in Germany, but also because of the many innovative firms locating there.

In the following years, Wolfsburg grows first to another hotspot, only to vanish almost completely by 2014. Yet, in 2016, this region is still visible, although it is not a very dense hotspot anymore. Berlin and Hamburg do not play major roles anymore. The main activity most constantly happens in the Ruhr area and in Munich, where the hotspots remain for the whole timeframe. Their density increases, up to values of 0.1 (Ruhr area) and 0.05 (Munich), and from 2008 on the density varies a little bit more towards the surrounding regions. The Ruhr area is a region with high density at the beginning of the 21th century, and it keeps its importance throughout the timeframe. Still, towards the more recent years, its density decreases, but not the geographical extent of its influence. This speaks for constantly evenly distributed patent publications, but fewer publications in total.

Contrariwise, Nuremberg and its surrounding region increase in density up until 2016, where the region reaches its maximum density of 0.03 in the timeframe observed. This is a development which especially accelerates in 2015 and 2016. By far the most interesting changes of density levels happen in the center of Germany, where the density values are rather low. This area is surrounded by small hotspots in Leipzig and Dresden, as well as in Hanover and Magdeburg. Besides the north eastern part of Germany, there seems to be a cold spot with few to no innovation activity happening. The level around Frankfurt (Main)-Stuttgart-Mannheim stays constant for the timeframe investigated. Only on the borders of the levels – depicted in the figures as contour lines – smaller changes are exhibiting variability in innovative activity's outreach, but the region proves to be a constant source of innovation.

In 2016, the heat map does not diverge so much from the past years' hotspot distribution (compare figure 6.7a). The Ruhr area is the strongest hotspot of innovation activity in Germany. Its density lies around 0.075, which is not the highest in the area's history, but the highest density for Germany in this year. Following in density level are Stuttgart and Frankfurt (Main), Berlin, and Mannheim. Almost

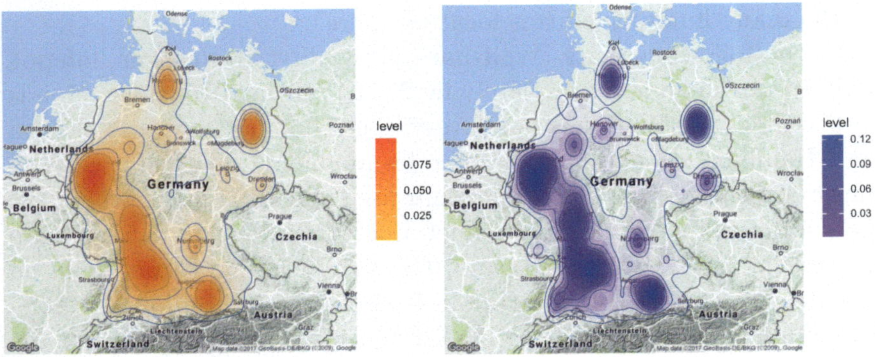

(a) All innovations. **(b)** Additive manufacturing.

Figure 6.7: Kernel density estimation heat maps for 2016. Darker shades illustrate higher density.

on an equal level are Munich and Hamburg. In general, the 2016 heat map shows an increased decentralization of innovative activity, compared to the years before. Though this could be the result of new types of innovation being able to be developed apart from big cities (more dispersed in the country), it could also be a manifestation of the general decrease in patents published and therefore in reduced innovation activity.

When comparing the situation independent of technology fields to the situation of AM related innovation, a similar, but by no means equal heat mapping structure emerges. Mainly, the density in total is higher. The levels of the contours relating the regions to another are more defined, therefore more concentrated and restricted to fewer regions. The number of defined hotspots is mostly equal, the regions favored in the prior description of general innovation activity again seem to be hotspots. Nevertheless, the distribution among involved regions is higher. As with all technologies, the Ruhr area is also the main hotspot of AM technology related innovation activity, and its impact is even bigger as density values are higher (around 0.12). The other main hotspots near Munich, Stuttgart, Berlin, and Frankfurt (Main) are also present in the heat map and on a similar density level, although their density does not reach the values of the greater Ruhr area. Still, the density level seems to reach out in the direction of the south west of Germany, towards the Lake Constance, and regions west of this area.

The main differences compared to the distribution of all innovative activity are the stronger pronunciation of hotspots, the all in all higher density that is restricted to fewer more defined regions. There is a certain lack of AM innovative activity in the north of Germany (west of Bremen) and in the center of Germany. The relation of Bielefeld and Hanover is different, as Bielefeld seems to be more relevant to AM than for innovation in general, which applies also to Hanover. Berlin and Munich are bigger hotspots, as well as Nuremberg. The density level of Frankfurt (Main) spreads more north towards Gießen and less towards Würzburg. On the axis from Frankfurt (Main) towards Stuttgart, Mannheim seems to be only of little importance, as the density level narrows onto the city, illustrating a lessened impact for innovation (compared to the ends of said axis). For 2016, the pattern observed for AM is less smooth than that for technologies in general. Whereas for all technologies a relatively evenly distributed innovation activity shows, this does not apply to AM, which seems more imbalanced. The influence of the Ruhr area southwards to Bonn is stronger, as the high innovation activity level extends in that direction. Freiburg (Breisgau) seems to be an important hotspot for AM, while that does not apply to all innovation per se.

All in all, the density of AM technologies is higher, but more distinctly patterned considering the regional hotspots. As with all technologies, in 2016 the AM map also shows a relatively decentralized pattern (compare figure 6.7b) and seems more irregular compared to earlier years. Still, the hotspots are located in the Ruhr area, and also Stuttgart and Munich persist. Nevertheless, innovation activity seems to confirm its allocation in the south west of Germany, leaving the east and north of Germany behind. This applies to innovative activity in all technologies, but especially to activities in AM, where

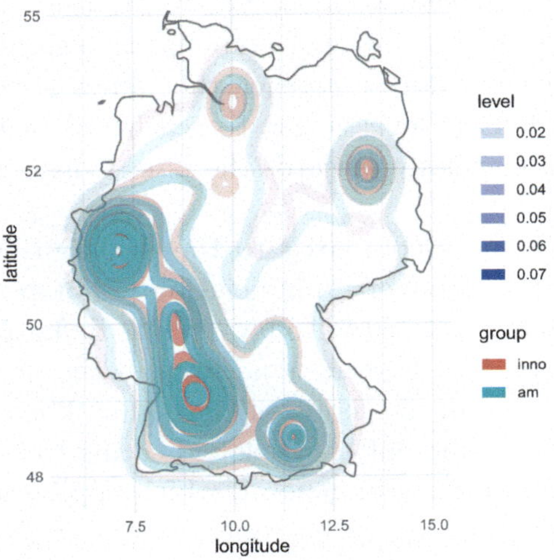

Figure 6.8: Overlay of kernel density estimation heat maps. The contour plots show the levels of all innovation (*inno*, darker lines) and innovation in additive manufacturing (*am*, lighter lines) in comparison for 2016. The contours show the extent of the distribution of activity, the lines fade out where density decreases.

the distribution is more defined, and regions can be determined more precisely.

In figure 6.8 the densities for all technologies and AM technologies are overlaid on a single map. AM innovations are illustrated by the darker contours, all innovation are the lighter contours below. The increasing transparency towards the outer contour lines shows the decreasing density levels. Where the density is highest, the contours are most saturated. The deviation of the density allocations of the two types of innovative activity is now easy to compare and supports the preceding remarks for figure 6.7. The distribution of AM innovations seems more restricted and locally restrained, albeit not much. It does not reach as far north towards the coastal region of the North Sea compared to innovation in general. There is no hotspot in Wolfsburg, Berlin is more important, and the central region of Germany is not as strongly covered. The axis from Stuttgart to Frankfurt (Main) is more important, as is the Ruhr area. Munich and the south eastern border of Germany are not as relevant. All in all, the notion of a slightly stronger concentration and a less broadened spread is supported.

Although the overlay seems to be relatively balanced, and both samples (all technologies and AM) appear relatively similar, this is not the case, as AM innovative activity is effectively a subset of all innovative activity. The heat maps with the contours and the contour plot of figure 6.8 have to be understood as a two-dimensional illustration of a three-dimensional relation. The hotspots in the heat maps are like the tops of a mountain, the contours function like geographical contours that symbolize different heights, which decrease towards the outer edges. Thus, the AM innovation has another distribution of hotspots not only because of the spatial location (latitude, longitude) but also because of other, different heights. Furthermore, the number of patents underlying the density calculation is smaller than those for all innovations, because of its subset-character.

When adjusting the bandwidths around the automatically chosen value (compare chapter 6.1 for detailed formal considerations in choosing this parameter, and e.g. Silverman (1986, pp. 44-47)), further characteristics of the density of innovative activity get visible in the heat maps (compare figure 6.9). For both the complete sample of all technologies and for the subset in AM technologies bandwidth parameters of 0.4, 0.75, and 1.5 are calculated. The values below 1 produce a more detailed map, whereas the latter value of 1.5 displays more cohesive levels.

Regarding all technologies, the smaller bandwidths allow a more precise localization as the regional centers where the densities are highest are discernible more clearly. Yet, this does not deliver new insights, as the heat map with an automatically generated bandwidth already results in relatively defined hotspots. The increased bandwidth of 1.5 depicts the higher level density relation. Here, the importance of the south and the west of Germany is the main proposition. Besides, the axis from the Ruhr area over Bielefeld, Hanover up until Wolfsburg poses a balancing counterpoint. The north and east of Germany still occupy no part on the innovation heat map.

Switching to AM technologies, the insights of the reduced bandwidth parameters are larger. The highest density in AM innovations in the Ruhr area occurs in Düsseldorf. A small hotspot also lies in Detmold, as well as the concentration of patenting activity points to Aalen to the east of Stuttgart. Another small region where AM innovation activity locates is Jena in the center of Germany, east of Erfurt, as well as a hotspot in Friedrichshafen at the Lake Constance appears on the map (compare figure 6.9e). Looking at the heat map with the highest bandwidth parameter, the south west of Germany is again the center of innovation of the whole country. As a contrast to all technologies, AM technology activity seems to stay even more in the south and does not reach up to Nuremberg that much. Also, the axis Ruhr area-Wolfsburg is separated, as the Ruhr area is forming a distinct hub. Moreover, Hamburg seems to play a more important role for AM than for technologies in general.

All in all, the picture drawn by the KDEs supports the view about the innovation landscape presented in section 4.4.

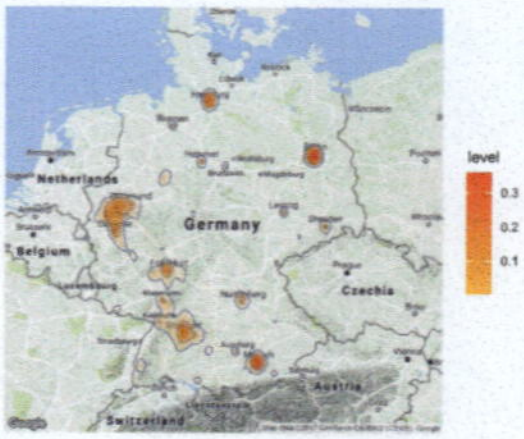

(a) All technologies, bandwidth 0.4.

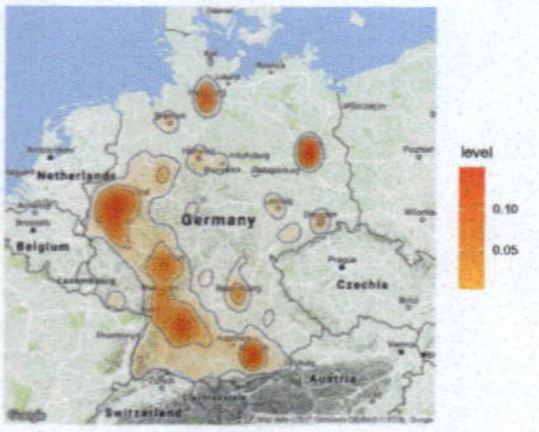

(b) All technologies, bandwidth 0.75.

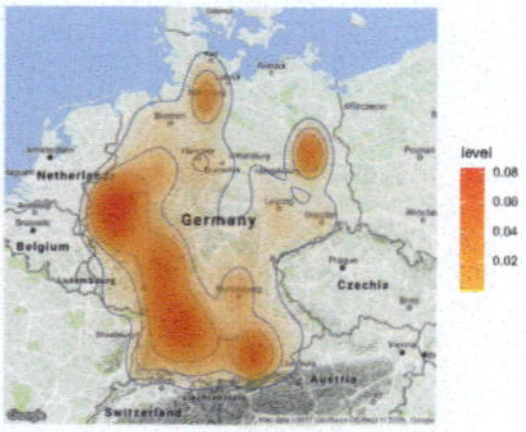

(c) All technologies, bandwidth 1.5.

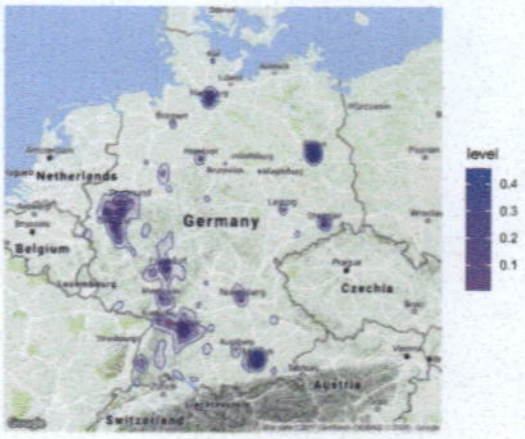

(d) AM technologies, bandwidth 0.4.

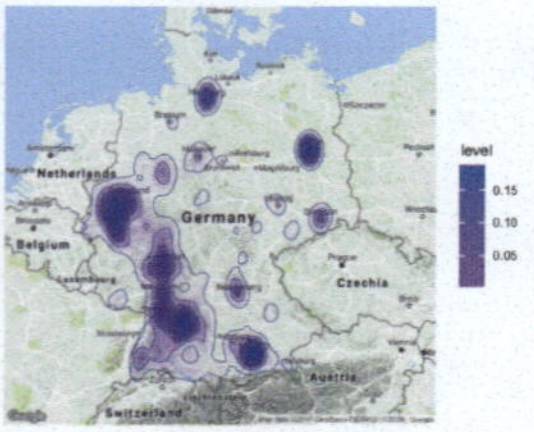

(e) AM technologies, bandwidth 0.75.

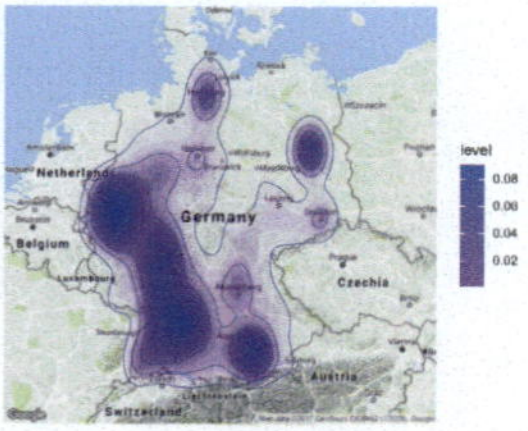

(f) AM technologies, bandwidth 1.5.

Figure 6.9: Kernel density estimation heat maps: bandwidth adaptions. For both all innovations and for additive manufacturing, different bandwidths lead to different heat maps. Darker shades illustrate higher densities. Increased bandwidth leads to smoother densities and to decreased distinctions.

7 Discussion and Conclusion

In this paper, innovative activity derived from patent publications is investigated. Innovative activity in all technologies is compared to activity in the highly innovative field of AM (3D printing). The aim is to discover different locational hotspots for this specific technology. This way it can be shown that depending on the type of innovation, other parameters may define their location and regional influence. Reasons for innovation therefore are distinct, as well as resources and importance of innovation for the region.

Comparing the allocations of innovative activity to the allocation of socio-economic indicators (compare figure 4.1), these explanations can be supported. The values for these exemplary economic indicators are from 2014. For innovation activity, patent publications data are from 2016. This is fitting, as it is assumed that the process of patenting normally takes some time. In the dataset used the major number of patents took two years from application to publication. Based on the explaining factors for this behavior, it seems to be justified that the values for e.g. economic indicators influence the innovative activity via the patents published in 2016.

Parallels between the innovation activity and the occurrence of high values in productivity (figure 4.1a), effective labor and investment can be drawn on a descriptive level. In districts where effective labor and consequently productivity are high, innovation activity measured by patents also seems to be high. The same applies for investment, where regions with high spending correspond to regions where inno-

I. Rhoden, *Space and Time in German Innovative Activity*,
https://doi.org/10.1007/978-3-658-28600-2_7

vation activities are also increased. But these considerations are not straightforward, as the direction of the effects of these innovation determining factors seems dichotomous. This can be seen as there exist regions with high values in productivity, knowledge intensity, and investment, where no innovation hotspots can be found. Nevertheless, as these factors support growth, their connection to innovation cannot be neglected and has to be analyzed further.

Mainly, the distribution of innovative activities in AM technologies (as a measure for high-tech innovations) diverges from the allocation of all technology activity. It is therefore possible that differing technology or industry fields need different conditions in their development. As innovation is a major contributor to growth, depending on which goals are to be reached, it can make sense to structure support for innovation for ultimately increasing economic growth. Concluding, the innovation activity exhibited in the field of AM is harbored more in the south and the Ruhr area. This portrays a more separated position for AM in innovative activity. Nevertheless, the main centers of innovation are also the centers of AM activity, although these two should not be treated as equal.

Concerning innovation promoting policy measures, under the premise that innovation impacts economic growth favorably, then if the effect of those means is to be maximized, high-tech innovations should be the focus. As the allocation of innovations in Germany differs slightly for high-tech innovations, this should be kept in mind when designing or administering policies.

Further possibilities for investigation concern the determinants of these different regional allocations of innovation activity. Another option is the analysis of effects in the development of AM technology. As the technology is relatively old with early technology-defining patents in the 1980's, it is possible to examine the partly recent events of the expiration of key technology patents and check if the expiration leads to a significant increase in (for instance) new patents. Based on the kernel density estimates and the general number of innovation activity in the period of 2000-2016, this is at the moment not visible via these methods. Either another approach is needed, or the expiration of key patents is still too recent. The latter reason seems feasible as the average time until a patent is published based on its registration, takes about two years. The effects could therefore show in a few years at most.

Part II

Regional Determinants of Innovative Activity – Geoadditive Modeling of Diverging Allocations

8 Introduction

The relevance of innovation for economic growth allows a multitude of different research on this topic. For adapting to the future, it is undeniable that innovation is the main driver for the globalized digitalization. Patents as innovation indicator are a readily available measure and thus often cited for modeling the innovation situation and dynamics.

Analyzing the innovation activity with respect to the underlying effects of covariates is the aim of this paper. Theoretically based determinants of innovative activity are examined to show which factor impacts innovation how much, and where exactly. With the help of a geoadditive model the reasons for the spatial clustering of innovation shall be explained.

The geoadditive model further allows not only to incorporate a spatial effect, but moreover the composition of nonparametric covariates together with linear regressors. This method is established and frequently used, for instance in scientific research concerning environmental topics (e.g. Bocci, Caporali, and Petrucci (2012)), medical questions or survival models (e.g. Kneib and Fahrmeir (2007)), agricultural or environmental issues (e.g. Cafarelli and Castrignanò (2011)), and other analyses.

As the concept is so flexible, it can be applied to a variety of problems. In regional innovation economics, this approach seems to be less common. In this paper, the impact of several theoretically relevant determinants of innovative activity is examined. This is executed by estimating a geoadditive semiparametric model with all determinants. The resulting effects are, on the one hand, presented generally in func-

I. Rhoden, *Space and Time in German Innovative Activity*,
https://doi.org/10.1007/978-3-658-28600-2_8

tion plots and, on the other hand, illustrated specifically regionally by mapping the effect strength onto the corresponding German administrative districts. This way, the contribution of each determinant can be observed in magnitude and with respect to each German district. Implications can consequently be made very precisely with regard to each location.

The paper is further structured as follows: The ninth chapter relates patents to innovation and illustrates the way patents can be used as an indicator of innovative activity. Moreover, the German economy is presented as the area of investigation. The importance of considering patents as a spatially related variable is also explained. In chapter 10, the theoretic implications of the predictors of the following analyses are delineated. All used covariates are explained by theory, and consequently their expected behavior within the estimation of the final geoadditive model is stated. In the following chapter, first an OLS model is estimated and analyzed as a starting point of more advanced analyses. Moreover, after considering the Moran I statistic, the method of geoadditive modeling is introduced. This is to account for spatial relations of the dependent variable and allows additionally to model the impact of covariates parametrically, as well as including nonparametric regressors. The estimates are brought into context and compared to their initial expected behavior. A short conclusion ends this paper.

For purpose of clarification, a *region* in the context of this paper is used throughout interchangeably with the concept of German administrative districts, meaning *Landkreise* and *kreisfreie Städte* on NUTS-3 level. Furthermore, the main investigation concept of the paper is *innovative activity*, which will also be referred to as innovation, innovation activity and is explicitly measured by the count of applicants of published patents.

9 Patents and Innovation

Innovation is the main driver of economic growth (Cooke et al. 2013, p. 3). It is recommended to be considered as a broad concept to account for all types of innovation and all processes related to its development (OECD 2005). Following the neoclassical view of Solow (1956), innovation is part of the system which allows entities to catch up to each other in the growth process. Nevertheless, innovation has accordingly not only an impact for developing countries or regions, but also for developed entities. (Fagerberg, Srholec, and Verspagen 2010, p. 835)

Other strands of literature follow the view of Schumpeter (1934) and proclaim technological innovation in a more endogenous way. Convergence does not happen accidentally but is the result of great exertion. (Ames and Rosenberg 1963)

For Schumpeter, technological progress is the sufficient condition for achieving productivity growth and therefore long-run economic growth. Improvement by technological progress uses knowledge in different forms, which can be combined and transformed to create new products or processes. Additionally, existing goods or services can be altered and improved. This view follows the neo-Schumpeterian approach for innovation. (Wolfe and Vatne 2011, p. 45)

Relying further on Schumpeter, the roots of innovation in firms in markets is also mentioned by the OECD (2005). Firms innovate for keeping up with the development and movement of the market. They therefore are intrinsically motivated to stay competitive and accelerate economic growth as a consequence (OECD 2005, pp. 28-29). The motivator of innovation can be increased demand, or scoring a finan-

I. Rhoden, *Space and Time in German Innovative Activity*,
https://doi.org/10.1007/978-3-658-28600-2_9

cial advantage compared to a competitor. Innovation, firms, markets, and economic growth thus are strongly interrelated and influence each other manifold.

Patents as an indicator of innovation have a long tradition. They are often criticized, but also supported, because the availability of data is unparalleled in its amount and accessibility. An overview about the advantages and consequences of patents as an indicator is proposed e.g. by Griliches (1998). Furthermore, in the German law for patents it is defined that for registering a patent, an invention has to be new, developed by inventive activity and imply a future commercial usability (PatG 1936, §1). The registration of a patent in Germany is binding for 20 years. This protection acts as spatiotemporal monopoly for the usage of the registered matter. The implied knowledge gain by publication itself can also foster incentives for future R+D. The German Patent and Trade Mark Office also stresses the ability of the patent to strengthen firms for global competition and their provision of a positive locational factor. Also, patents can increase the chances of a firm for new cooperation or financial investments. Knowledge transfer via technology transfer can consequently promote general economic growth. (DPMA 2018)

In this paper, the implied commercial use of the patent classifies what is important for using the patent as innovation indicator (e.g. Kürtössy 2004; Smith 1992, p. 386).

9.1 Germany's Economy and the Innovation Sector

Up until 2016, the German economy increased growth in GDP onto 1.9%. However, over the prior three years growth did not rise much. After GDP growth was at a historical low with almost -6% in 2009, resulting from the global economic crisis, the economy recovered immediately in the following year with a value of over 4.1% in GDP growth. Since 2012, a trend towards increasing growth can be observed, although it only adds up to about 0.3%. Anyhow, labor productivity has decreased slightly in the last years, amounting to 0.6% in 2016 compared to 2015 with 0.8%. Gross wages and the share of wages of national income increased, or respectively remained constant. (Statistisches Bundesamt 2018a)

Considering Germany's position within the innovation context, the European Union's EIS (and RIS) proclaim Germany as one of the innovation leaders in Europe, next to Scandinavian countries and the United Kingdom (EC 2016b, p. 17). According to these reports, Germany exhibits above average performance in the fields of innovators and firm investments, both of which are important for fostering growth through innovation. This is although the innovation index has dropped in recent years relative to the EU average, but remains 21% above the other EU members. (EC 2016a, p. 51)

Subdividing these statistics and looking at the regions within Germany, the south performs especially well (EC 2016b, p. 16). To be considered as innovation leader, a high number of patents have to be published, which are the result of extensive research and innovative efforts. Mostly, patents in key enabling technologies, e.g. in advanced manufacturing, are reflected here (Berger et al. 2017, p. 10). Patent applications registered at the European Patent Office or the World Intellectual Property Organization have world market relevance and have risen by 9% in the timeframe from 2000-2013. Onto each million inhabitants in Germany falls the number of 372 published patents, whereas the European average amounts to only 154 and the United States of America account for 216 (BMBF 2017, p. 14). Furthermore, the revealed technology average-index by the RIS states the positive specialization of Germany for several technology fields and classifies Germany as innovation leader. Here, not only the southern regions stand out, but also regions in e.g. North Rhine-Westphalia. (EC 2016b, pp. 23-25)

The German government with its High-Tech-Strategy (BMBF 2017, p. 14) aims to support these favorable developments by recognizing the importance of innovative contributions to the economy in Germany. Investment in R+D accounted for 3% of GDP in 2015, which marks a new peak. Company investment thus increased by 10% compared to 2014 and compared to 2005 it even expanded by 60%. As new paradigm, R+D investment shall now always amount to at least 3% of GDP per year, which is a goal adapted from the European Strategy 2020 by the German Federal Ministry of Education and Research. (BMBF 2017, pp. 12-13))

Generally, these and further measures delineated in the High-Tech-Strategy and its European prequel shall encourage sustainability, security and efficiency. These efforts also result ultimately in innovation. The governmental initiative is asserted in the *Innovation Atlas* issued by Prognos (Berger et al. 2017).

Competition among the innovators on the global market is the main concern, and this is furthermore where the connection to neo-Schumpeterian approaches can be found. Accelerating competition can only be mastered by increased innovative activity. To allow a cohesive growth, as the EU stipulates it, all regions shall have equal opportunities. Germany therefore has to strengthen structurally disadvantaged regions as well as prospering districts, if the position as innovation leader shall be retained. Here, not only the government, but also the federal ministries and regional administrative districts are challenged. (Berger et al. 2017, p. 56)

In figure 9.1 it is apparent that although the distribution of values among the districts is very diverse, a clear separation between eastern and western districts is still prominent for some indicators. Thus, the German reunion of 1990 is still noticeable. However, depending on the indicator used, the distribution is more or less equal. A general separation of east and west Germany is therefore not per se present.

Regarding innovation measured by patent publications, clear emphasis is placed onto the south and west of the country. Largely, the positive impression of German innovative activity declared by governmental agencies and the EU is not reflected in every federal state or administrative district. There exists a visible incline of innovative activity from the north towards the south, and from the east towards the west, and from the metropolises towards the periphery. Innovation in Germany seems to develop mostly in the automotive industry, which is concentrated in few cities or regions and these are possibly

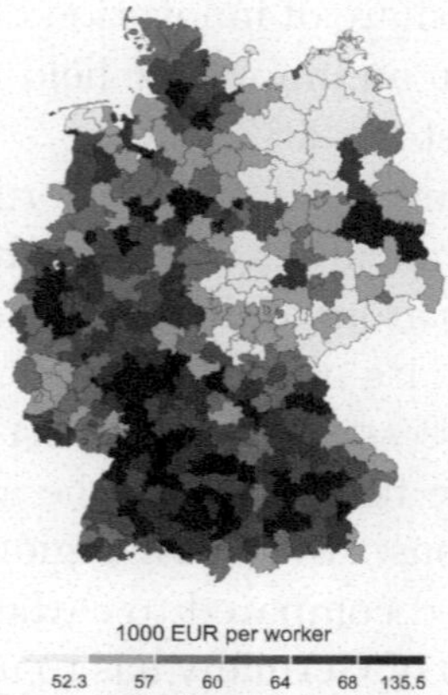

(a) Spatial distribution of productivity.

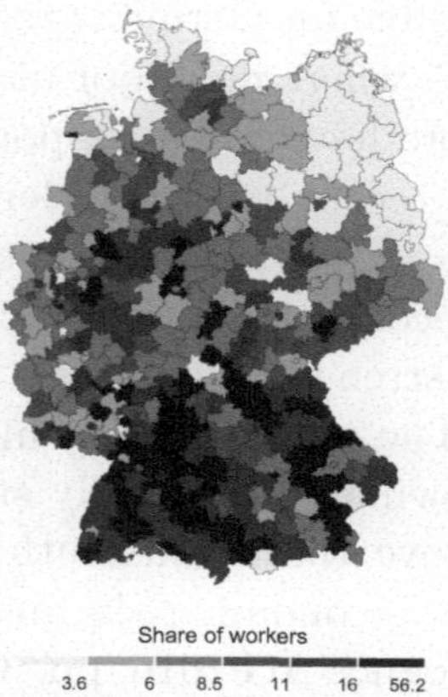

(b) Spatial distribution of knowledge intensity.

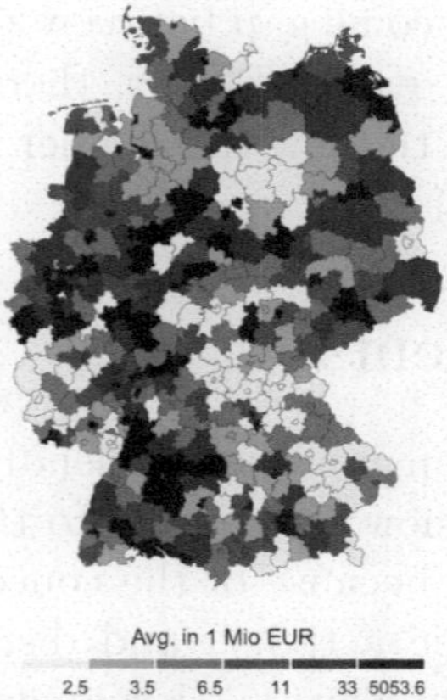

(c) Spatial distribution of R+D funding.

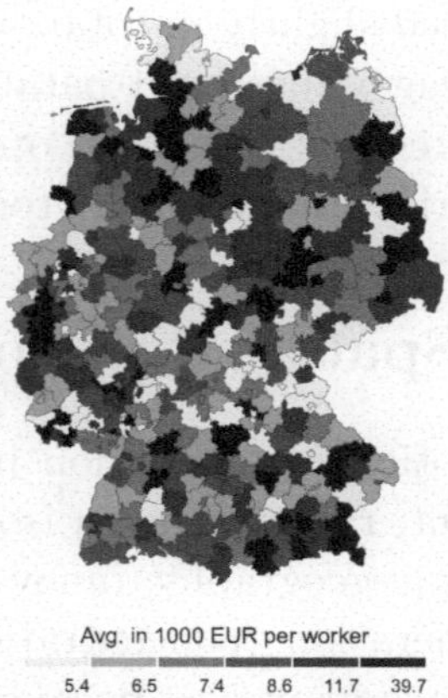

(d) Spatial distribution of investment.

Figure 9.1: Exemplary innovation determinants for 2014. These determinants are used (among others) as covariates in the analyses. Here, the dispersion of the values across Germany can be observed.

responsible for Germany reaching the 3% share of innovation of GDP. Regions where no major industry leader in an innovative field resides therefore have to be supported. (Berger et al. 2017)

In a recent ranking, German regions are positioned according to criteria of sustainable digitalization and an indicator of micro- and macroeconomic figures. Included are indicators of digitalization, economic strength, dynamics, labor market data as well as other covariates. The result shows which regions possess the best opportunities for growing economically successful in the future. Here, the authors can prove the north-south slope of regions. Southern regions face only few economic risks and even improved compared to earlier studies (Prognos AG 2016, pp. 3-6). The north of Germany has to manage rather decreasing possibilities to keep up with the accelerated development of today's digitalization. However, wealth in Germany also increased slightly in total, although the income gap between low and high wages increased parallel. To put it exaggeratedly, there exist either regions with good opportunities or those with a higher future-based risk projection. (Prognos AG 2016)

9.2 Spatial Relations of Patents

The notion of innovation happening in an innovation-friendly environment, rather than in isolation, is not new. According to the new economic geography, innovation happens because of the concepts of agglomeration (concentration of economic activity) and dispersion (market advantages because of market influence). (Krugman 1990, p. 484)

Often, innovation concentrates in clusters of economic activity because of positive scale economies in production processes (Marshall 1890). In the field of localization and urbanization effects, either mass production effects by centralization can be achieved, or consumers can be served better by diversified suppliers in a competitive environment. (Krugman 1990)

Depending on the industry, its age in the industry life-cycle and the degree and effect of tacit knowledge, the concentration of innovative activity is different (Feldman and Audretsch 1999). Moreover, innovation tends to concentrate where knowledge is situated. Knowledge spillovers happen mostly locally and they decline with increased distance from their place of origin. Also, they spread out with time. (Feldman and Audretsch 1996; Jaffe, Trajtenberg, and Henderson 1993) Moreover, innovation is not distributed spatially evenly, as it clusters in specific areas (Acs, Anselin, and Varga 2002). The distinctiveness of the localization of innovative activity is considerable and especially salient between urban and peripheral regions. As Feldman finds, innovation differs according to economic distinctions and behaves similarly. (Feldman and Kogler 2010, p. 384)

This characteristic of innovative activity – to follow along spatial conditions – is also explained in the economic geography of innovation and the behavior of innovation to spill over is extensively analyzed (compare e.g. Ratana (2007)). As Marshall (1890) established, industries which are related to another, cooperation on the market and specialized labor are the main reasons for the concentration of innovation. Also, intangible externalities in knowledge transfer realized by exchanging tacit knowledge are the major factor for clustering and increasing knowledge bases (Maskell and Malmberg 1999, p. 171). This is supported by the inherited property of tacit knowledge to only thrive via short distance communication (Gertler 2003). Conversely, in recent research a reduced importance for the local dimension of knowledge has been stressed. It is professed that because of the digitalization and advanced technologies locality is not as relevant to the transmission of knowledge anymore. Thus, innovation would not only necessarily succeed that much in clusters. As Morgan (2004, p. 4) explains, time, on the one hand, can replace the local component in the innovation equation, because of information being on hand always and everywhere. On the other hand, it is illustrated that knowledge is too diverse to be independent from space at all times. Information and therefore knowledge can be uncoupled from space, but the comprehension of it cannot. Again, tacit knowledge is not fungible over all digital communication channels. (Morgan 2004, pp. 3-7)

Nevertheless, as innovation is fostered by the digitalization and its possibilities, it still does need an analog transfer of ideas (Feldman and Kogler 2010, p. 393). As Storper (1997) puts it, the impact of innovation does not only depend on dispersion, but also on diffusion. The empirical evidence on the matter of local ties of innovation is also ambiguous (for an overview see e.g. Morgan (2004)). (Morgan 2004, p. 17)

10 Theoretical Foundations

10.1 Covariate Theory

As the positive contribution of innovation to regional economic growth is unquestioned, it can thus be seen as a key to achieving economic growth and therefore welfare (Acs, Anselin, and Varga 2002, p. 1069). Innovation itself is involved in almost every economic activity (Bell and Pavitt 1993; Kline and Rosenberg 1986) and can be understood in a very broad sense of its actual meaning (Fagerberg, Srholec, and Verspagen 2010) . Determining what innovation is influenced by in the first place can be done via an analysis where publicly available covariates are regressed onto the dependent variable. This then illustrates what controls innovation activity. Another possibility is to obtain information about innovative activity by surveying firms about their R+D output (and the revenue thereof) and their inputs in R+D (mainly their organizational structure, resources, and institutional arrangements). A short general overview can be found in Fagerberg, Srholec, and Verspagen (2010, p. 846). Not all variables are observable either way, so in this paper only a curated selection is employed.

To delineate further what influences innovation itself, several factors are reviewed to have an impact. Indicators for innovation stem from early ideas of technological convergence processes in the tradition of Solow's (1956) neoclassical model and the already mentioned

I. Rhoden, *Space and Time in German Innovative Activity*,
https://doi.org/10.1007/978-3-658-28600-2_10

Schumpeterian (1934) approaches. Here, special exertion is necessary, along with altered organizational and institutional circumstances, to cultivate innovation in the widest sense (Ames and Rosenberg 1963). In catching up on technological progress in general, it is necessary to adopt what the technology is made of. This means if technology is labor intensive, increased labor and possibly expedited employment of specialists can increase advances in technology, and therefore innovation. (Gerschenkron 1962, p. 7)

Another relevant concept is by Abramovitz (1986), who stresses the social component of innovative output. Here, competence of labor through education, managerial experience, capable financial institutions and resources, honesty and trust as well as macroeconomic stability are the prevailing aspects. Related are concepts of adaptivity of new knowledge, which are presented by Cohen and Levinthal (1990). Firms where innovation happens have to be able to assimilate knowledge in the form of new ideas and concepts and utilize it. For this to occur an existing stock of knowledge has to be expanded by learning. All this is mostly realized by human capital, which is how this aspect will be measured in this analysis. Human capital here will be indicated by the share of workers in knowledge intensive industries (mostly high-tech industries like pharmaceuticals, chemical industry, electronics, automotive, or data processing). Also taking effect in this is the ability of firms to invest in R+D and to supply the technological endowments to realize innovations. To account for this possible effect, firm investment is incorporated into the model.

Resources have to be used efficiently. Not only does this apply to domestic relations of firms, but also to international activity, which is seen as an indicator of successful efficient managing of resources. These considerations will therefore be proxied by the domestic and foreign turnover of firms. (Lall 1992)

A further important factor is the size of the firm, as smaller firms are often impeded to innovate as the bureaucratization and the costs of patenting can hinder creativity (Ahuja, Lampert, and Tandon 2008). Moreover, market structure seems to also have an influence, as increased market power allows to invest more into R+D, which is shown by Blundell, Griffith, and Reenen (1999). Both values can be approached by substituting a firm's turnover, as it is assumed that bigger firms generate more turnover. Moreover, firm size is also important for e.g. Kim, Kim, and Flacher (2012), or Sanyal and Cohen (2009). Another measure used here is the share of Small and Middle Enterprises (SME) related to the number of all types of enterprises, where a negative effect for SME regarding innovation is expected (Löfqvist 2012; Pantano 2014).

Also correlated to innovative activity is the general economic situation, as innovation leads to growth and in a way reflects economic development (Fagerberg, Srholec, and Verspagen 2010, p. 849). As a variation, not GDP, but productivity measured as GDP per worker is used here, to check for economic concentration effects.

To account for general agglomeration effects, population density is used and expected to act in favor of innovation. This is based on Krugman's considerations for geographical relations of economic activity. It is assumed that firms locate where labor is available, and that labor thus locates where jobs are and money can be spent. Firms also seek these agglomerations, for instance in favoring proximity to market demand. (Fujita, Krugman, and Venables 1999)

Further research in determining the conditions for the development of innovation (in a wider sense) is for example presented by Tavassoli (2015) who stresses the importance of firm engagement in international relations, as this openness seems to be a major factor in delineating a firm's propensity to innovate.

The OECD (2005), as well as Blanchard et al. (2012), think that skilled labor is as important as an unsaturated market. Further proponents for a positive influence of human capital are, among others, Cuerva, Triguero-Cano, and Corcoles (2014), who determine this effect only for so called non-green innovations.

Additional determinants are investigated by Horbach (2008), who separates possible factors into supply and demand side effects. Again, technological capabilities and market structure are important. These can be covered by the covariates already mentioned. Additionally, expected demand is also taken into account, which is expressed in this analysis by an approximate measure for market potential.

For their analysis, Divisekera and Nguyen (2018) divide impact factors into innovation inputs (among others, human capital and funding) and institutional factors. Here, especially the role of the industry and its characteristics are mentioned, as the authors investigate a case for the tourism sector. In deriving this, the role and share of the industry in Germany is used as a proxy for the industrial structure in the analysis of this paper, as it is assumed that most innovation is emitted by the secondary sector. All factors imply a positive effect onto innovation activity.

As incentivized by the government supporting innovation, funding for firms in structurally weaker regions in Germany is included in the analysis. An important goal for the government is supporting growth through several policies via different channels. This is in addition to EU funding. Among the German panoply of instruments for funding is the GRW policy (Die Bundesregierung 1969), which is eligible for firms in structurally disadvantaged regions. This way, growth in the long-run shall be promoted. Especially the GRW as a regional policy can interfere in possibly harming market outcomes and adjust welfare to reach a more equalized level. Societal needs and spatial disadvantages in lacking regions can thus be counterbalanced. (Eckey 2008, p. 169)

Including the GRW in the model for estimating innovation makes sense, as the result of funding innovation and knowledge can increase output and moreover, marginal productivity of input factors (Eckey 2008, p. 220). Thus, a positive effect is expected, although funding is only eligible in economically deprived regions, which could counteract innovative activity.

Further funding by the Federal Ministry of Education and Research is also seen to be responsible for increasing innovation as the ministry intends to do so via allocating the money. The funds used here in the analyses comprise average funding per year allocated, in million EUR and contain funded projects of R+D relevant education, public services, technology and innovation itself. Also included are university-related projects and knowledge-generating and interdisciplinary fundamental research. The money is by several sponsors, among them German Federal Ministries of Education and Research, of Economic Affairs and Energy, for the Environment, Nature Conservation and Nuclear Safety, of Transport and Digital Infrastructure, of Food and Agriculture, and the Federal Ministry of Justice and Consumer Protection. (Die Bundesregierung 2019; BMBF 2017)

10.2 Hypotheses

To sum up the preceding chapter, the following hypotheses with their corresponding effect onto innovative activity can be constructed:

- Industry is expected to have a positive impact.
- Knowledge intensity is expected to have a positive impact.
- Policy funding is expected to have a positive impact.
- Investment is expected to have a positive impact.
- Productivity is expected to have a positive impact.
- Market potential is expected to have a positive impact.
- Openness is expected to have a positive impact.
- Agglomeration is expected to have a positive impact.
- Firm size is expected to have a positive impact.

11 Modeling

The variables used in this paper are listed in table 11.1. The data for the dependent variable innovative activity are by the German Patent and Trademark Office (DPMA 2017) and are measured as the count of patent publications per administrative district in 2016. All further data are by the German Bundesinstitut für Bau-, Stadt- und Raumforschung (Federal Institute for Research on Building, Urban Affairs and Spatial Development) (BBSR) (2018), Eurostat (2018), and by the Regional Database Germany (Statistisches Bundesamt 2018b). The covariates date from 2014, which is two years before the datum of the patent data, as it takes roughly two years until a patent is published after registration. This can be determined by comparing the date of application and publication of the patent. The unit of observation are German regions on NUTS-3 level, which yields 402 administrative districts (working with administrative borders of 2014). All data are logarithmized.

Table 11.1: Variable declaration. In this table all variables used are listed.

Shortcut	Variable	Description
		Dependent variable for 2016
innov	Innovative activity	Logarithm of the number of published patents

Table 11.1 – *Continued on the next page*

I. Rhoden, *Space and Time in German Innovative Activity*,
https://doi.org/10.1007/978-3-658-28600-2_11

Shortcut	Variable	Description
		Indices
adminid	Spatial index	Number of administrative district to identify regions, reference year: 2014
		Covariates for the year 2014
clus	High-tech clusters	Dummy for high-tech clusters supported by policies by German BMBF and BMWi
inst	R+D institutes	Dummy for non-university research organisations
grw	Policy	Logarithm of the sum of GRW funding (incl. EFRE funds), long term 2005-2014
fund	R+D funding	Logarithm of allocated (R+D) funds, mainly by the German BMBF
inv	Investment	Logarithm of average investment per worker (worker who is subject to social insurance contributions)
gdpem	Productivity	Logarithm of GDP per worker (working population)
ppot	Market potential	Logarithm of regional population potential (population per area in a radius of 100 kilometers)
ind	Industry	Logarithm of the share of workers in the industry (workers who are subject to social insurance contributions per 100 inhabitants of age 15-65)
know	Knowledge intensity	Logarithm of the share of workers (workers who are subject to social insurance contributions) in high-tech industry

Table 11.1 – *Continued on the next page*

Shortcut	Variable	Description
open	Openness	Logarithm of average foreign turnover per worker (worker who is subject to social insurance contributions)
popd	Agglomeration	Logarithm of population density (population per square kilometer)
sme	Firm size	Logarithm of share of SME, (SME: 10-249 employees per firm) 2013
turn	Firm size	Logarithm of average turnover per worker (worker who is subject to social insurance contributions)

To check for the relation of the theoretically derived predictors towards the dependent variable, two-dimensional scatter plots are analyzed. These are depicted in figure 11.1. If the scatter plot points to the relationship being seemingly linear, the corresponding model term will be linear as well. Where the relationship is rather undefined or could possibly best characterized by a nonparametric curve, this is factored in accordingly. What is still to consider is the skewed nature of patent data, although the log-transformation has counterbalanced this (see figure 11.2). The most dense concentration of the dots is largely located in the lower values of the predictor, as for example with industry share (figure 11.1h) or productivity (figure 11.1c). The relation between the index for knowledge intensity and for R+D funding seem to be upward sloping for higher innovation activity. This can also be said about almost all coefficients. Exceptions seem to be investment, turnover and the share of SME. The most different from all plots seems to be the share of SME, where the direction of the possible relation cannot be predicted in advance.

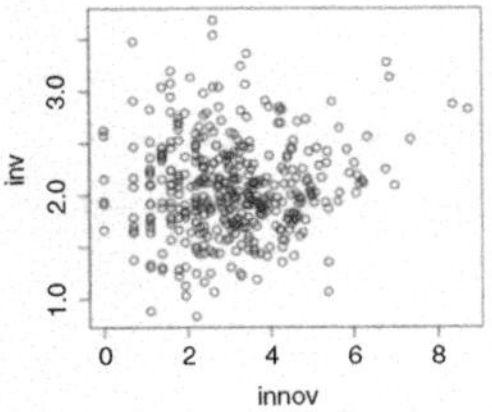

(a) Investment.

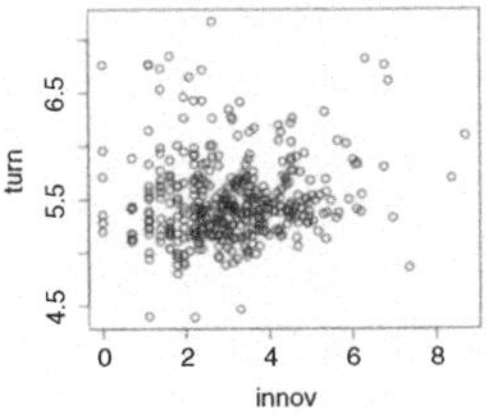

(b) Turnover.

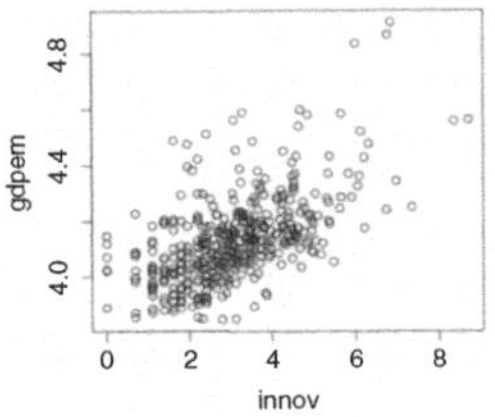

(c) Productivity.

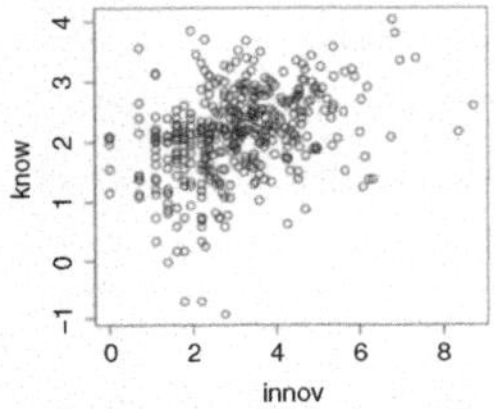

(d) Knowledge intensity.

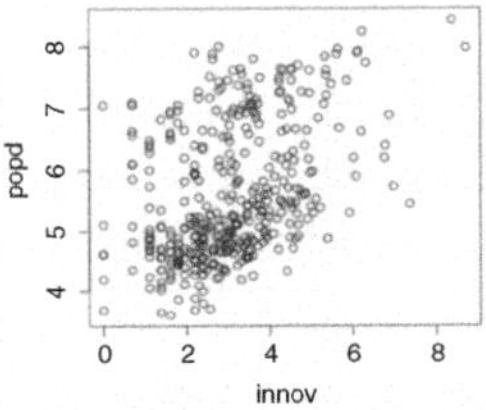

(e) Population density.

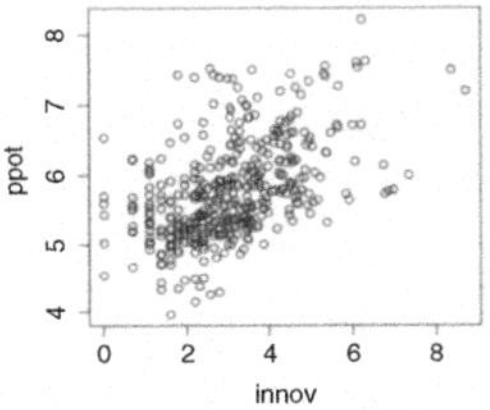

(f) Market potential.

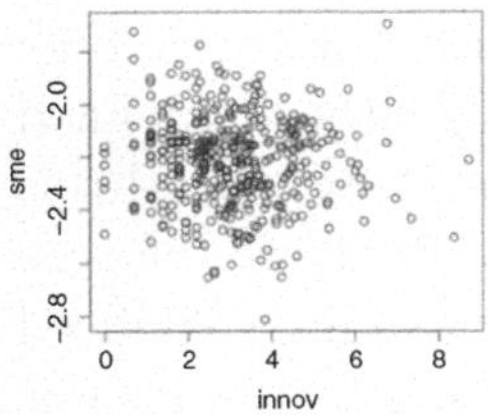

(g) Share of SMEs.

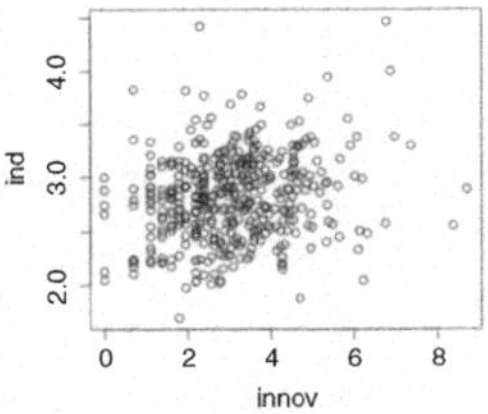

(h) Industry share.

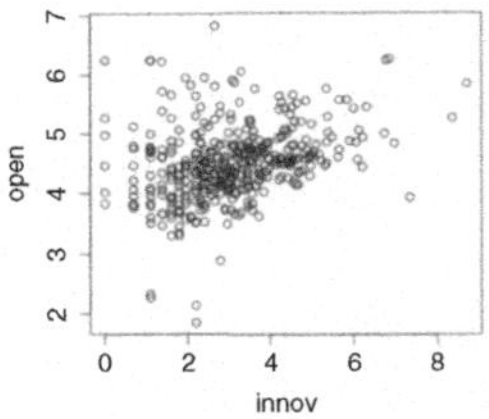

(i) Foreign turnover.

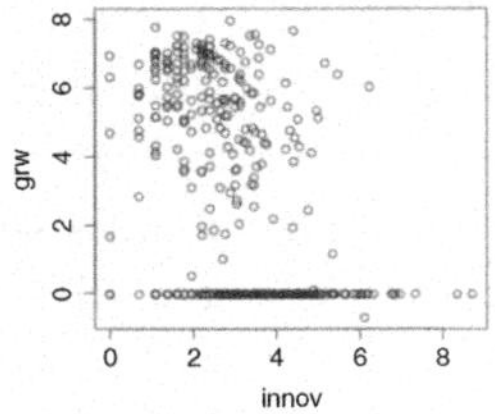

(j) GRW funding long term: 2005-2014.

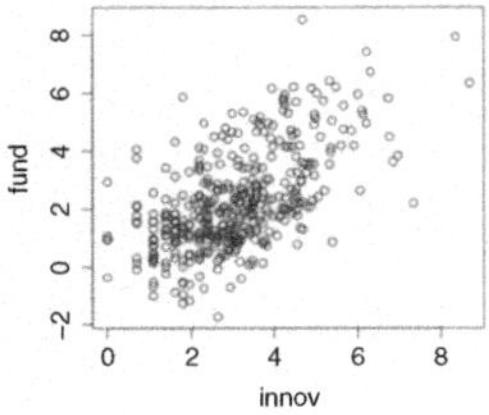

(k) R+D funding.

Figure 11.1: Correlation scatter plots for all covariates. The plots allow to delineate assumptions about the relations of the covariates towards the dependent variable.

11.1 OLS

Because of the variables' impacts mostly not seeming to be too clearly linear or nonlinear, OLS estimation forms the first reference for finding a fitting model. Additionally to the coefficients mentioned in figure 11.1, dummy variables accounting for the structure of the industry and for knowledge intensity of a district are included. The dummy for an existing high-tech cluster in a region is $clus = 1$, and $= 0$ otherwise. The clusters are supported by the cluster excellence strategy by German federal ministries (BMWi 2018). The dummy delineating if a district includes a federal R+D institute is $inst = 1$, and $= 0$ otherwise. These institutes include major research institutes by the Fraunhofer-Gesellschaft, the Helmholtz Association, the Leibniz Association, the Max-Planck-Gesellschaft as well as R+D institutes of the German state (BMBF 2018b).

The basic data structure can be observed in table 11.2.

The OLS model (1) states significant (0.01 '*', 0.001 '**', 0 '***') influences for several coefficients.

First, **productivity** has a significantly positive influence on patent publications. When productivity increases by 1%, then innovative activity two years later increases by 0.02%.

Long term **GRW funding** in the years of 2005-2014 also has a significant impact, but a negative one. If funds increase by 1%, innovative activity decreases by -0.008%. This can possibly be explained by the characteristics of the regions where firms are receiving GRW funds over a long period of time, because the funds are only allocated to regions lacking in economic performance. Therefore, innovation in these regions also could be hampered, as other issues are also pressing. Furthermore, GRW funding aims not specifically for an increase in innovation but is rather an instrument inducing investment in general. (Die Bundesregierung 1969)

Market potential has another significant influence. As it increases by 1%, innovation also increases by 0.005%. The demand side of the market therefore seems to have another considerable impact

Table 11.2: Variable statistics.

Statistic	Mean	St. Dev.	Median	Min	Max
adminid	8293.00	3766.00	8233	1001	16077
innov	3.10	1.40	3.00	0.00	8.70
clus	0.14	0.34	0	0	1
inst	0.21	0.41	0	0	1
grw	2.60	2.90	0.00	−0.69	8.00
fund	2.20	1.70	1.90	−1.70	8.50
inv	2.10	0.46	2.00	0.83	3.70
gdpem	4.10	0.16	4.10	3.80	4.90
ppot	5.80	0.71	5.70	4.00	8.20
ind	2.80	0.40	2.80	1.70	4.50
know	2.10	0.74	2.10	−0.92	4.00
open	4.50	0.63	4.50	1.90	6.80
popd	5.60	1.10	5.30	3.60	8.40
sme	−2.20	0.17	−2.20	−2.80	−1.70
turn	5.50	0.39	5.40	4.40	7.20

onto innovation. It could be explained by firms needing to innovate because of aiming to provide customers with their goods.

Other covariates with significant impacts are **industry share** and **R+D funding**, which impact innovation positively. Also, the existence of high-tech clusters in a district has a positive effect. Negatively affecting innovative activity is **population density**, which illustrates the strength of agglomeration of a region, as in regions where many people live, decreasing marginal returns of scale in production, and thus in innovation, could be happening.

No significant impact on innovation has the existence of an **R+D institute** in a region, as the locational dummy is not significant. However, as the sign indicates a negative relation, the presence of such an institute is per se no prove for innovation happening. This could point to the fact that innovative activity is here measured as

Table 11.3: OLS estimation results.

	Innovative activity in 2016	
	(1)	(2)
Dummy for high-tech cluster	0.33	0.33
Dummy for R+D institute	−0.12	
GRW funding	−0.08**	−0.10**
Firm size (Share of SMEs)	−0.67	
Knowledge intensity	0.05	
R+D funding	0.45**	0.42**
Investment	−0.08	
Openness	0.14	
Firm size (Turnover)	−0.38	
Population density	−0.26*	−0.35**
Industry share	0.80**	0.81**
Productivity	1.60**	1.40**
Market potential	0.47**	0.61**
Constant	−7.90**	−7.40**
Observations	402	402
R^2	0.61	0.60
Adjusted R^2	0.60	0.59
Note:	*p<0.01; **p<0.001; ***p<0	

patents and not every innovative activity needs to result in a patent. (Griliches 1998)

However, regarding the estimated value of the coefficients, urban regions seem to be preferable for the allocation of patenting activities. **Knowledge intensity** and **openness** (measured via foreign turnover) are per se positive as well, but not significantly so. General **investment** also has a negative effect, which may show the fact that the investment variable also includes investments not related to innovation, but rather contains spending for tangible assets. Those could appear not to be particularly related to innovation.

The impact of firm size, although not significant as well, is rather ambivalent. On the one hand, the coefficient for firm **turnover** is negative. If it increases, innovation decreases. This seems counter-intuitive, as high turnover proclaims bigger firms, which should be more capable of spending money on innovative activity. On the other hand, the **share of SME**, as expected, has a negative impact onto innovation activity. If there are relatively many SME in 2013, patents decrease with respect to 2016. This could be reasoned by the high efforts needed to file a patent application, monetary and non-monetary. This contrasting relation of either large firms not innovating more, the larger they get, and SME which also seem to be disadvantaged in innovating, suggests giving it a closer look in future work. However, even as both variables are indicators for firm size, they are measured differently, as the indicator for SME uses the number of employees in a firm, and the variable for turnover uses monetary measures of size.

Model (2) replicates the OLS model (1) but includes only the significant predictors from the prior estimation. Significance holds mostly constant, whereas the values change slightly. The size of the impact seems mostly similar. Nevertheless, the impacts are in general small, so the effects onto innovative activity are visible and significant, but not big. The model fit also does not change significantly between both specifications.

Moran's I As in chapter 9.2 explained, innovation and therefore patents have an undeniable spatial relation. As a result, the dependent variable of these analyses has to be tested for locational relevance. Otherwise, the estimation omits important effects for the explanatory potential of the model. A first step in examining the spatial nature of patents is to test the variable for spatial autocorrelation. A common measure for this is the Moran I statistic (Moran 1950) that tests for the hypothesis of non-existent spatial autocorrelation. If the Null is rejected, the present spatial autocorrelation confirms the degree of association of the values in the patent variable.

The result of the Moran statistic shows significant spatial autocorrelation. Further analyses accordingly have to consider the locational connection of the dependent variable. OLS estimation does not account for this, so another approach has to be executed. Taking the OLS estimation model, enhancing it by a spatial effect and allowing for possibly nonlinear effects of the covariates leads to a geoadditive model in the context of a GAMM.

11.2 Geoadditive Model

11.2.1 Derivation

The term geoadditive model as such has been introduced in a larger context by Kammann and Wand (2003). This approach follows the idea of structured additive regression, where the estimator is not necessarily parametric anymore. It is replaced by a flexible semiparametric predictor that can encompass linear and nonlinear regressors (Kneib and Fahrmeir 2007, p. 33). This way, additive models (T. J. Hastie and Tibshirani 1990) can be combined with geostatistical smoothing or interpolation; e.g. with a method called *kriging*. Due to this it is possible to geographically map effects of the regressors on the outcome while controlling for nonlinear impacts of the covariates (Kammann and Wand 2003, p. 2). Information in the model can therefore not only be explained by spatial variation, but by additional factors as well (Bocci 2009, p. 19). All in all, the geoadditive modeling approach facilitates incorporating nonparametric effects for time scales and continuous covariates (with varying coefficient terms) as well as spatial effects and random intercepts and / or slopes (Kneib and Fahrmeir 2007, p. 207). A geoadditive model reveals consequently not only where spatial variation happens but can also tell why it happens. It is important to account for nonlinearities by executing a semiparametric framework, as parametric restrictions are often making the estimation of relations difficult. The semiparametric characteristics can be satisfied by adding smoothed functions for some of the explaining covariates. Moreover, a geoadditive model is the resulting model if a smooth surface of space (via geo-coordinates) is taken into account via kriging. Thus, spatial heterogeneity is considered. The predecessors of the geoadditive model are the Generalized Additive Model (GAM) and the Generalized Linear Model (GLM). (Basile, Benfratello, and Castellani 2012, p. 29)

Following Kammann and Wand (2003, p. 5), with y as dependent variable and a set of j with $j = 1, ..., s$ predictors x_j, the general additive form is:

$$y_i = \beta_0 + \sum_{j=1}^{s} f_j(x_{i,j}) + \epsilon_i \tag{11.1}$$

Here, the functions f_j are unspecified, but smooth. To implement these smooth functions, usually smoothing the functions via splines is applied. Splines can approximate unknown functions by connecting different polynomials at their junctions, called knots. The final spline function depends on the chosen base, the location and number of its knots. Here, the importance lies in choosing the splines to achieve a good fit, which is largely determined by the characteristics of the knots. As with the bandwidth in the case of KDE, the model's degree expressed by its knots controls the amount of smoothing. Too many knots undersmooth the model, to few knots oversmooth it. As is shown in Hastie (1996), a smaller number of knots is computationally favorable and often leads to the same results as using more knots, as lower rank models lack the less significant knots of full rank models (Bocci 2009, p. 4). Using penalized splines, which is common (Kneib and Fahrmeir 2007, e.g. Basile, Benfratello, and Castellani 2012; Umlauf et al. 2015; Kammann and Wand 2003; Bocci 2009), in this approach and also preferred by Kammann and Wand (2003), the number of knots selected is somewhat larger, but maintained at a fixed level. Compensating for this, the impact of the knots is restricted via added penalty to the general least squares fitting of the model. The model with penalized splines is therefore (Kammann and Wand 2003, p. 5):

$$y_i = \beta_0 + \beta_{x_j} x_{j_i} + \sum_{j=1}^{s} \sum_{p=1}^{P_{x_j}} u_p^{x_j} (x_{j_i} - \kappa_p^{x_j})_+ + \epsilon_i \tag{11.2}$$

The variables $u_p^{x_j}$ are penalized knot coefficients with $u_+ = u$ if $u < 0$ and $u_p^x = 0$ otherwise. $\kappa_1^{x_j}, ..., \kappa_{P_{x_j}^{x_j}}$ are knots for x_j. The knots are moreover treated as random effects in the mixed model. It can be shown that in this case the penalized least squares approach is equal to the best linear unbiased predictor. (Kammann and Wand 2003, p. 5)

As Hastie (1996) illustrates, penalized spline additive models use only few knots and therefore belong in the category low rank smoothing. To arrive at a geoadditive model, the before-mentioned additively structured model has to be combined with kriging which itself is declared as linear mixed model. Kriging-modeling can be expressed as

$$y_i = \beta_0 + \beta_1^\top \boldsymbol{g}_i + S(\boldsymbol{g}_i) + \epsilon_i \tag{11.3}$$

where $\boldsymbol{g}_i \in \mathbb{R}^2$ constitutes the geographical location vector and $\{S(\boldsymbol{g}_i) : \boldsymbol{g} \in \mathbb{R}^2\}$ is a zero-mean stationary stochastic process. For further derivations it is referred to Kammann and Wand (2003).

The final geoadditive model is then

$$y_i = \beta_0 + \sum_{j=1}^{s} f(x_{j_i}) + \beta_1^\top \boldsymbol{g}_i + S(\boldsymbol{g}_i) + \epsilon_i \tag{11.4}$$

where the first part is the additive structure containing the predictors, and the latter part holds the geographical kriging model (Kammann and Wand 2003, p. 8). The model can be expressed completely in matrix notation.

For count data that is heavily skewed it is necessary to use a generalized geoadditive model (Kammann and Wand 2003, p. 15). Because of the log-transformation of the patent data (see figure 11.2), this can be omitted, so that the normal geoadditive model can be

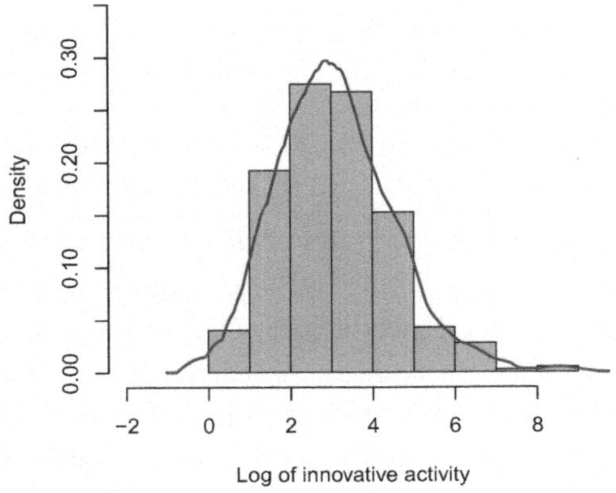

Figure 11.2: Histogram of innovative activity in 2016. Data are logarithmized. Additionally, a density curve smoothing the histogram is illustrated.

used. Reason for this is that the distribution of the dependent variable *innovative activity* is approximately normal, so a method which is based on Gaussian random fields and penalized splines can be applied (Kammann and Wand 2003).

As with KDE, the amount of smoothing in a geoadditive model is also critical, as both penalized splines and kriging are forms of smoothing. Kammann and Wand (2003), in following Hastie and Tibshirani (1990), suggest that smoothing via Maximum Likelihood (ML) also leads to reliable results.

Model Specifications As in (Brezger, Kneib, and Lang 2005) and related publications mentioned, there exist mainly three approaches to estimating such a Structured Additive Regression (STAR) model (to which the geoadditive model belongs as well), namely MCMC, REML and a combined selection and estimation method, STEP (stepwise regression). For this paper, the REML method will be preferred.

As it is illustrated in the methodology manual of the *BayesX* program (2018a, p. 5), it takes a frequentist approach to a mixed model representation. In general, STAR models are GLMs based on flexible, structured additive predictors. The variance parameter (or smoothing parameter) in the REML approach is assumed to be an unknown constant, which is estimated via REML. The coefficients are determined via penalized likelihood. A possibility for interpretation is that the estimates can either be interpreted as empirical Bayes estimates, but also as regular penalized likelihood estimates. The latter approach will be followed here. The predictors can include smooth effects that may be nonlinear, two-dimensional surfaces, are spatially correlated, or show varying coefficients. Further possibilities are spatially varying effects or random intercepts/slopes containing cluster effects. Thus, geoadditive models can be expressed with STAR models. (Umlauf et al. 2015, pp. 5-7)

11.2.2 REML Estimation

Starting with the model specification of the OLS model in chapter 11.1, for some of the variables a nonlinear context is assumed. This seems to apply mostly to coefficients industry share, knowledge intensity, openness, population density, turnover and share of SME (compare figures 11.1h, 11.1d, 11.1i, 11.1e, 11.1b, 11.1g). Nevertheless, these assumptions have to be investigated, as the model specification with the best Akaike Information Criterion (AIC) value is chosen to be the final model (Umlauf et al. 2015, p. 7). The OLS model without spatial effects exhibits an AIC of 1062.47.

The model specification selected for REML estimation in the STAR model context is:

$$\begin{aligned} innov_i \sim Normal(&dummies_i \\ +linear\,covariates_i + &nonlinear\,covariates_i \\ &+spatial\,effect, error\,term) \end{aligned} \tag{11.5}$$

with

$$dummies_i \sim clus_i + inst_i \tag{11.6}$$

$$linear\,covariates \sim grw_i + fund_i + inv_i + open_i + gdpem_i + ppot_i \tag{11.7}$$

$$\begin{aligned} nonlinear\,covariates \sim f_1(ind_i) + f_2(know_i) + \\ + f_4(popd_i) + f_5(sme_i) + f_6(turn_i) \end{aligned} \tag{11.8}$$

$$spatial\,effect \sim f_{spatial}(district_i) \tag{11.9}$$

where $district_i$ is the identification number of the administrative district, which relates the model geographically and therefore expresses the spatial model component. In the estimation, the centroid of the district is calculated by referring to a map provided simultaneously.

The model is formulated and estimated with *BayesX* via `R2BayesX` in `R`:

$$\begin{aligned} \texttt{innov} \sim \texttt{clus} + \texttt{inst} + \texttt{grw} + \texttt{fund} + \texttt{inv} + \texttt{open} + \texttt{gdpem} + \texttt{ppot} \\ + \texttt{sx(ind)} + \texttt{sx(know)} + \texttt{sx(popd)} + \texttt{sx(sme)} + \texttt{sx(turn)} \\ + \texttt{sx(district, basis} = \texttt{"geokriging", map} = \texttt{districts)} \end{aligned} \tag{11.10}$$

The estimation of the model with REML is executed in several steps. Based on the theoretically derived model, specifications regarding a parametric or nonparametric incorporation of the covariates are investigated. Extensive testing leads to the assumption that half of the covariates can be factored in nonparametrically, which increases model fit. However, this is mostly due to the sparse instrumentation of the higher values of the covariates. Because of the high frequency

Table 11.4: Estimation results of the geoadditive model, part 1. This table contains the results for the parametric effects. The estimation method used is REML.

Covariate	Estimate	Std. error	t value	Pr(>|t|)	
(Intercept)	-9.26	1.99	-4.65	0.00	***
clus	0.31	0.15	2.07	0.04	*
inst	-0.12	0.14	-0.89	0.37	
grw	-0.08	0.03	-2.75	0.01	**
fund	0.38	0.04	9.50	0.00	***
inv	-0.09	0.10	-0.84	0.40	
open	0.16	0.13	1.22	0.22	
gdpem	2.09	0.44	4.72	0.00	***
ppot	0.44	0.19	2.33	0.02	*
Signif.:		0 '***'	0.001 '**'	0.01 '*'	

Table 11.5: Estimation results of the geoadditive model, part 2. This table contains the results for the nonparametric effects. Additional estimation statistics are also presented. The estimation method used is REML.

Covariate	Variance	Smooth Par.	df
sx(adminid)	0.17	3.4	22
sx(ind)	0.05	12.2	5
sx(know)	0.01	133.3	3
sx(popd)	0.01	52.1	4
sx(sme)	0.01	45.9	4
sx(turn)	0.01	164.2	2
Scale estimate:	0.6		
N = 402	df = 52	AIC = 245	BIC = 453
method: REML		distribution: Normal	

of few patent publications in the districts, here, the prediction can be more accurate than for districts exhibiting a high number of patent publications. Supported is this analysis by examining the confidence bands. Where they drift apart from the curves, interpretation is to be treated with care as the prediction here may not be reliable.

The results of several estimations lead to the model specified in equation 11.5. Discarded specifications contain nonparametric investment and nonparametric GRW funding, as the relation seems to be linear anyways. Considering the other covariates, the respective construction derived from the scatter plots is apparent and fitting directly. The best AIC amounted to 245, which is remarkably lower than with the OLS model. This is due to the possibility of nonparametric variable construction which allows a more flexible model fit. Still, productivity and R+D funding have shown to be linear in every tested model specification.

For the parametric part (compare table 11.4), **productivity** is again highly significant. Increased productivity increases innovative activity by 0.02%. **R+D funding** influences innovation by 0.004%. **GRW funding** impacts the dependent variable by -0.0007% and is also highly significant. This can be a phenomenon of decreasing marginal returns for funding. However, as the funds are allocated only in regions classified as structurally weak, this could explain the steep fall in innovative activity.

Additionally, **market potential** and the dummy for **high-tech clusters** are also significant and positive, albeit on a slightly lower level. Not significant, but influencing in a negative way is again investment, as well as the dummy for **R+D institutes**. **Openness** is also not significant, but the coefficient has a positive sign. All in all, the direction of the coefficients is the same as in the OLS estimation. During model testing, the linear incorporation of productivity, R+D funding and GRW funding leads in almost all specifications to highly significant estimates. In their direction of influencing innovation activity they correspond to the effects observed in the OLS model.

The corresponding plots for the parametric estimation results (see figures 11.3 to 11.6), are split in two separate parts for each covariate.

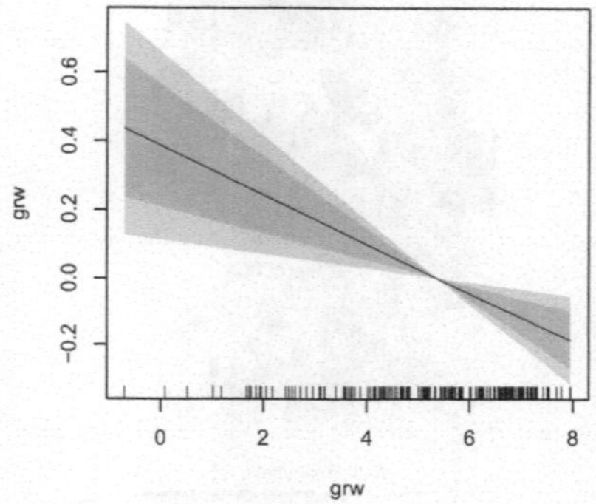

(a) Estimated effect.

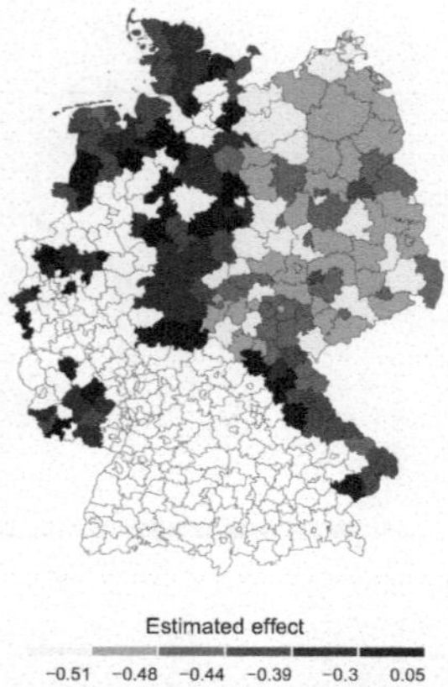

(b) Spatial distribution of the effect.

Figure 11.3: Estimated effects for covariate GRW funding. Parametric effect.

In the left part (part (a)) of the figures, the function plots show the strength of the effect (on the y-axis with confidence intervals) in the regions, ordered from regions with low values of the covariate towards regions with high values of the covariate (on the x-axis from low to high). As the relations are of parametric nature here, the functions are linear and slope either upward or downward.

The right element (part (b)) of the figures shows the spatial distribution of the effect on a map with all German administrative districts. Where the color is dark the covariate explains more variation of innovative activity than in lighter colored regions, where the importance of that determinant seems to be reduced. These notions correspond to the effect of the covariate being higher or lower. Regarding these geographic choropleths, the strength of the effect can directly be compared among regions and the visual allocation on the map is a useful clarification. Moreover, implications and interpretations are thus less abstract.

Considering the strong negative effect GRW funding has onto innovative activity, this effect even accelerates, the more funding a region

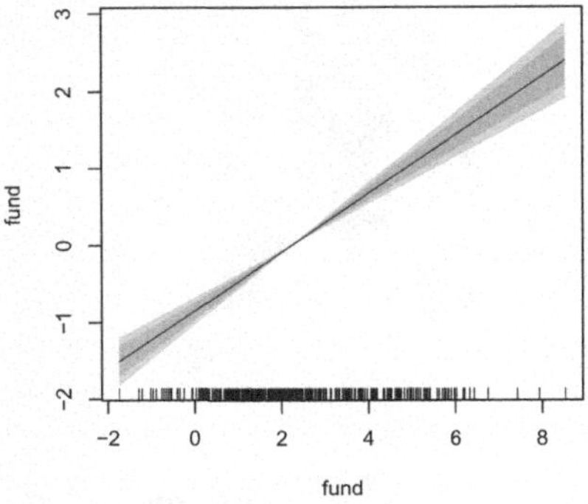

(a) Estimated effect.

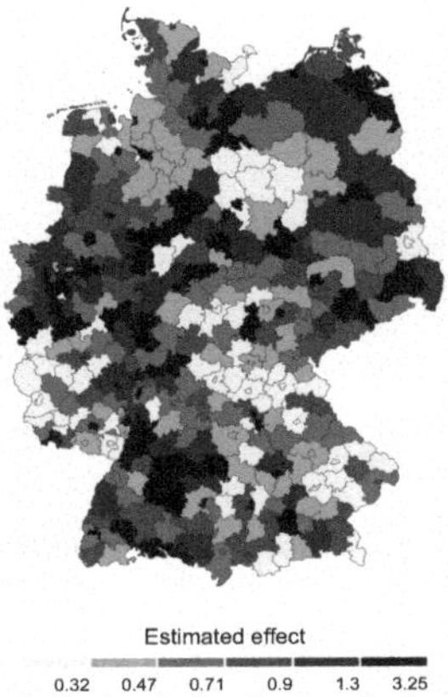

(b) Spatial distribution of the effect.

Figure 11.4: Estimated effects for covariate R+D funding. Parametric effect.

gets. In figure 11.3b, the regional dispersion of that effect can be observed. Where the districts are colored darkest, the effect deviates most from the mean value estimated. The map is incomplete, as not in all German administrative districts firms are eligible for obtaining funds (this is based on a regions' status of funding eligibility; only in classified regions firms can apply for funds). In former East Germany, where highest funding sums are allocated, the effect on innovative activity seems to be rather small. This corresponds to the right part of figure 11.3a. On the contrary, regions in the western and northern part appear to be affected more positively. Here, the covariate exudes more explanatory content for the relation towards innovation.

For the covariate of R+D funding, mostly by the BMBF, the effect is more positive, the more funds the firms in a region obtain. Regarding figure 11.4b, the effect of funding is dispersed relatively evenly throughout German districts. There are some areas consisting of several districts, where R+D funding does not seem to matter much for explaining innovation activity. This is for example in the area around Stendal and Lüchow-Dannenberg or around Bayreuth

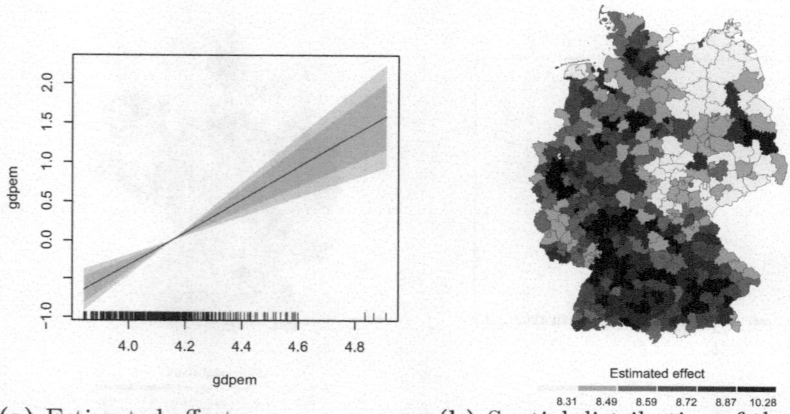

(a) Estimated effect. (b) Spatial distribution of the effect.

Figure 11.5: Estimated effects for covariate productivity. Parametric effect.

and Dingolfing-Landau. Hotspots are for instance in the west around Stuttgart or from Paderborn towards Hanover.

The effect of productivity on innovative activity is positive and increasing. Nevertheless, for average productivity the effect lies around zero. The regional visualization of the effect distribution in figure 11.5b shows highest effects for west and especially for south Germany. Hotspots are in the Ruhr area and south towards Cologne, and the axis from Frankfurt (Main) to Stuttgart is marked by high explanatory potential of productivity for innovation as well. This applies also to the area around Munich and for Hanover as well as for Hamburg. Weaker effects on innovation prevail in the eastern parts of Germany, mostly in the state of Mecklenburg-Vorpommern. Here, productivity does not contribute to disclosing innovative activity. The only exception in former East Germany are the districts of Teltow-Fläming, Dahme-Spreewald, and Cottbus / Spree-Neiße directly south of Berlin. These districts exhibit a high impact on innovation.

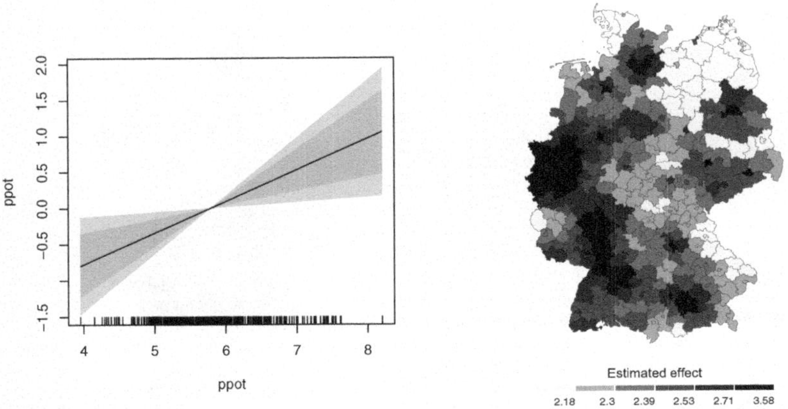

(a) Estimated effect. (b) Spatial distribution of the effect.

Figure 11.6: Estimated effects for covariate market potential. Parametric effect.

For market potential, the general effect onto innovative activity is again around zero for average regional values of market potential. With increasing potential, the impact increases. As in figure 11.6b illustrated, the construction of the covariate of market potential is obvious, as the effect seems to be regionally smoothed and fading out over the regions. Market potential is proxied as the measure of the amount of population which is reachable in a radius of 100 kilometers. The strongest effects are estimated for western parts of Germany. The whole greater Ruhr area is a hotspot, where the market potential holds a big share in explaining innovative activity. This effect fades out slowly towards the south and north west. Again, the region from Frankfurt (Main) towards Stuttgart is a hotspot, with the surrounding districts exhibiting slightly reduced effect strength; until the effect almost completely fades out (compare e.g. eastwards to the center of Germany to the area around Hildburghausen). The Bavarian border to Czechia is also less important, same as almost all of Mecklenburg-Vorpommern and the northern parts of Brandenburg.

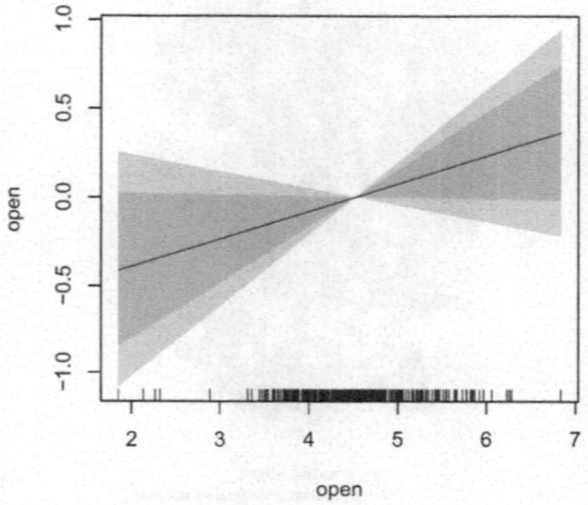

(a) Estimated effect.

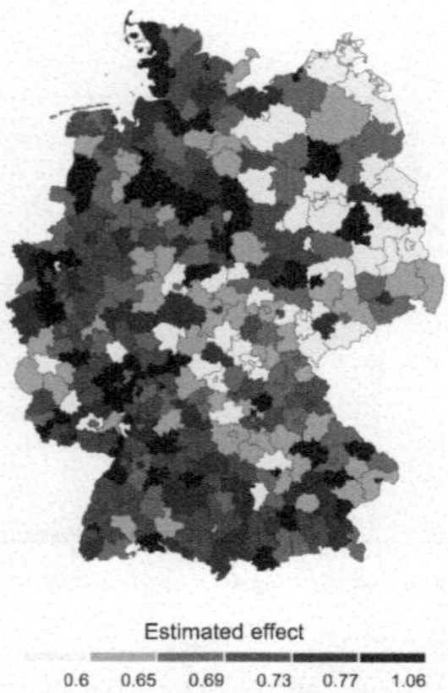

(b) Spatial distribution of the effect.

Figure 11.7: Estimated effects for covariate openness. Parametric effect.

The covariate openness is approximated by foreign turnover in the districts. The effect is parametrically modeled, yet the resulting estimated function shows wide confidence intervals to both margins. These could point to nonlinearity of the covariate, but that specification did not prove valuable in an earlier estimation. The intervals are relatively wide because of the few values to the upper and lower bounds. The effect of openness on innovative activity could also well be stagnating with increasing foreign turnover. The size of the effect would then lie around zero, thus the impact could be negligible. The values for openness in the regions are relatively concentrated around the mean, with only few outliers towards lower or higher values. Regarding figure 11.7b, the localized distribution of the effect is mostly even for German districts. Hotspots where the covariate achieves higher importance for the relation onto innovation are dispersed throughout Germany. Only the cold spots, where the effect is least pronounced (and affecting innovative activity negatively), seem to locate more in the eastern parts of the country. A few districts in the center of Germany exhibit decreasing effects of openness, such as the Landkreis Kassel or Vogelsbergkreis. Some districts in the east-

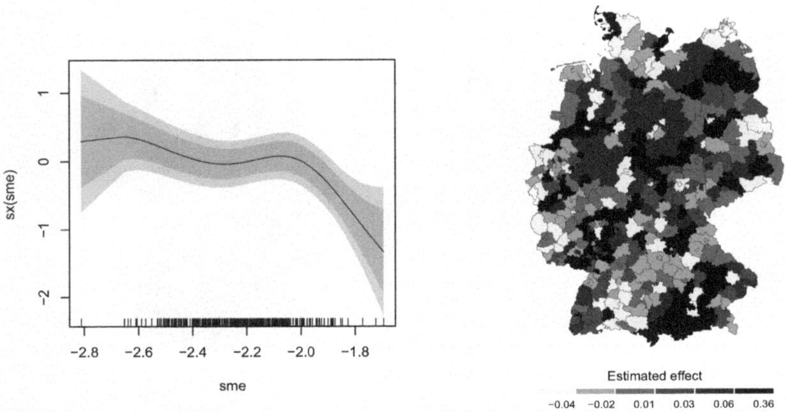

(a) Estimated effect. (b) Spatial distribution of the effect.

Figure 11.8: Estimated effects for covariate share of SMEs. Nonparametric effect.

ern areas of Bavaria or in Saxony and north at the Polish border are also cold spots.

Considering the nonparametric estimation results of table 11.5, again side by side plots for the covariates are available in figures 11.7 to 11.12. The interpretation is similar; on the left (part (a)), function plots shows the strength and variation of the effect for the regions. On the right (part (b)), a spatial rendition of the effect is projected on the administrative district's map. Darker colored regions show a higher effect and relevance for innovative activity, whereas lighter colored regions illustrate lower effects.

For the share of SME, which can also indicate the firm size effect onto innovation, the effect decreases relatively consistently linear with the rise of the share. The bigger the share of SME in a region, the less innovation activity is brought to the public. This effect is slightly less pronounced for regions with a smaller share of SME and decreases stronger, the higher the share of SMEs in a region is. Again, this speaks for small firms not having the capabilities of patenting that much. Regarding the spatial distribution of the effect in figure 11.8b,

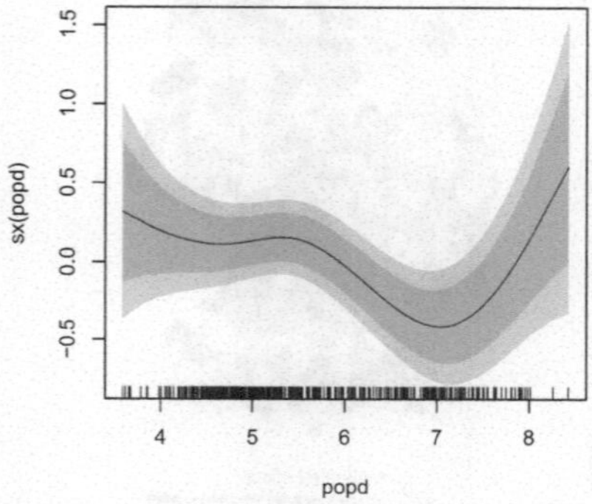

(a) Estimated effect.

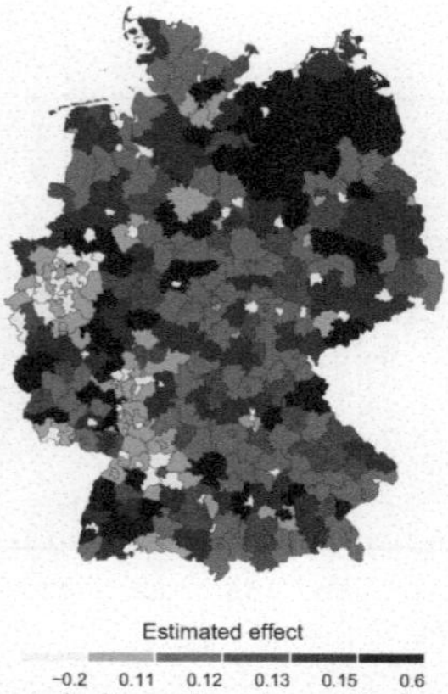

(b) Spatial distribution of the effect.

Figure 11.9: Estimated effects for covariate population density. Nonparametric effect.

the hotspots where the effect is biggest do not seem to reside in the big cities, but moreover slightly alongside the fringes of those regions. This view can also be supported by fact that some of the major medium sized cities seem to be on the lower end of the importance-scale, compare e.g. Bonn, Wolfsburg, Osnabrück, or Eisenach. Here, the effect of the share of SME for explaining innovation is rather low. Nevertheless, the distribution of the effect is rather dispersed over Germany, with the exception of some small clusters of the same impact size.

Regarding the nonparametric estimates, the impact of population density is roughly u-shaped. For the less densely populated regions, there is a decreasing effect onto innovation activity. The impact is then constant until a density of 403.43 (log-value 6) and then decreases further. This applies until a population density of circa 1096.63 (log-value 7) is reached. Afterwards, the innovative activity in densest regions increases the more densely a region is populated. Acknowledging the relatively stable confidence bands, this seems to argue in favor of a cluster effect. For population density, the spatial

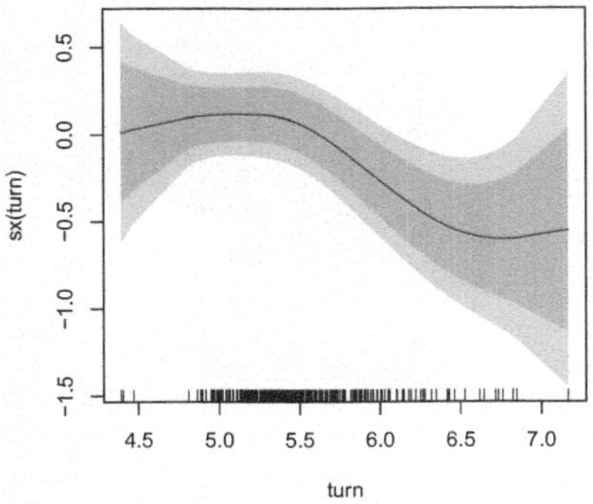

(a) Estimated effect.

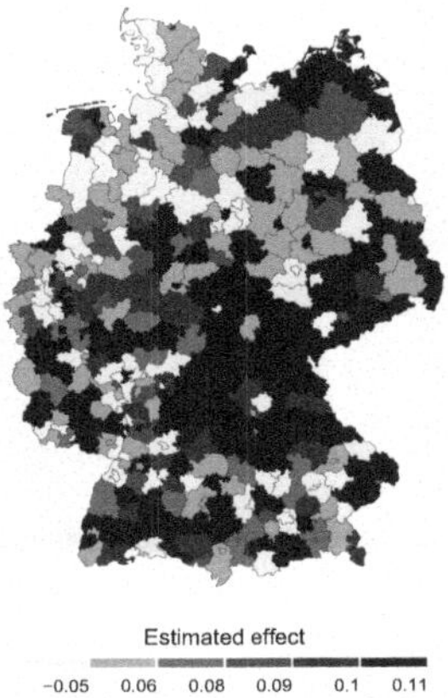

(b) Spatial distribution of the effect.

Figure 11.10: Estimated effects for covariate firm size. Nonparametric effect.

distribution of the effect is rather separated (compare figure 11.9b). Most regions lie somewhere in the middle of the effect's scale, near an impact close to zero onto innovative activity. More compelling is the allocation of hotspots and cold spots. Whereas the hotspots manifest in a few districts all over Germany (for example in Calw, Heidenheim, Erzgebirgskreis, Hildesheim, and Segeberg), a big cluster of the strongest effect exists in Mecklenburg-Vorpommern, where in almost all regions population density has great importance for innovative activity. Contrariwise, in the metropolises and cities of Germany, population density is less important, as those (often very small districts) yield some of the lightest spots on the map. In these cities, population density is not a major innovation-determining factor.

For turnover as firm size indicator the behavior of the estimated curve is constant for regions with low values of turnover per employee. With increasing turnover, innovation activities decrease slightly, until for larger sums the patenting variable stagnates again. Companies with average turnover therefore seem to be hindered in publishing their inventions and innovating. However, for very small and for

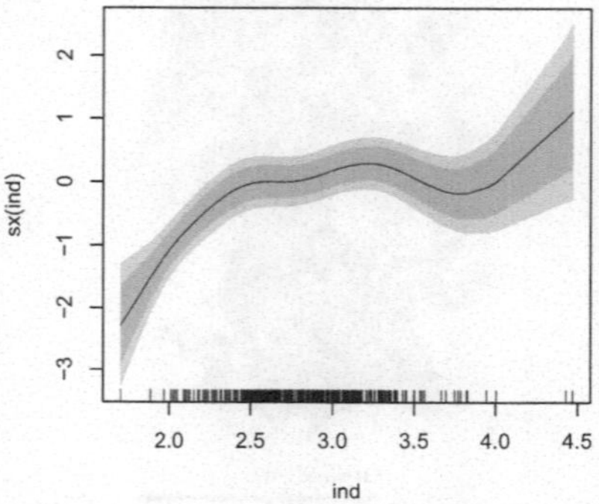

(a) Estimated effect.

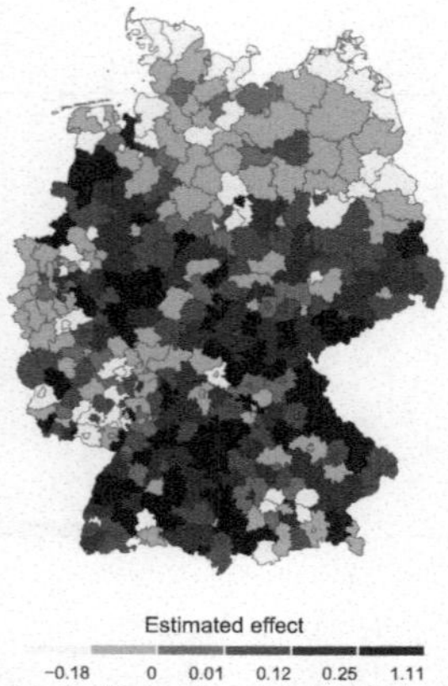

(b) Spatial distribution of the effect.

Figure 11.11: Estimated effects for covariate industry share. Nonparametric effect.

very large firms the effect is not significantly determined, as the confidence bands are wide enough to allow for diverging curves. Yet, the importance of firm size is not given in a relevant amount as the effect is rather small. Focusing on the spatial distribution of the effect in figure 11.10b, the effects estimated are very small and revolve only slightly around zero. The hotspots are mostly located in the center of Germany and spread somewhat widely. The coastal area at the Baltic Sea is a large hotspot area, also the regions in the Schwarzwald. Cold spots are scattered all over the country, with some clustering in the north west. All in all, the spatial manifestation of the effect is rather diffused.

Another non-monotonic curve is plotted for industry share. For low shares of employees in the industry in a region and with rising shares the innovation activity increases as well. This is up to relatively average share, where the relation is rather stagnating. At an industry share of 54.6 (log-value 4) there is a dip in the effect on innovation activity, as the latter declines with further rising shares up to this value. Following then is an increasing effect onto innovation

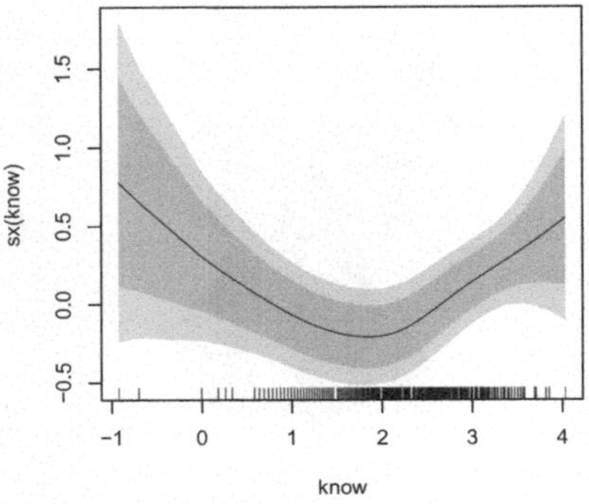

(a) Estimated effect.

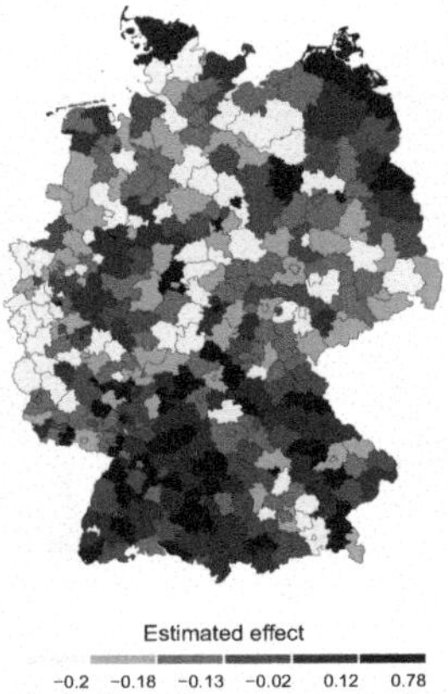

(b) Spatial distribution of the effect.

Figure 11.12: Estimated effects for covariate knowledge intensity. Non-parametric effect.

with increasing industry share. Still, as the frequency of values is very low towards the end of the scale, it is recommended to not place too much importance on those relations. Comparing the function plot with its spatial pendant (see figure 11.11b), the dispersion is relatively even over the country, with an exception to the north-east. In Schleswig-Holstein and Mecklenburg-Vorpommern, effect strength is low. Nevertheless, a few districts in the south of Germany (e.g. Erding or Tuttlingen) also exist. Here, industry share is not relevant to influence innovation decisively. Larger importance of industry seems to allocate at the Czechian border, in the districts around Bamberg, around Unterallgäu, Hochsauerlandkreis and the Emsland.

The effect of knowledge intensity on innovation activity is u-shaped. For regions with small shares of workers in the high-tech sector a negative effect on innovation is estimated. For an average knowledge intensity of circa 7.39 (log-value 2) the effect is smallest, before it increases and impacts innovation positively with increasing knowledge intensity in regions. This supports the expected relation that higher knowledge intensity in administrative districts in Germany leads to higher innovative activity as well. As this applies not for regions with below-average knowledge intensity, but the confidence intervals are relatively broad, this could be investigated closer. In figure 11.12b, the spatial distribution of the estimated effect is illustrated. Hotspots in knowledge intensity explaining innovation reside mostly in the south of the country and are relatively scattered and independent from other districts. Besides these hotspots (e.g. Landkreis Regensburg, Ostalbkreis, Groß-Gerau, Main-Spessart) some regions in the outer north (Nordfriesland and Schleswig-Flensburg) and in the east (Vorpommern-Rügen and Vorpommern-Greifswald) exhibit higher importance for knowledge intensity in innovation. Generally, the west and north of Germany are rather on the lower end of the scale of the estimated effect strength. Regions where knowledge intensity seems to have less relevance are for instance Prignitz, Heidekreis, Oldenburg, Steinfurt or Göttingen.

In general, the nonparametric effects are mostly fitting the model and the confidence intervals are largely narrow (which is also confirmed by the estimated variances). Checking residual model diagnostics, the fit seems to be reasonable considering the nature of the data. Partial residuals do not indicate major misspecification or misinterpretation of the relation between the variables. The Normal distribution chosen for the estimation is also indicated as plausible, whereas a slight improvement considering accounting for slightly heavier tails could be possible.

The spatial residual effect of the model on innovative activity can be observed in figure 11.13b. In the darker areas the spatial effect is higher than in the lighter areas. This coloring corresponds to hotspots (dark) and cold spots (light) in innovative activity. As a geoadditive model considers spatial variation via extracting the effects from the residuals, the map shows the remaining residual variation among the regions. Where the variation is high, the model did not account for all present effects to the full extent. These regions appear to be characterized by further influencing factors which contain potential for spatial explanation of regional innovation activity.

As the geographic pattern is very distinct, it becomes obvious that the spatial effect is non-negligible and there still seem to be factors influencing the regional innovation distribution that remain hidden in the residuals. This confirms the result of the Moran statistic of spatial autocorrelation. In darker regions the effect on innovative activity deviates positively from the mean estimated value. This corresponds mostly to the regions commonly known as highly innovative. The areas northeast to the Ruhr area, in the southern region around Lake Constance and the coastal area at the Baltic Sea are hotspots of activity. In those regions, innovation activity prospers and reinforces itself. Further regions benefiting are the region around Nuremberg towards the direction of Dresden. In these regions there exist further factors influencing the innovative activity that are not yet included in the geoadditive model. However, this does not automatically result in absolute high activity, which is illustrated by the comparison with figure 11.13a.

Negatively influenced are the Saarland, Erfurt in the federal state of Thuringia, and the region near Passau. Furthermore visible is the relatively consistent dispersion of the mapped spatial residuals. With exception of the Saarland, which deviates most strongly from the mean, the hotspots and cold spots are not very pronounced. Therefore, the model seems to account properly for the spatial autocorrelation. Considering the extreme cold spot near the Saarland and Mannheim towards Frankfurt, some undisclosed covariates influence innovation seemingly negative and should be added to the model to account for complete spatial autocorrelation. In absolute magnitude, the estimated spatial residuals are not too large, pointing again to a relatively reasonable model fit.

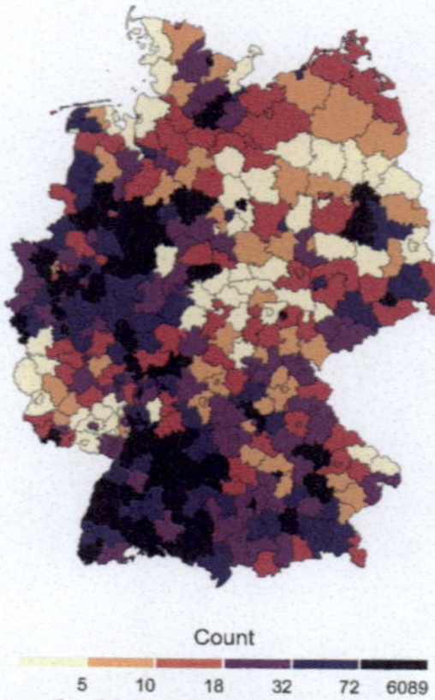

(a) Spatial distribution of innovative activity in 2016.

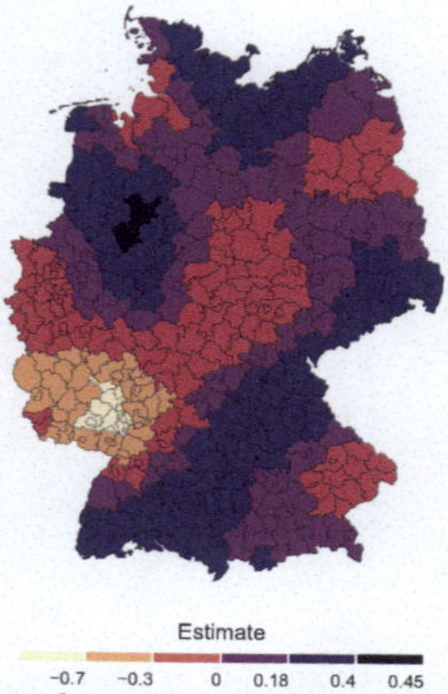

(b) Spatial residual effect of innovative activity via geoadditive kriging.

Figure 11.13: Comparison of spatial distributions of innovation. Spatial residuals estimated by the REML model are compared to the general spatial variation inherited in innovative activity.

12 Conclusion

In the prior analyses several theoretically relevant covariates are examined regarding their influence on innovation activity proxied by patent publications. In this connection, the covariates obtained for all 402 administrative districts are taken mainly from 2014. Data for innovative activity are measured as patent publications from all regions, where at least one patent is published in 2016. By allowing a two-year time-lag between endogenous and exogenous variables the average duration of the patenting process is factored in. This way, the effect of the factors influencing the innovation process is accounted for additionally.

All in all, the estimated effects for innovative activity are very different, but clearly not accountable for by an exclusively linear model. The inclusion of a spatial dimension in the geoadditive model also is indispensable, as the OLS model is not able to account for any spatial variation and the inclusion of the latter gives valuable insights. The effects of the geoadditive model mainly follow those of the OLS model. However, neglecting spatial autocorrelation may lead to the model not being reliable when making assumptions about the actual effects.

The spatial effect of the model is further considered appropriate, as the mapped residuals do not show extreme deviations from the mean value. The necessity of incorporating spatial autocorrelation therefore is reasonable.

The geoadditive model proves as useful tool for investigating the spatially dependent structure of innovation activity. In figure 11.13a the log-transformed dependent variable – innovative activity – is il-

I. Rhoden, *Space and Time in German Innovative Activity*,
https://doi.org/10.1007/978-3-658-28600-2_12

lustrated to show the regional distinct pattern of activity in 2016. The respective distribution heightens the necessity of the geoadditive model specification. This becomes especially obvious when regarding the spatial effect of the dependent variable in figure 11.13b. Here, a strong regional pattern which favors certain regions can explain the different allocation of the innovation activity. The spatial kriging approach extracts the spatial autocorrelation from the dependent variable in the model by rearranging the data. Spatial dependencies cannot be omitted, as they form a considerable part of the model.

This is supported by reflecting on to the effects of the predictors of the geoadditive model. Parametric covariates are GRW funding, R+D funding, investment, openness, productivity, and population potential. Except for investment and GRW funding, all covariates express a positive effect on innovation activity. Most significant are the positive effects on innovative activity exhibited by productivity and R+D funding. Innovation therefore seems to benefit in productive regions where R+D funds are allocated as well. In contrast to R+D funding, GRW funding seems to impact innovation negatively. As these funds are only eligible in regions which are structurally lacking (and therefore eligible by design), this points to innovation not being the focus in these regions as well. It is that where economy prospers, innovation also thrives.

Investment and openness do not support innovations in that way and seem to be rather irrelevant. Considering the nonparametrically modeled covariates, the following can be stated: Regions with firms with many employees in knowledge intensive industries also benefit by exhibiting a higher amount of innovative activity. More highly skilled workers, which are needed in those firms, seem therefore prone to creating this innovation by fostering the publishing of patents and therefore innovative activity. This can illustrate a direct link between knowledge and innovation.

The indicators for the size of a firm, measured by the share of SME and firm's turnover, exhibit similar curves. These show that the impact of these regressors influences the innovation activity negatively with increasing values of the regressor. When many SME are in a region or when firms turnover increases, innovation is impacted negatively. This points in two directions: Many small firms innovate less, and firms with high turnover (bigger firms) are also creating less innovation. Firm size is therefore ambiguous and cannot stand alone in explaining innovative activity.

The effect of population density is stagnating for less densely populated regions. Contrastingly, once a certain higher value of the predicting variable is reached in a region, e.g. if a firm is located in a particularly dense area, the impact on innovation is positive.

The impact of industry share is starting as inverted u-shape, at least for smaller to middle values of the regressors. With small values, the innovative activity increases first, then peaks rather flatly. Then the curve of the effect of industry share falls sharply. Summing up, the larger the share of workers in industry in a region, the more positive the effects on innovation are. In industry, most of the patents seem to be published, leading to higher innovative activity.

Considering the resulting effects, there appear several possible leveraging options for improving upon regional (innovation) policies. Options can be derived from either covariates or spatial effects. As one example, funding for SME could be increased, so that innovating is more affordable. Another possibility could be incentivizing in regions with high population density, as there seem to be unused potentials in innovative activity which could be improved upon. Additionally, policy support for regions not being as innovative as the leading regions could be strengthened, for instance by creating policies targeting innovative investments in the north or east of Germany and specializing on these regions.

All estimated effects for each covariate are additionally mapped onto the respective German administrative districts. This way, the impact of each covariate can be determined for each district. Where the effect is higher, the relevance for the relationship towards innovation is also larger, and vice versa. Innovation promoting policy can then directly be derived for each individual district. Where the effect on innovation is high for a determinant in a region, policies can boost innovative activity by applying means to that district in accord with the respective covariate. Alternatively, funds can be applied to compensate in regions where innovative activity is lacking and the effects of a determinant are rather lower.

Nevertheless, further modeling possibilities exist, be it by investigating spatial econometrics or by including further predictors. A time dimension could also be included, as innovative activity changes over time. A spatiotemporal modeling approach could therefore bring new insights.

Part III

Innovative Activity over Space and Time – Spatiotemporal Modeling of Innovation Promoting Factors

13 Introduction

Innovation is a main driver of economic growth, as it is almost always able to impact growth favorably. In examining innovation as a growth factor, the determinants of innovation itself have to be considered more closely. This way, policy can aim better at stimulating innovation and consequently, economic growth. (Dosi 1982, p. 160; BMBF 2017)

Innovation is a regionally dependent concept, as it is proven to spill over locally and favor certain regions. Additionally, economic growth and growth in innovation are dynamic processes which have to be contemplated over time. (Audretsch and Fritsch 2002)

Questions to be covered in this paper are the explicit explanation of innovative activity in Germany by several theoretically based socio-economic determinants. It is examined to which extent which determinant influences innovative activity and where it does so. Moreover, as a conclusion of these investigations, innovation promoting policies are matched to administrative districts. This is based on the estimated effects for the modeled determinants.

In this paper innovation is integrated in a system based on endogenous growth concepts in space over time. This multidimensional approach is appropriate, as technological innovation is the result from the interaction of social, economic and geographic factors on the technological frontier. (Oinas and Malecki 2002, pp. 102-103)

Furthermore, it is not only possible to explain which factors influence innovative activity and to which degree, but also where in Germany the individual determinants for innovation exert the most strength. A direct interpretation on the level of German adminis-

I. Rhoden, *Space and Time in German Innovative Activity*,
https://doi.org/10.1007/978-3-658-28600-2_13

trative districts (*Kreisfreie Städte* and *Landkreise*) for innovation-determining covariates is possible. It can be detected exactly in which district a certain covariate explains how much of the variation in innovative activity. This way, implications for innovation policy can be concluded and policies can be matched extremely closely to administrative regions.

The analysis carried out in this work will be based on Bayesian reasoning, as this allows interpreting the results as probability ("credible") intervals and facilitates using prior knowledge about determinants of innovative activity. Moreover, the specification of the model, its results, and the prior specification all hold valuable information about the relationship that leads to innovation. (Arrow 1969, pp. 30-31)

Generally, spatiotemporal models are found in many different fields of research, as they are not a fixed modeling concept. They rather consider time and space explicitly in building the model (Finkenstädt, Held, and Isham 2006, pp. 152-154). Applications can be found in environmental research (e.g. Patrick, Harvill, and Hansen (2016) or Paci, Gelfand, and Holland (2013)), epidemiology (e.g. Blangiardo et al. (2013) or Knorr-Held (2000)), biology (e.g. Gilman et al. (2015) or Zuur and Camphuysen (2012)), and in many more fields.

As time series models using panel data are a frequently applied model approach, the augmentation of this practice by introducing an explicit spatial reference and the corresponding Bayesian modeling of innovation determinants can be a further contribution to the field of empirical innovation and growth economics. The explicit consideration of a geoadditive model in the field of regional economics (with application possibilities for economic policies supporting innovation and economic growth) as a modeling approach has, as executed here, not been persecuted before.

The paper is further structured as follows: After introducing innovation as time and space dependent concept, in chapter 14 a theoretical basis is laid down, stressing the origins of innovation and growth theory. Concluding, hypotheses for the expected effects of innovation influencing covariates are pointed out. In chapter 15, the data is presented and examined more closely. Then the modeling approach for the relationship between innovation and determinants is explained.

Furthermore, the specification and the exact implementation in R (R Core Team 2019) is delineated. The results are interpreted afterwards in chapter 16, where the influences of the covariates as well as the temporal and spatial effects are analyzed. The hypotheses of chapter 14 are also answered here. After a short model discussion, final remarks and interpretations for the results conclude the paper.

A *region* in the context of this paper is used throughout interchangeably with the concept of German administrative districts, meaning *Landkreise* and *kreisfreie Städte* on NUTS-3 level. The concept which is investigated is *innovative activity*, which will also be referred to as innovation, innovation activity and is explicitly measured by the count of applicants of published patents.

14 Theoretical Framework

14.1 Innovation as Time-Space Relevant Concept

The positive impact of innovation on economic growth is unquestioned. In the field between growth theories and agglomeration concepts innovation is a main driver of growth itself (Acs and Varga 2002, p. 132). Additionally, innovation itself is also dependent on growth, as growth can create an innovation-friendly environment by providing incentives to invest. Nevertheless, the strength and direction of these connections are not easily determined. (Dosi 1982, p. 147)

As innovation as a measure is readily available via patent data, analyses on this factor influencing growth and on its determinants themselves are possible. In standard growth theories innovation as technological progress is the key discerning concept (Bertuglia, Lombardo, and Nijkamp 1997, p. 17). For this paper, the endogenous theory of growth shall be the basis. Mainly Romer (1990; 1994) as well as Aghion and Howitt (1998) shaped the growth process with technological progress not to be exogenous, but endogenous. The model-inherent technological progress is a non-rival and partially excludable good, produced by individual actors following market incentives to achieve profit by innovation. Therefore, knowledge is intentional and moreover, deliberately controllable. (Romer 1990, pp. 74-77)

Furthermore, patenting inventions can exclude others from benefiting from the technology so that firms are able to absorb costs for R+D. These means qualify as monopolistic powers on the market.

I. Rhoden, *Space and Time in German Innovative Activity*,
https://doi.org/10.1007/978-3-658-28600-2_14

Despite the invention being patented and replication therefore being permitted, knowledge is still able to spill over, as the patent is a public document. Technological progress therefore consists of two parts, a public part, here named A, which is the existing stock of knowledge and an excludable part, named H, which is human capital in R+D. If A increases, then H will also boost productivity. (Romer 1990, p. 83)

As Acs and Varga (2002, p. 140) state, in innovation geography this is not possible because of the tacitness of new knowledge. H is therefore locally tied. In the standard model by Romer, spatial considerations are not included, whereas several other works by e.g. Baldwin and Forslid (2000), Cheshire and Magrini (2000), Englmann and Walz (1995), and Walz (1997) provide considerations of augmenting the basic model of endogenous growth. Martin and Ottaviano (2001, p. 948) present the connection between growth and agglomeration as well, focusing on the cyclic behavior of growth through innovation, which is accelerated by agglomeration of knowledge, thus making innovation economically more feasible, which also leads to growth increases. Their model is based on Krugman's (1990; 1991) cost linkages, replacing the causation and agglomeration processes by inserting endogenous growth. Growth here leads then to geographic agglomeration by market interactions, so that geography matters for economic growth, even if no spillovers of knowledge happen. (Martin and Ottaviano 2001, pp. 947-949)

To illustrate this further, figure 14.1 shows the innovation generation process based on the concept of the production function, depending on technological progress A, human capital H, capital stock K and labor L. Growth and innovation impact each other and the connection is positive for either of them (e.g. innovation increases growth and vice versa). The technological component consisting of A and H is divided into a global and a regional part. Those are further influenced by globalization as well as institutions and moreover, by several other variables which will be included in the model used here. The regional part is covered by considering innovation among regions. This implies the necessity of considering spatial effects. The

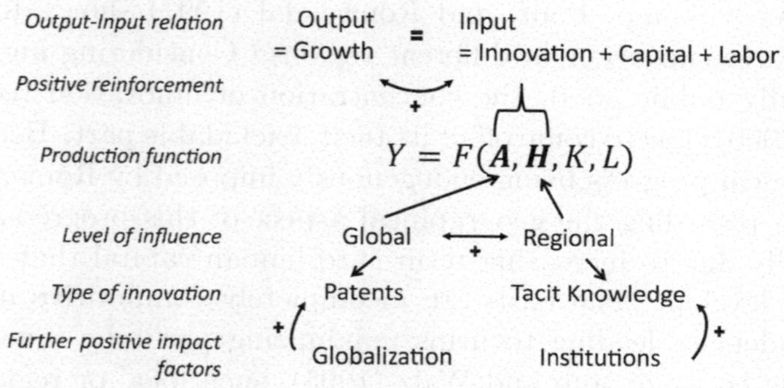

Figure 14.1: Theoretic model summary. In this illustration, the connection of several theories relevant in the context of this work are presented. Arrows show the direction of influence, a plus-sign stands for a positive influence. On the left part, the descriptions of the elements on the right are listed. (Romer 1990).

global part is inherent in the dependent variable of the model to be estimated, innovation activity (as proxied by patents). The outcome variable will be determined by patents, more precisely by the number of applicants of patents. One declared applicant (or participant) (in the development) of the patent equals one innovation activity. The latter are measured as dependent variable throughout the paper.

Accruing from Romer (1990, pp. 74-75), patents can be understood as standing for global knowledge transmission. A patent can be looked at by everyone and thus pose the base for creative adaptions and new ideas. The focus here lies on the spatial aspect of innovation, so the regional component reflected by knowledge passed on locally (H) and its impact on innovative activity are the main concern. All in all, the regional disparity of knowledge (effectively: innovative activity) is thus able to influence the outcome of innovative activity itself.

An important factor in this is the diffusion of knowledge over regions. As Nijkamp, Poot, and Rouwendal (1991) show, diverging growth rates can occur in different regions. Considering knowledge as partially public good, the concentration of innovation (compare Porter (2000)) has to come off of its tacit, excludable part. Because of technological progress being endogenously imposed by Romer's models, when regarding the geographical aspect of this progress, this is supposedly due to increasing returns to human capital that agglomerations develop. The basis are incompletely competitive monopolistic tendencies leading to firms maximizing profit by innovations. According to Englmann and Walz (1995), such local or regional external economies can also be caused by technological spillovers, not only by market size or pecuniary externalities. This therefore defines regional growth models including technological change as main driver. (McCann and Oort 2009, p. 24)

Spatial considerations today are not questioned anymore in the theories of economic growth and technological change, as they affect those directly and indirectly (Bertuglia, Lombardo, and Nijkamp 1997, p. 223). As Krugman (1991) recognizes, regions matter far more than nations. According to Acs, Anselin, and Varga (2002, p. 1070), space plays a major role in analyzing innovation activity. The distribution of knowledge is regionally distinct, as transmission of knowledge seems to influence where innovation happens. Clear regional patterns should consequently emerge and thus be identifiable and explicable.

Generally, the concept of innovation or knowledge to spill over from a region to another represents the basis of agglomeration concepts. Clustering of innovation is therefore evident and expected. Not only spillovers between firms in a region (*Marshall-Arrow-Romer externalities*), but spillovers from outside a sector (*Jacobs externalities*, (Jacobs 1969)) are combined in this model. Furthermore important are costs for transactions between the firms (Scott 1988), which, if low, facilitate knowledge exchange. These factors will be included in the model via covariates.

14.2 Hypothesizing on Innovative Activity

Following the general model of the former chapter, the influences on innovative activity are specified in detail. The endogenous model for growth, which is augmented to also apply to explaining innovation in figure 14.1, mainly names globalization and institutions in the broadest sense as impacting factors. Nevertheless, some general influences will also enter the model.

Productivity As such, productivity will be considered in the model as explaining factor. It is assumed that productivity influences innovation as well as an increase in economic growth in a region is also expected to increase innovative activity in the same region (Bos, Economidou, and Sanders 2013, p. 86). As McCann (2016) resumes, innovation and productivity are also connected via R+D. Pointing to Schumpeter (1934) and to Nelson and Winter (1982), innovation is part of the output of technological possibilities, and can reinforce productivity in a circular motion, where innovation brings profits that are then invested in R+D which leads, again, to innovation. Therefore, in regions with high productivity, innovative activity is also expected to be higher than in regions with less productivity. This can lead to productive regions innovating more, and thus being more productive as well. Romer (1990) and Aghion and Howitt (1998) also support this point of view, stressing a positive correlation between innovation and productivity.

Openness Starting with globalization, this can be delineated via foreign turnover. The higher the share of turnover generated abroad, the more active the firm is in innovating. This also corresponds to general openness which fosters gains from trade. Nevertheless, it is possible that this influence is also correlated with firm size, for instance, when the latter is measured via turnover in general. Higher turnover offers possibilities for investing more in innovation. (Hitt, Hoskisson, and Kim 1997)

Knowledge intensity Another factor which can impact innovation is the share of employees in knowledge-intensive industries. Those industries belong to the high-tech sector, which in its nature is often seen as the strongest sector with respect to innovative activity. If in a region there is a high share of workers in these industries, it is assumed that innovation per se is also higher compared to sectors where less knowledge-intensive industries are located. The important role of the high-tech sector in spawning innovation is widely renowned. Furthermore, the human capital bound in this variable is the key factor in technological progress for growth according to Romer (1990). (Ketels and Protsiv 2016)

High-tech clusters When naming knowledge intensive industries, also pointing in a similar direction are the location of high-tech clusters. Where those specific clusters exist, a higher innovation output is naturally assumed as the clusters contain mostly high-tech firms and institutions. Clusters are often reinforced because of special funding by federal or state policies based on their contribution to growth via innovation. Examples for such clusters in Germany are the *Hamburg Aviation* cluster in Hamburg, the *BioEconomy Cluster* in the state of Saxony-Anhalt or the *Cluster Electric Mobility South-West* in the state of Baden-Württemberg near Stuttgart. These examples are all part of the *Excellence Measure* by the German Ministry for Education and Research and belong to so-called leading-edge clusters which are especially high-technological. (Ketels and Protsiv 2016; BMBF 2015)

R+D institutes As clusters mostly consist of firms specialized in high-tech located together with research infrastructure, as another important representative for innovation all major German R+D institutes are also factored in. The considered institutions are for example institutes of the Max-Planck Society, the Fraunhofer Gesellschaft, or other internationally acclaimed institutes. (BMBF 2018a)

Furthermore, as R+D is a part of innovation itself, it is related to various other factors impacting innovation. The presence of R+D institutes needs highly-educated personnel, which is often attracted by factors of social overhead capital, meaning cultural and educational facilities, which are also often found in agglomerated regions. (Davelaar and Nijkamp 1997, pp. 32-33)

R+D funding Additionally to the cluster status of a region, where the cluster may or may not have been the result of administrative funding policies, explicit funding for R+D is also included in the model. The average sum of R+D funding by the Federal Ministry of Education and Research per year of the funding timeframe indicates, if a region is considered an innovation hub (BMBF 2017). It is expected accordingly that higher funding sums correspond to increased innovative activity. (Baumol 2002; Cai and Zhou 2014, p. 240)

Firm size Besides innovation specific factors, further general socio-economic influences on innovation activity exist. As patenting is rather expensive and consumes not only financial resources but also non-monetary expenses like personnel, larger firms are suspected to be more solvent than smaller firms (Arundel 2001, p. 613). Furthermore, firms which generate more turnover are here perceived to be larger and can often spend more on R+D. The spatial dispersion of larger and smaller firms also impacts innovative activity (Davelaar and Nijkamp 1997, pp. 21-22). Thus, firms with higher turnover are presumably larger and therefore expected to have a higher propensity to innovate. This propensity can then be measured in increased submission of patents. (Mohnen, Mairesse, and Dagenais 2006)

Urbanization and market potential Focusing on locational factors, regions where a high population density prevails and therefore also a high market potential exists shall also show increased innovative activity. This is due to Krugman and general agglomeration theories. Firms locate where they find employees and market structures to distribute their goods. Where goods are produced, workers move to, so this demand linked causality is an explanation for those regions also being favorable to innovative activity. Another reason is the smaller cost of transportation of goods for firms, so they tend to locate near each other. These concentration processes can also explain the formation of clusters where the conditions prove fruitful for firms. (Marshall 1890, p. 271; Fujita, Krugman, and Venables 1999, pp. 4-5)

Industry The industry share is, nevertheless, an example for applied theories of agglomeration externalities. The higher the share of employees in the industry sector, the higher the innovative activity, as most patents consider some kind of (high-)technological application. The latter are most often developed in firms in the industrial and especially high-tech sector of the economy. (Janger et al. 2017, p. 35)

Time effect Lastly, all covariates and their expected influences are investigated with respect to their behavior over time and over space. Innovative activity declines over the modeled timeframe, as the absolute counts of the data show. This could be due to higher global pressure on leading, high-innovative industries. Globalization increases competition and furthermore, highly qualified workers could be accepting more challenging jobs abroad (BMWi 2017, pp. 29-32). This relation should also show in the estimated effects, as the model takes this decline into account to avoid overstating.

Spatial effect Additionally, the impact of space is considered via allocating each variable to its corresponding administrative district in Germany. It is expected that this can unmask regional effects besides the concentration of innovative activity already contained in clusters. Moreover, a strong regional connection is anticipated, as innovation is bound to several factors (some of them are explained in the preceding paragraphs) which thus determine it. (Breschi 2000; Krugman 1991; Jaffe, Trajtenberg, and Henderson 1993)

Concerning the exact spatial allocation of the effects of the covariates, the distribution of the impacts among the districts follows mostly the expectations of the covariates mentioned prior. For example it is assumed that innovation manifests where high productivity prevails, and locates less so where productivity stagnates. Thus, in districts where the latter is high, innovative activity – supposed it is positively impacted by this covariate – can be analytically explained by it to a large degree. Therefore, all estimated effects are not only plotted in function plots with corresponding credible intervals, but also on a choropleth map of all 402 German districts.

15 Modeling the Innovation Relation

15.1 The Data

In the following analyses a set of patent publications from 2009 to 2016 is examined (DPMA 2017). Patents as indicator for innovation can be criticized, as Scherer (1965, p. 1098) for instance states. Innovation as such encompasses more than the inventions which are patented at last; and innovative action may not always result in a patent. Though, patents are the main data source available when measuring technological progress, as there exists a distinct connection between them and R+D efforts of firms. Those result in innovation and can therefore be classified as innovative activity further on. (Griliches 1990, pp. 335-336)

The variables used are listed in table 15.1.

Patent data in this paper is used for approximating innovative activity. One unit of innovative activity corresponds to exactly one applicant of a published patent (reference date is the publication date). As patent data is highly skewed to the left, leaving very few administrative districts with extremely high publication counts, the values are logarithmized to approximate the normal distribution. Additionally, as it is assumed that innovative activities need time to result in a published patent, a two-year time-lag accounts for this duration. It is the average interval from the application of a patent until its publication. This information is also contained in the dataset. Innovations

I. Rhoden, *Space and Time in German Innovative Activity*,
https://doi.org/10.1007/978-3-658-28600-2_15

(published patents) of 2016 therefore result from innovative efforts in 2014. The dependent variable innovative activity is dated back for the purpose of the calculations accordingly, so that they match the exogenous variables covering the timeframe with 2014 as the latest year.

To further elaborate on the covariates used, table 15.1 explains what makes up the proxy of a covariate. For *productivity*, the values are constructed taking the log of GDP (in market prices) in 1,000 EUR per worker. For *knowledge intensity*, employees in the following fields are considered: manufacturing of chemical and pharmaceutical products, of data processing devices, electronic and optical products, electrical equipment, engineering and the production of automobiles and automotive parts, and other vehicle construction sectors. For the covariates *openness* via foreign turnover and *firm size* via turnover, the values are the average sums in the sectors of mining and general manufacturing in 1,000 EUR per worker. These are either for recipients of deliveries and services in foreign countries (openness) or in Germany (firm size).

The values for the covariate *industry share* are constructed using the share of workers in the industrial sector of all inhabitants in a region of working age per 100 inhabitants. Sectors considered here are mining, general manufacturing, energy and water provision, and waste services. For *population density*, the number of inhabitants in a region is divided by the area of that region in square kilometers. The *market potential* is calculated via regional population potential. This is measured by the sum of a region's population in 1,000 inhabitants for the range of 100 kilometers linear distance, weighted by the area in square kilometers. This way, possibilities of spatial interaction can be indicated. If a high amount of population is reachable in the area surrounding a region and infrastructure is facilitating mobility, contact potential in a region is also high.

Considering the covariate *R+D funding*, values are obtained from the funding database of the German Federal Ministry of Research and Education. The sums are the average funding per year allocated in million EUR. The values contain funding profiles for projects in the following fields: R+D relevant educational spending, R+D for public services, technology and innovation funding, special university-related programs and university construction, and knowledge- generating and interdisciplinary fundamental research. Participating in allocating the funds are several project sponsors, mainly the German Federal Ministries of Education and Research, of Economic Affairs and Energy, for the Environment, Nature Conservation and Nuclear Safety, of Transport and Digital Infrastructure, of Food and Agriculture, and the Federal Ministry of Justice and Consumer Protection. (Die Bundesregierung 2019)

Table 15.1: Variable declaration. In this table all variables used are listed.

Shortcut	Variable	Description
		Dependent variable for the years 2011-2016
innov	Innovative activity	Logarithm of the number of published patents
		Indices
adminid	Spatial index	Number of administrative district to identify regions, reference year: 2014
yearid	Temporal index	Year of data obtained, time series identifier
		Covariates for the years 2009-2014
gdpem	Productivity	Logarithm of GDP per worker (working population)
know	Knowledge intensity	Logarithm of the share of workers (workers who are subject to social insurance contributions) in high-tech industry

Table 15.1 – *Continued on the next page*

Shortcut	Variable	Description
open	Openness	Logarithm of average foreign turnover per worker (worker who is subject to social insurance contributions)
ppot	Market potential	Logarithm of regional population potential (population per area in a radius of 100 kilometers)
ind	Industry	Logarithm of the share of workers in the industry (workers who are subject to social insurance contributions per 100 inhabitants of age 15-65)
popd	Agglomeration	Logarithm of population density (population per square kilometer)
turn	Firm size	Logarithm of average turnover per worker (worker who is subject to social insurance contributions)
fund	R+D funding	Logarithm of allocated (R+D) funds, mainly by the German Federal Ministry of Research and Education
clus	High-tech clusters	Dummy for high-tech clusters supported by policies by German Federal Ministries of Research and Education and of Economic Affairs and Energy
inst	R+D institutes	Dummy for non-university research organisations

The dummy for clusters is based on the cluster excellence strategy by federal ministries in Germany. These contain several cluster networks which are funded by federal government and federal states. Furthermore, clusters are from all fields of the industry and technology and can also be financed by the private sector (BMWi 2018). The dummy for R+D institutes contains the major research institutes located in Germany. These are institutes by the Fraunhofer-Gesellschaft, the Helmholtz Association, the Leibniz Association, the

Max-Planck-Gesellschaft, as well as R+D institutes of the German state (BMBF 2018b).

Table 15.2: Variable statistics.

Statistic	Mean	St. Dev.	Median	Min	Max
innov	3.20	1.40	3.00	0.00	8.90
adminid	8293.00	3763.00	8233	1001	16077
yearid	2012.00	1.70	2012.0	2009	2014
gdpem	4.10	0.17	4.10	3.70	5.00
know	2.20	0.72	2.20	−1.60	4.00
open	4.40	0.65	4.40	0.10	6.80
ppot	5.80	0.71	5.70	4.00	8.20
ind	2.80	0.40	2.80	1.60	4.50
popd	5.60	1.10	5.30	3.60	8.40
turn	5.40	0.39	5.40	4.20	7.20
fund	2.20	1.70	1.90	−1.70	8.50
clus	0.14	0.34	0	0	1
inst	0.21	0.41	0	0	1

All exogenous covariates used in the model are by the German BBSR (2018), Eurostat (2018) and by the Regional Database Germany (Statistisches Bundesamt 2018b) and date from 2009 to 2014. The data matches the regional structure of the patent data. As for 13 districts some values for foreign and domestic turnover as well as for investment are not available for some years of the investigation timeframe, those have been imputed via predictive mean matching. The dataset is used in its complete form, as it is refrained from removing outliers in the patent counts. The imputation of the missing values is executed via `R`-package `mice` (van Buuren and Groothuis-Oudshoorn 2011). Further transformations are executed by taking logs of all variables in the dataset to produce normally distributed coefficients, which facilitates use of the program *BayesX* (Belitz et al. 2015). Summary statistics are displayed in table 15.2.

15.2 Model Specification

The model applied is a geoadditive model with additional time dimension, which constitutes a spatiotemporal modeling approach. Compared to geoadditive models in the sense of Kammann and Wand (2003), the main discerning component is an added time series. This allows to check for time related variance of the covariates that also interacts with spatial influences in the model. The resulting estimates are suitable for showing if innovative activity has a space and a time varying behavior at the same time. Spatiotemporal models can be derived from the family of (and executed as) GAMMs.

Those descend from GAMs (Hastie and Tibshirani 1990), which are able to model linear as well as nonlinear covariates by applying splines to smooth nonlinear functions (Wood 2004). With this approach, linear as well as nonlinear effects of covariates on the dependent variable can be estimated, so this approach increases modeling flexibility and, correspondingly, model fit. (Wood 2017)

Also, the distribution of the response variable innovation activity can be considered appropriately. Because this variable descends from patent publications, which naturally follow a very skewed distribution (Fahrmeir, Kneib, and Lang 2009, p. 33), a negative binomial or Poisson distribution can be neglected only because of the log-transformation.

The model is geoadditive because of one or more influences of spatial variables accounting for the geographic origin of the data. It is recommended to use a flexible modeling approach like mixed modeling that can account for differing effects appropriately. As a mixed model also allows nonparametric covariates, the resulting fit of the model can be improved, and the estimates are expected to be more definite. (Kneib and Fahrmeir 2011, p. 334)

Here, the locational effect is included in the model because the dataset is divided into administrative districts. As each district is not only a geographic location, but also a municipal decision, the interpretation of results is manifold. (Kammann and Wand 2003, pp. 2-3; Wood 2017)

Innovative activity $innov_{i,t}$ with districts $i = 1, ..., 402$ in years $t = 1, ..., 6$ is to be explained by several covariates $X_{i,t}$ and $C_{i,t}$ with a normal parameter distribution. The model is as follows:

$$\begin{aligned} innov_{i,t} &\sim Normal(\nu_{i,t}, \epsilon) \\ \nu_{i,t} &= f_{spatial}(district_i) + f_{time}(year_t) + f_3 X_{i,t} + C_{i,t} \end{aligned} \tag{15.1}$$

Innovative activity consists of an additive predictor $\nu_{i,t}$ that varies over region i and time t and an error term ϵ, which all follow the normal distribution. The additive predictor contains a spatial effect $f_{spatial}(district_i)$ via geographic coordinates of the district boundaries, which accounts for the spatial correlation in the data and is combined with boundary information about the location of the districts. $f_{time}(year_t)$ represents the time trend of the data that accounts for temporal correlations. Further nonlinear covariates with additional smoothing are incorporated via $f_3 X_{i,t}$, while $C_{i,t}$ consists of linearly modeled covariates. (Kneib and Fahrmeir 2011, p. 340)

The corresponding smooth functions applied to the covariates are based on penalized regression splines. Splines present functions of some kind (for example cubic polynomials), which form, assembled at their end points (so called knots), the final curve which is used to describe the data. The spline-based smooth shall represent the data, but not result in a curve too wiggly to derive any interpretative effect. (Wood 2017, pp. 215-219)

As ML (or REML) estimation methods are limited concerning the estimation of such complex mixed effects models, fully Bayesian estimation is executed accordingly (Gelman et al. 2014). This way, probabilistic statements for every value in the model can be derived and prior knowledge about parameters can be specified, which facilitates the estimation and can result in accurate estimates. With ML, this is not necessary, as this branch of estimation methods relies on repeated samples only, which are independent of any prior beliefs. With Bayesian statistical reasoning, external knowledge influences the data, which can lead to better estimates (considering the quality of the external knowledge is good; otherwise the estimates are no worse than those of ML estimation processes). (Gelman et al. 2014; Kruschke 2015) .

The model is estimated via *BayesX*, which furthers not only REML estimation but MCMC estimation as well. *BayesX* allows to use common `R`-syntax and is interconnected with standard plotting possibilities and diagnostics. The probability intervals resulting of the estimation allow interpretations about the estimated posterior distribution, which arises from the prior information and the likelihood (the data). The range of values of the probability interval states the uncertainty of the model and can be interpretated relatively intuitively. In general, the probability information gained from the results is conditional on the observed values. The 97.5% probability interval for instance explains the range of values on the posterior distribution in which an unknown parameter, given the data, may lie with 97.5% probability. (Gelman et al. 2014, p. 11)

15.3 Programmed Application

The precedingly explained model can be implemented in `R` via the package `R2BayesX`. The exact underlying construction of the estimation procedure can be obtained from the manuals of *BayesX* (Belitz et al. 2018a; Belitz et al. 2018c; Belitz et al. 2018b). The general structure follows a GAM with a space and a time effect, modeled as additive (non-)parametric terms. Nonparametric terms are smoothed via the function $sx()$. This is a smooth nonlinear function, which is based on the function $s()$ and uses penalized splines as smoothers. The number of knots is automatically selected and suitable for most regression problems. (Umlauf et al. 2015, p. 14; Wood 2003; Wood 2004; Wood 2017)

In detail, the following is the general construction of the spatial and the temporal term. The spatial effect is modeled depending on the index of the regional administrative district, which locates the observations in Germany via a map object (which contains the boundaries of the districts in form of geographic coordinates). The spline used is a geospatial spline, which accounts for the locational aspect of the data. The temporal effect can also be included via the function $sx()$, but as data exploration did not point to the term being incorporated best as nonparametric term, it is constructed as a linear additive term.

$$\begin{aligned} sx(district_i, base - spline = geospatial, map = districts) + year_t \\ = sx(adminid, map = districts) + yearid \end{aligned} \tag{15.2}$$

The final model comprises the spatiotemporal model with geographical and temporal effects as well as nonlinear and linear covariates. Also included are dummy variables for the districts with main offices of R+D institutes ($inst = 1$ if an institute is located in a region, $= 0$ otherwise) and a regional cluster identifier ($clus = 1$ if a region contains promoted high-tech clusters, $= 0$ otherwise):

$$\begin{aligned} \texttt{innov} \sim dummies + nonlinear\,covariates + linear\,covariates \\ + spatial\,effect + time\,effect \end{aligned} \tag{15.3}$$

with

$$dummies \sim \texttt{clus} + \texttt{inst} \tag{15.4}$$

$$\begin{aligned} nonlinear\,covariates \sim \texttt{sx(know)} + \texttt{sx(fund)} + \texttt{sx(inv)} \\ + \texttt{sx(open)} + \texttt{sx(popd)} + \texttt{sx(ind)} + \texttt{sx(ppot)} \end{aligned} \tag{15.5}$$

$$linear\,covariates \sim \texttt{turn} + \texttt{gdpem} \tag{15.6}$$

$$\textit{spatial effect} \sim \texttt{sx(adminid, base - spline = "geospatial",} \\ \texttt{map = districts)} \tag{15.7}$$

$$\textit{time effect} \sim \texttt{yearid} \tag{15.8}$$

The final specification regarding whether a covariate is modeled linearly or nonlinearly is based on visual inspection of the data beforehand. When the relation towards the dependent variable is seemingly linear, this is modeled accordingly and then the overall model fit is analyzed with regard to general model explanation. Therefore, covariates for turnover and productivity are modeled linearly. All other terms (except the dummy variables) are incorporated nonlinearly. The spatial effect is based on two-dimensional geospatial penalized splines. The estimation uses the coordinates of the district's centroids constructed from a map of all German districts. (Umlauf et al. 2015, p. 15)

The time trend is also a linear factor in the model, as the relatively short timeframe of the analysis does not give indications for irregular behavior of the data over time. A nonlinear modeling approach here does not add to the explanatory content.

As the Bayesian reasoning allows, priors can be specified accordingly. These inform the data and, if reasonably chosen, can benefit the sampling. Generally, with *BayesX* priors are implicitly assumed via the type of spline applied for a term. For the default specification, it is relied on penalized splines for the covariates. The priors are shaped by the assumption about the degree of smoothness of the function $sx()$ and follow a gamma distribution. (Belitz et al. 2018a, pp. 11-13)

16 Analyses and Outcomes

The results of the MCMC estimation with 50,000 iterations (and a burn in period of 10,000 wherein samples are discarded) and 4 chains are shown in tables 16.1 and 16.2. The number of observations is 2412, as for the 402 districts data for six years is utilized. The mean and the standard deviation stated together with the probability intervals give information about the posterior probability calculated. The latter is based on the prior information available and on the dataset. The mean stated in the table for each covariate is the mean estimated by sampling over the prior and the likelihood by employing MCMC. The probability interval states the respective percentage with which the posterior (the estimated mean) lies in that interval. For the covariate *gdpem* the mean is estimated as 1.22 and it lies below 1.59 with a probability of 97.5%. For the other covariates, the intervals look also sensible. Merely the intervals of the intercept, the region identifier *adminid* and the smooth $sx(popd)$ for population density express a little higher uncertainty by showing somewhat wider intervals. *Sigma*, the scale estimate of the variance of the model, is denoted with a mean of 0.46 and the 97.5% probability interval lies below 0.48. The interval is narrow and seems reasonably.

I. Rhoden, *Space and Time in German Innovative Activity*,
https://doi.org/10.1007/978-3-658-28600-2_16

Table 16.1: MCMC estimation, parametric coefficients. These are the results of the estimation for the linearly modeled coefficients.

			Credible intervals		
Covariate	Mean	Std. Dev.	2.5%	50%	97.5%
(Intercept)	173.88	18.90	135.81	174.16	210.75
clus	0.31	0.06	0.16	0.31	0.44
inst	-0.14	0.06	-0.25	-0.14	-0.03
turn	-0.32	0.08	-0.48	-0.32	-0.16
gdpem	1.22	0.19	0.85	1.21	1.59
yearid	-0.09	0.01	-0.10	-0.09	-0.07
N = 2412		burnin = 10,000	iterations = 50,000		
		method: MCMC	family: Normal		

Table 16.2: MCMC estimation, smooth term variances. These are the results of the estimation for the nonlinearly modeled coefficients. All terms are smoothed with penalized splines, the scale estimate shows the variance of the model.

			Credible intervals		
Covariate	Mean	Std. Dev.	2.5%	50%	97.5%
sx(adminid)	6.85	2.21	3.66	6.47	12.17
sx(fund)	0.81	0.76	0.04	0.61	2.81
sx(ind)	0.78	0.88	0.06	0.48	3.35
sx(know)	0.06	0.08	0.00	0.04	0.26
sx(open)	0.05	0.05	0.00	0.04	0.19
sx(popd)	2.61	1.92	0.20	2.19	7.44
sx(ppot)	0.09	0.08	0.02	0.07	0.30
		Scale estimate:			
Sigma	0.46	0.01	0.43	0.46	0.49
N = 2412		burnin = 10,000		iterations = 50,000	
		method: MCMC		family: Normal	

16.1 Interpretation and Assessment of Effects

In figures 16.1 to 16.8 the results of the estimation are plotted. All linear and nonlinear effects are included. Furthermore, the spatial effects of each covariate are shown next to the estimated general effects. This way it is apparent where in Germany a covariate exerts the biggest effect in the estimation. Regions where a single covariate has an increased importance can be determined. In general, the plots (part (a) of the figures) show on the x-axis from left to right the regions with low values in the respective covariate to high values in that covariate. The corresponding frequency of regions for a value is indicated by a rug plot on the x-axis. For example, on the left a region which exhibits a lower productivity is marked, on the right regions with higher productivity are illustrated (compare figure 16.8a). On the y-axis the effect on the dependent variable innovative activity is plotted. Considering the nonlinearly modeled covariates, the 80% and 95% probability intervals are relatively close to the estimated curve. Only for small and very large values of the covariate the bands diverge somewhat more, which is due to sparse data in those ranges. In the spatial illustration (part (b) of the figures) regions are colored darkest where the effect of the determinant is highest, and colored lightest where the effect deviates negatively from the mean.

Dummies for high-tech clusters and R+D institutes The inclusion of the dummies for innovation clusters and for research institutes into the model improves model fit overall, as the divergence information criterion is smaller with incorporated dummies. Also, the residual spatial variation is slightly smaller, as the dummies seem to be able to reduce residual spatial variation. This points to those influences being an important factor in innovation activity. Regions where research institutes or (industrial) clusters of high-tech firms are located contribute significantly to innovative activity in Germany.

Knowledge intensity For employees in knowledge intensive industries (compare figure 16.1a), there are few regions with low knowledge

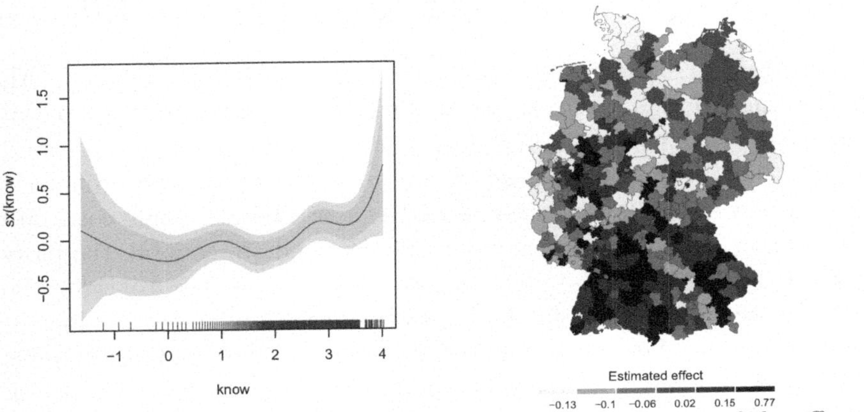

(a) Estimated effect. **(b)** Spatial distribution of the effect.

Figure 16.1: Estimate for knowledge intensity.

intensity in the sample, as the values cluster in the range of higher knowledge intensity to the right of the x-axis. This is also illustrated by the wider credible intervals on the left, which narrow towards the right, where more data is available. There is a slightly increasing trend to observe, although there are substantial fluctuations up and down. For regions with small values of knowledge intensity, the effect on innovative activity is slightly decreasing, then varies slightly up and down with increasing intensity. Finally, in regions with high knowledge intensity there is illustrated a positive impact onto innovative activity. Nevertheless, the fluctuations are omittable as they do not have major impacts and vary around a relatively constantly increasing mean value. Regarding figure 16.1b, the highest influences of the covariate on innovative activity are exclusively in the south and west of Germany. This applies, for instance, to the administrative districts of Tuttlingen, Oberallgäu, Lahn-Dill-Kreis, or Soest in North Rhine-Westphalia. Less important for explaining innovation is knowledge intensity, for example in Aachen, Landkreis Leipzig, or Fulda.

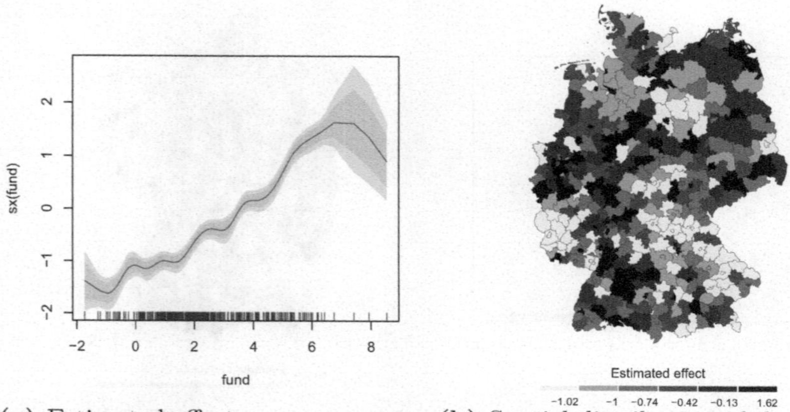

(a) Estimated effect. (b) Spatial distribution of the effect.

Figure 16.2: Estimate for R+D funding.

R+D funding For the covariate expressing funding in administrative districts (compare figure 16.2a), the expected positive effect on innovative activity can be confirmed. Here, regions with lower values of funding are more frequent. For those regions with small rates of funding, there seems to be a decreasing effect on innovation, as the effect is negative. With increasing funding, the effect on innovative activity seems to increase as well, which confirms that funding in education and research benefits innovative activity. Additionally, the more funding – not only by the Federal Ministry of Education and Research – firms in a region get, the more profitable the effect on innovation appears to be. For highest amounts of funding, the effect seems to be decreasing again, but this applies only to few regions. The most potential in explaining innovative activity is relatively dispersed over German districts (compare figure 16.2b). It is achieved in e.g. Aachen, Bremen, Main-Kinzig-Kreis, Stuttgart, or Bautzen. Less influence, for example, seems to be given in the western (border) part of Rheinland-Pfalz, or at the eastern Bavarian border to Czechia.

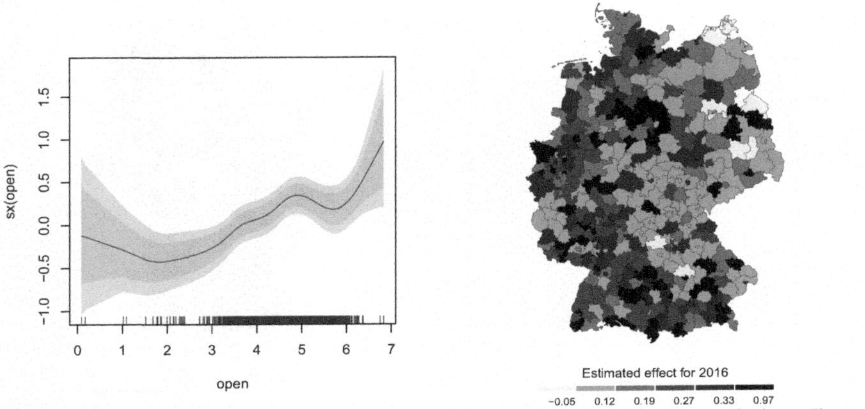

(a) Estimated effect. **(b)** Spatial distribution of the effect.

Figure 16.3: Estimate for openness.

Openness Considering openness measured by the share of foreign turnover, the picture is ambivalent. For the indicator (see figure 16.3a), the effect is constant for regions exhibiting less turnover, whereas for regions with higher shares in turnover, the effect on innovative activity is positive and increasing. Especially for the districts with firms showing high turnover, the effect is strongly positive. Most districts lie in the middle range, benefiting from a slightly positive effect. Considering figure 16.3b, the influence of openness is relatively evenly dispersed across Germany, while higher contributions seem to be made in districts in the western part of the country. Some hotspots are for example in Düsseldorf or Regen, but also in Celle or Hanover. Cold spots are in Eichstätt or Vorpommern-Rügen, but as with the hotspots, there are few, as most regions do not diverge too far from the mean.

Firm size Turnover in total (figure 16.4a) as indicator for firm size is modeled linearly, as a nonlinear function did not add to the model fit substantially. The relation to innovative activity in regions is strongly negative. This means that the more turnover a firm in a

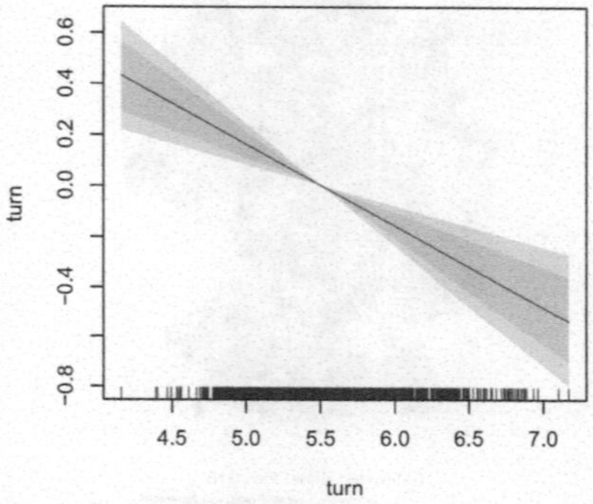

(a) Estimated effect.

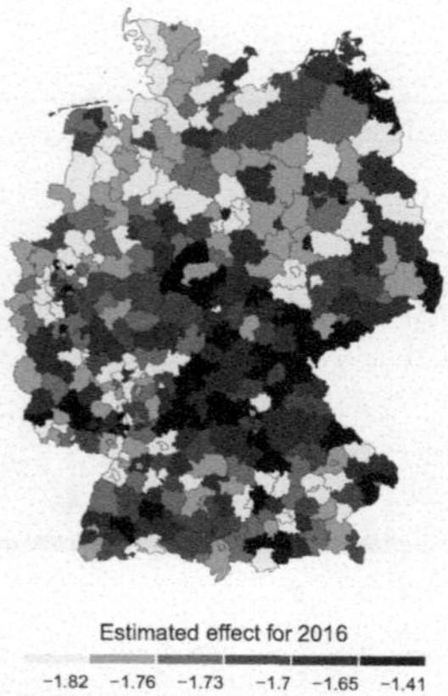

(b) Spatial distribution of the effect.

Figure 16.4: Estimate for firm size.

region displays, thus the larger a firm is, the more adverse the effect on innovation seems to be. Larger firms therefore do not suggest higher innovation counts. The contribution of firm size in the estimation leads to some hotspots mostly in the eastern regions and in the middle of Germany (compare 16.4b). Here, firm size contributes higher to innovative activity than in western parts of the country. Highest values are achieved in e.g. Görlitz, Vogtlandkreis, Bad Kissingen, or Northeim. Less importance for innovation by firm size can be noted in Recklinghausen, Ammerland, the greater Munich area, or Göppingen.

Population density For population density as an indicator for agglomerated space, the effect is difficult to interpret, as its estimate is relatively volatile (compare figure 16.5a). Regions in all ranges of population density are present, so that the credible intervals are, with few exceptions, relatively narrow. Districts which present low population density first have a positive, then immediately a negative effect onto innovative activity. The more densely a region is popu-

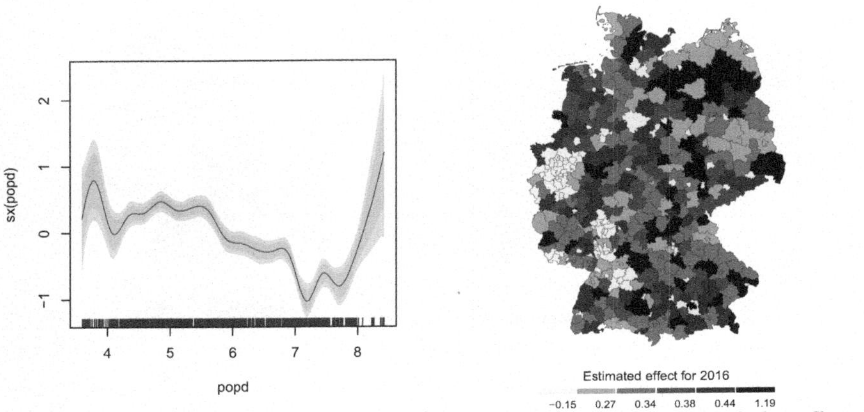

(a) Estimated effect.

(b) Spatial distribution of the effect.

Figure 16.5: Estimate for population density.

lated, the effect remains relatively constant before it declines strongly. For stronger agglomerated regions the effect fluctuates up and down, and the effect on innovation seems to be negative. For regions in that special range of population density (densities around 1808.04), this characteristic points to an impediment to innovation. Nevertheless, the most densely populated regions suggest a sharp increase in innovative activity. Checking for the importance of the covariate among regions, the picture is quite dispersed, but with a clear pattern (compare figure 16.5b): In agglomerated regions the importance is throughout small and deviates from the mean in decreasing direction. For example, cold spots are the Ruhr area, in most bigger cities as Bremen, Hamburg, Kaiserslautern, Dresden, and in the area surrounding Munich. On the contrary, Munich itself is a hotspot, where population density seems to matter highly for explaining innovative activity. Further hotspots are Trier, Bautzen, Freudenstadt, or the northern districts of Brandenburg.

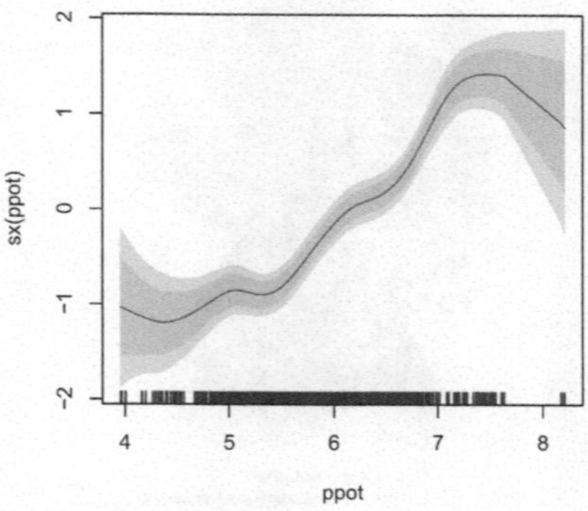

(a) Estimated effect.

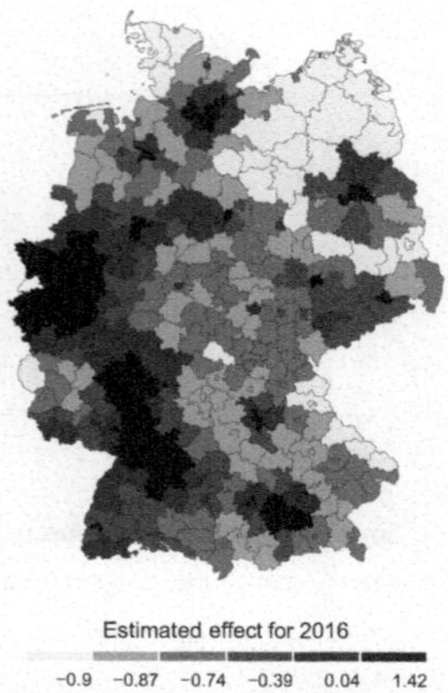

(b) Spatial distribution of the effect.

Figure 16.6: Estimate for market potential.

Market potential Contrariwise, the effect of market potential (figure 16.6a), expressed through population potential, is first relatively constant, but then increases significantly the higher the market potential rises and increases above zero. Regions with largest potential then suffer a declining effect, as innovative activity seems to be negatively impacted there. This could be related to the situation in agglomerated regions. Regarding the spatial importance of the effect in figure 16.6b, the nature of the covariate gets obvious: As market potential is a measure containing information about the population potential in a region with 100km radius, the resulting estimated effect is also somewhat smoothed over the regions. Hotspots are in the north western part of North Rhine-Westphalia, the Frankfurt (Main)-Stuttgart-axis, and the metropolis spaces of Munich, Berlin, and Hamburg. In these regions the market potential is high and the effect onto innovation follows this. Negative deviations from the mean and therefore lower importance occurs in regions in Mecklenburg-Vorpommern, the northern regions of Schleswig-Holstein, and the eastern parts of Bavaria.

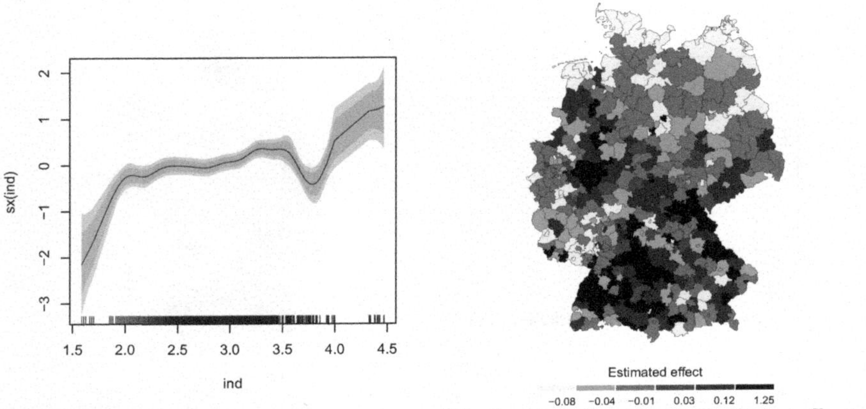

(a) Estimated effect. (b) Spatial distribution of the effect.

Figure 16.7: Estimate for industry share.

These regions also correspond to regions with lower absolute market potential.

Industry The industry share of a region, measured by the share of employees in firms of the industry sector, has an overall constant impact onto innovative activity (see figure 16.7a). As regions with very low (very high) industry shares are relatively rare (the rug plot concentrates in the middle part of the x-axis), the strongly increasing effects there should not be valued too highly. For regions with average industry shares there seems to be no distinctively positive or negative impact considering innovative activity. For some regions with almost highest shares, there appears to be a dip in the effect, meaning that for some districts with larger shares the effect is rather variable. In sum, the effect seems to be negligible. Regarding figure 16.7b, a higher effect of industry share on innovative activity is mostly scattered over districts in the south of Germany. Hotspots are for instance the area south west of the Hochsauerlandkreis, the area

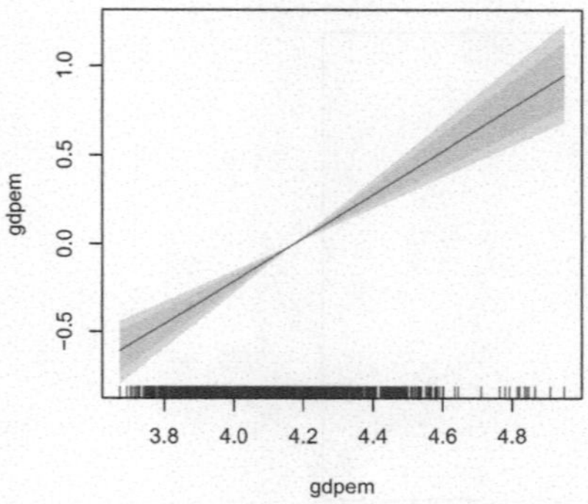

(a) Productivity.

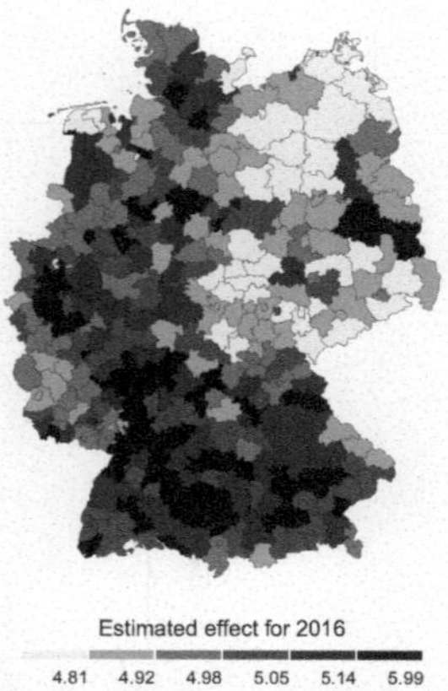

(b) Estimated separated effect of productivity.

Figure 16.8: Estimate for productivity.

around Schwäbisch Hall, or Hof. The north and north east are rather unimportant for innovation, as the values there are mostly lower.

Productivity A positive effect on innovation activity is observed the higher the productivity in a district increases (figure 16.8a). The relation is modeled linearly and increases constantly. Higher productivity seems to go hand in hand with higher innovation. Higher innovation could then lead to increased productivity as well, accelerating and influencing itself repeatedly. Towards the right end of the scale the credible intervals widen, as only few regions exhibit largest values in productivity. Nevertheless, the effect is clear. In figure 16.8b the spatial representation of the effect is shown. Again, the west and especially the south are favored in terms of importance of productivity for the model. Hotspots of importance coincide with areas of innovative activity, as e.g. the region from Frankfurt (Main) towards Stuttgart or the region of the Ruhr area towards Cologne. Also, Munich, Bremen, and Hamburg are important here. Less influ-

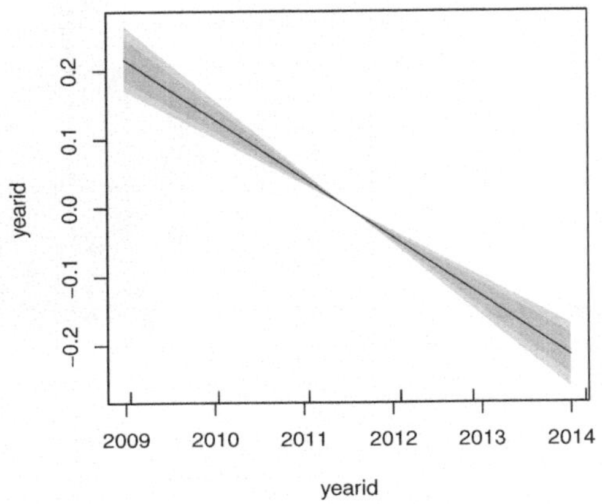

Figure 16.9: Estimated effect of time on innovation. The relation is modeled parametrically.

ence applicable is exuded by Mecklenburg-Vorpommern, the southern fringe of Saxony, and the coastal area of the Baltic Sea.

The effect of time on innovative activity (illustrated in figure 16.9) is modeled linearly. The timeframe consists of six years, from 2009 to 2014 (or 2011 to 2016 respectively). No smoothing is necessary, as the relation is decreasing and best explained linearly. Overall, the estimated effect of time is negative. This is not surprising, considering the general decline in innovative activity measured in absolute numbers over the timeframe. The effect thus corresponds to the actual development of innovative activity in absolute terms, which confirms the validity of the model and is an expected result.

Regarding the spatial effect shown in figure 16.10, there seems to be a relatively strong variation over space. As this is the core component of the geoadditive model, here the residual spatial autocorrelation is plotted. Hotspots of activity are marked dark, cold spots are colored light. Where the map is colored flat, the effect corresponds to

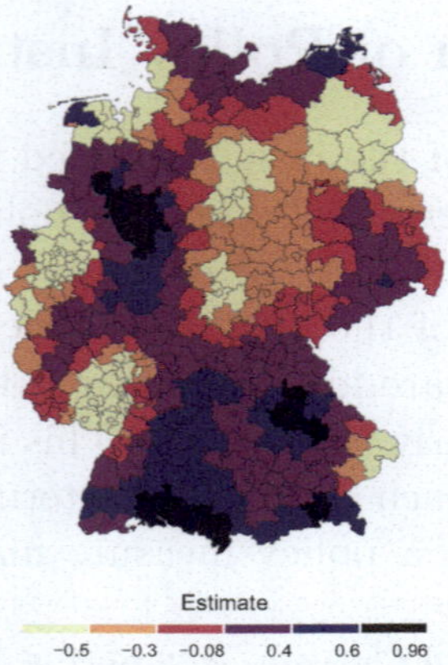

Figure 16.10: Spatial effect of innovative activity. The map illustrates the spatial residuals produced by the spatiotemporal model (2009-2016) and contains leftover variation which is not accounted for by the covariates used.

the mean, as hotspots and cold spots are deviations from the latter. Hotspots are in the region around Münster, Bielefeld, and further down south towards Kassel and Marburg. Also indicating higher activity are some districts at the North and Baltic Sea coasts, as well as in Saxony and north of Dresden. Almost completely marked as a hotspot area is the southern part of Germany, with regions around Stuttgart, at the Bodensee, the southern border of Germany, and in the eastern districts near Nuremberg.

Notable cold spots are on the coast of the North Sea in Lower-Saxony, around Berlin, in the Ruhr Area, near Aachen and Passau, as well as there happens to be a cold valley in the northern center of Germany. All regions deviating from the mean appear in small clusters of administrative districts, often with the most extreme deviation in the middle. This points to a fading effect into the surrounding regions. Thus, when a region exhibits innovative activity strongly deviating from the mean, its effect, whether positive or negative, decreases, the farther this region is. Nevertheless, the magnitude of these deviations is not overly large, as it ranges from circa -1 to +1.

16.2 Application of Policy Instruments

A possible application of the insights gained in the previous section can be made by fitting regional economic policy programs to the estimated regional effects. Part (b) of figures 16.1 to 16.8 illustrates the regional allocation of the estimated effects. Regions where the effects of the covariates are lower, compared to regions where the effects are higher, are clearly identifiable. This information is available for each region and for each covariate / determinant and can be used when considering where a policy measure may be introduced most effectively and efficiently.

In this section, selected German regional policies are presented and matched to regions, taking simultaneously into account to which economic area the funding measures apply. Consequentially, for each relevant policy, regions where it should best be applied can be listed. The aim of this is the desire to realize the potential for an increase of innovative activity. Regionally relevant policies can increase innovation not only by promoting innovation itself, but additionally by indirectly funding determinants of innovation, matched to each individual region.

As Untiedt et al. (2016) state, regionally relevant funding in Germany is not solely limited to structurally weak regions but follows general economic growth principles as well. It is furthermore diverse, often with overlapping aims, instruments, and scope of action, and affects several economic branches simultaneously. (Untiedt et al. 2016, pp. 139, 250)

With the help of the funding database by the German Federal Ministry for Economic Affairs and Energy (BMWi 2019k), a selection of possible choices for funding measures is made. The programs and the corresponding level of operation are described briefly in table A.2 in chapter 18.4 in the appendix (see also for further references on the programs). Some programs for regional support are available for all regions and federal states in Germany, whereas others are only eligible to firms in a certain federal state.

The measures are then matched to the estimated coefficients from the spatiotemporal model of section 16. This is achieved in table 16.3. Based on the estimated coefficients for the covariates of the model for innovation activity, the corresponding spatial level on which the policy operates, the measure itself, and some arbitrarily selected regions for which this measure could be used, are listed.

The policy measures can either support a region where the effect for a covariate is above average – in a hotspot – so that an already innovative region gets strengthened even more. This focuses on boosting innovative performance (see column *Reinforce effect*). Alternatively, a region where the effect is lower than average – a cold spot – can be supported, so that innovative activity across all regions happens to be more balanced (see column *Compensate effect*). For both types of impact some exemplary regions are listed. For all other regions being estimated with a similar value, this procedure can be applied as well, as the selection of regions is arbitrary and not exhaustive.

Generally, the effects on innovation are highest where the absolute value of a covariate is also highest. If a region is for instance highly productive, then the effect on innovation is also highest in that region.

Contrariwise, for covariate effects of *firm size* (measured by turnover) there is a diverging effect apparent: The higher the firm size, the lower the effect onto innovation, until the effect of highest firm size in a region has a negative effect on innovation. To reinforce a positive effect onto innovation, regions where the effect of firm size is high, should be funded – these are regions where absolute firm size is low. To compensate regions with low effects, i.e. funding specially supporting SME can be applied.

This scheme also applies for covariates *population density* and *market potential.* There is a switch of direction in the estimated curve illustrating the effect (compare figures 16.5a and 16.6a). For population density, the effect is lowest where the absolute value of the determinant is not minimal or maximal, but in between. To reinforce the effect of the covariate on innovation, regions with either very low or very high population density should be selected for allocating funding. To compensate, policy can use the potential leading to an increase or a decrease in population density, as both directions lead to higher effects onto innovation. For market potential, the effect is highest where the absolute value is almost maximal. To reinforce funding effects on innovation, not the regions with highest market potential should be selected for funding, but regions with a value slightly below. To compensate, regions with either very low or very high market potential can be selected, either boosting potential or lowering it slightly.

The mentioned policy programs are, because they tend to aim at innovation in general, rather broadly applicable to the estimated coefficients. For example, the *go-Inno* funding program is targeted mainly at SME, but as it aims for increasing innovative capacity, it adds to increasing effects for the covariate *R+D funding* as well as to the covariate *firm size*. The selection of the funding programs is also arbitrarily chosen and not exhaustive, as well as its association with a corvariate is not exclusive. (BMWi 2019k)

Table 16.3: Regional policy measures per estimated effect. This table contains regionally relevant funding programs for supporting regions in Germany and matches them to the estimated effects of the spatiotemporal model. The aim is to increase innovative activity. Either weak regions can be compensated by applying measures, or strong regions can be supported to increase performance. For further references to the programs see the appendix, chapter 18.4. (BMWi 2019k).

		Example regions	
Covariate	Program name	Reinforce effect	Compensate effect
Knowledge intensity	CONNECT Education-Research-Innovation	Eisenach, Traunstein	Düsseldorf, Münster
	Education bonus	Ingolstadt, Soest	Dessau-Roßlau, Stendal

Table 16.3 – *Continued on the next page*

Covariate	Program name	Example regions Reinforce effect	 Compensate effect
	Funding for innovation by universities and R+D institutes	Emden, Holzminden, Wolfsburg	Göttingen, Oldenburg, Osnabrück
	Funding for innovative professional education	Göppingen, Ludwigsburg, Reutlingen	Freiburg
	go-Inno	Leverkusen, Warendorf	Helmstedt, Gera
	Knowledge transfer funding	Saarlouis, Saarpfalz Kreis	Merzig-Wadern, Saarbrücken
R+D funding	CONNECT Education-Research-Innovation	Freiburg, Karlsruhe	Höxter, Ostholstein
	Development of digital technologies	Münster, Kiel	Eifelkreis Bitburg-Prüm, Freudenstadt
	Funding for innovation by universities and R+D institutes	Braunschweig, Oldenburg	Harburg, Wittmund
	Funding for regional development	Darmstadt, Gießen	Hersfeld-Rotenburg, Odenwaldkreis
	Funding for research, innovation and technology	Berlin	-

Table 16.3 – *Continued on the next page*

Covariate	Program name	Example regions	
		Reinforce effect	Compensate effect
	go-Inno	Erfurt, Leipzig	Garmisch-Partenkirchen, Memmingen
	INVEST - Funding for venture capital	Dresden, Frankfurt (Oder)	Kleve, Tirschenreuth
Openness	Foreign trade funding	Flensburg, Lübeck, Neumünster	Ostholstein
	Market development program	Koblenz, Lörrach	Elbe-Elster, Neustadt Bad Windsheim
	Program for Internationalization	Berlin	-
	Trade fair presentations	Hanover, Nienburg, Wolfsburg	Leer, Wittmund
Firm size	Foreign trade funding	Potsdam, Vorpommern-Greifswald	Munich, Regen, Uckermark
	INVEST - Funding for venture capital	Kassel, Landkreis Kaiserslautern	Konstanz, Zweibrücken
	go-Inno	Bad Kissingen, Hof	Hagen, Frankfurt (Main)

Table 16.3 – *Continued on the next page*

Covariate	Program name	Example regions	
		Reinforce effect	Compensate effect
	Market development program	Dessau-Roßlau, Vogtlandkreis	Eisenach, Leipzig, Wittenberg
	Personnel transfer	Bonn, Bottrop, Herne, Wuppertal	Bochum, Cologne, Recklinghausen
	Trade fair presentations	Braunschweig, Northeim	Ammerland, Emsland, Gifhorn
Population density	Experimental urban development	Berlin, Mecklenburgische Seenplatte	Chemnitz, Dresden
	Funding for sustainable urban development	Lahn-Dill-Kreis, Schwalm-Eder-Kreis	Frankfurt (Main), Offenbach
	Urban development funding	Grafschaft Bentheim, Rendsburg-Eckernförde	Hanover, Schwerin
	Urban renewal funding	Hochsauerlandkreis	Bonn, Cologne, Ruhr area, Städteregion Aachen

Table 16.3 – *Continued on the next page*

Covariate	Program name	Example regions	
		Reinforce effect	Compensate effect
Market potential	Funding for private railway siding	Braunschweig, Bremen, Erlangen	Cham, Rhön-Grabfeld
	Funding for municipal roadmaking	Erfurt	Ilm-Kreis, Nordhausen
	INVEST - Funding for venture capital	Berlin, Dresden	Freyung-Grafenau, Vorpommern-Rügen
	State program for rural development	Herford, Stormarn	Cottbus, Nordfriesland, Schleswig-Flensburg
	Urban renewal funding	Cologne, Bonn, Ruhr area	Höxter
Industry share	Funding for research, innovation and technology	Baden-Baden, Coburg, Germersheim	Erding, Leipzig
	Funding for regional development	Kulmbach, Wolfsburg	Oldenburg, Potsdam-Mittelmark
	INVEST - Funding for venture capital	Erlangen-Höchstatt, Ulm	Helmstedt, Lüneburg

Table 16.3 – *Continued on the next page*

Covariate	Program name	Example regions Reinforce effect	 Compensate effect
	Personnel transfer	Remscheid, Siegen-Wittgenstein	Oberhausen, Rhein-Sieg-Kreis
	Regional funding program of the Saarland	Saarlouis, Saarpfalzkreis	Regionalverband Saarbrücken, Sankt Wendel
Productivity	EFRE NRW - production funding	Cologne, Gütersloh	Bottrop
	Funding for research, innovation and technology	Bergstraße, Reutlingen	Havelland, Salzlandkreis
	INVEST - Funding for venture capital	Dahme-Spreewald, Hamburg	Aurich, Ludwigslust-Parchim
	Personnel transfer	Duisburg, Münster	Bottrop
	Regional funding program of the Saarland	Regionalverband Saarbrücken	Neunkirchen, Sankt Wendel

16.3 Model and Residual Diagnostics

In the course of finding an appropriate model for the purpose of estimating regionally diverging effects, several specifications were tested. The final model explained in section 15.3 has been estimated with MCMC and 50,000 iterations. The trace plots for the coefficients do not show any specific pattern, which suggests that the MCMC sampling did not experience any problems. The autocorrelation for the model parameters is also close to zero, indicating that no major autocorrelation is not accounted for by the model. Plots can be found in the appendix (compare chapter 18.4 in the appendix). Furthermore, the model has seemingly converged, which is indicated for by checking repeated estimations of the same models. Throughout the paper, the results of just one model are shown, whereas the other repetitions exhibit extremely similar values.

Among the variations in the variables concerning (non-)linearity and comparing the model fit, other specifications are checked as well. As the main geoadditive model has to incorporate not only spatial, but also temporal autocorrelation, the dataset is additionally evaluated year by year. This is to discover changes in the resulting spatial pattern over the timeframe which can therefore point to the relevance of the whole spatiotemporal model of section 15.3.

Thus, when comparing the spatial residuals over time, a change in the pattern of innovation distribution in the model error is clearly visible. In figure 16.11 the changes between the spatial residuals of separate models for each year are illustrated. A model with data only for one year is compared to a model for another year, and the percental change in the spatial residuals is mapped back onto the regions. Where the regions are colored light, a negative change in the residuals occurs, the darker the colors are, the more positive this change is. In figure 16.11a the spatial model residuals for 2010 are compared to those of 2009. The regions in the west of North-Rhine Westphalia, in the Saarland, and in Rhineland-Palatinate have increased in their estimated residual values from 2009 to 2010. Figures 16.11b to 16.11e are showing the changes each from the preceding year, figure 16.11f points out the changes over the whole timeframe 2009-2016.

The changes range over a relatively broad spectrum of values. The regions marked darkest for instance often symbolize a positive change of several hundred percent. In general, most characteristicly is a pattern dividing Germany in roughly four parts, this can be observed especially well in figure 16.11d. The region around Frankfurt (Main) seems to be the middle, with extensions south towards Stuttgart and up north towards Hamburg. From west to east there seems to be a horizontal axis from Cologne towards Chemnitz.

Considering all figures, the most homogeneous areas are in the federal state of Bavaria. The other regions change back and forth, leaving an overall notion that regions where most positive changes happen are directly next to those with the most negative changes. These breaks in the landscape of residuals suggest that the consideration of the time dimension is highly relevant, as changes occur so significantly.

As these figures show the changes in residuals, a positive change thus stands for an increase in characteristics not accounted for completely by the model. In these regions, special situations seem to have developed, towards where the explanatory potential of the model cannot reach. Lighter colored areas indicate negative changes in the residuals, therefore reducing the residuals in that area and connoting a gain in explicability.

Especially the region around the Saarland and the southern border of Germany, north of Nuremberg, and large parts of the northern half of the country, as well as the regions on the coast of the Baltic Sea, differ strongly in their representation over the years (compare figure 16.11f). Including a year effect in the model seems therefore reasonable, as the remaining model specification is held constant here (and the time dimension is the only missing factor). The maps of the absolute spatial residuals can be found in figure A.3 in the appendix (compare chapter 18.4 in the appendix).

Considering the spatial effect mapped in the model's residuals (compare figure 16.10), there is still a distinct pattern evident. This points to relevant effects not contained in the model but accounted for in the residuals. Therefore, further specific variables could be added to increase the explanatory content of the model. Nevertheless, the data already used could also be reexamined and possibly refined, as another selection of variables into the model might benefit the fit. The inclusion of covariates is determined theoretically, which would possibly be altered by focusing only on empirical relevance. Still,

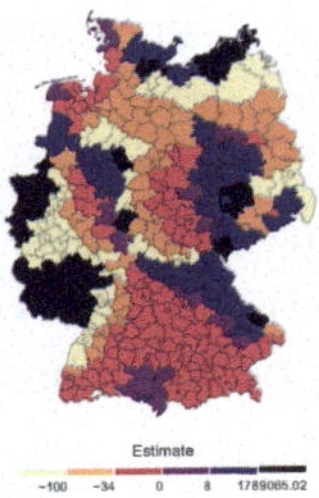

(a) 2009 to 2010.

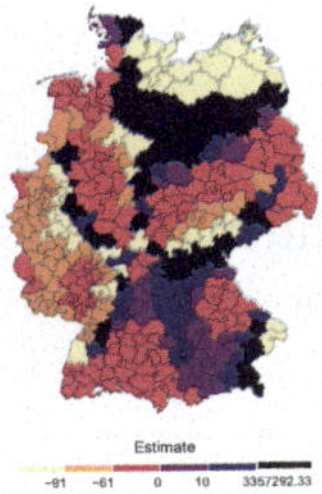

(b) 2010 to 2011.

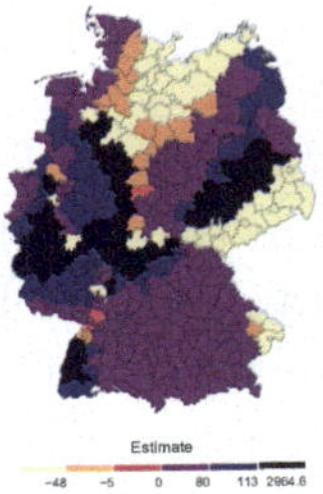

(c) 2011 to 2012.

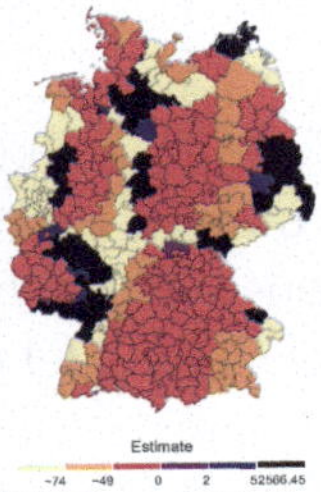

(d) 2012 to 2013.

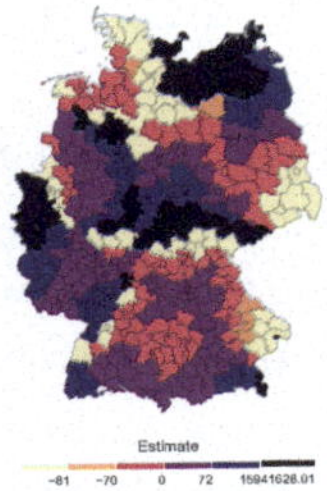

(e) 2013 to 2014.

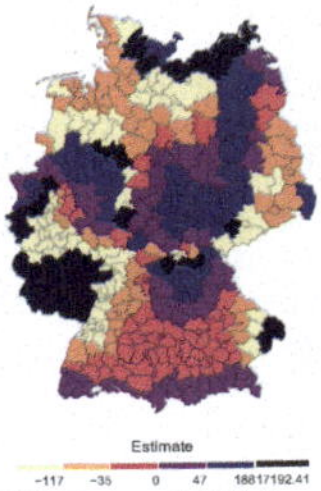

(f) 2009 to 2014.

Figure 16.11: Change in spatial residuals per year: 2009-2014. The maps show the change in percent in the spatial residuals by estimating a separate model for each year. The changes in the patterns suggest a time-variance of the relation of the covariates on innovative activity. Darker areas are positive changes, lighter areas are negative changes.

the variation in the residuals is only slight, as the hotspots and cold spots deviate only over a reasonably small range around the mean. Residual spatial disparity is consequently accounted for sufficiently. Additionally, as the hotspots are mostly in regions with increased economic growth and higher population density, the model points to those being the regions where most innovation-favoring determinants are still rather unknown. Contrariwise, this means that for regions being more peripherally located, most reasons for spatial innovative activity happening are already acknowledged for. Therefore the allocation of German innovative activity is covered to a reasonably good extent and a whole lot of innovation determining factors is explicable.

A possible extension, albeit another conceptual modeling approach, is the use of Bayesian multilevel modeling. The spatial and temporal effects can be constructed so that they serve as a group effect, structuring a hierarchical model instead. The resulting model can be estimated via Hamiltonian Monte Carlo in Stan (Carpenter et al. 2017), which outperforms MCMC considering efficacy and is also able to discover spatiotemporal effects in innovative activity. The model interpretation is different though, as the main spatial component is not recovered via the residuals but is inherent in the model structure. In future work, this could add to the explanation of spatiotemporal context in innovative activity.

17 Conclusion

The concept of innovation as depending on space and time is shown throughout this work. The incorporation of a spatial relation by considering each value for a certain district specifically has proven beneficially for the determination of innovative activity, as it is now possible to explain hotspots and cold spots in innovation with the help of certain covariates. Adding a spatial dimension proves significant, as the effect for administrative districts in the model estimated is by far the largest in absolute magnitude.

The resulting map of innovative activity has to be considered as illustration of residual variation, where exogenous factors are already included. In Germany, the main hotspots of innovation locate in the south western administrative districts, with some small exceptions for the region in eastern Westphalia, around Bielefeld, or some regions in Saxony. Here, innovation is especially active, and it is still to be examined what further drivers of innovation exist in those regions. The standard covariates used in this analysis do not seem to explain all spatial variation of innovative activity in Germany. Thus, there is still potential for further analyses.

As in chapter 14.2 delineated, the effects of the covariates considered are throughout expected to be positive regarding innovation activity. Now closing in on those hypotheses, the estimation in chapter 16 can give answers.

Innovation activity is affected positively in regions where high knowledge intensity exists and R+D funding is allocated relatively high, compared to the regional average. General openness is also regarded positively towards innovation activity. High productivity also ben-

I. Rhoden, *Space and Time in German Innovative Activity*,
https://doi.org/10.1007/978-3-658-28600-2_17

efits regions considering their innovation activity, as well as those regions lie in rather agglomerated areas with high market potential. A region's share of workers in industry does not seem to have an extremely significant impact. The influence of population density varies strongly around zero. Firm size, on the contrary, seems to have a strong decreasing effect onto innovation, as regions with firms of larger size are not exhibiting any advantages in innovative activity. Here, regions with many small firms seem to benefit, as innovative activity is higher there, but the effect is strongly decreasing with rising firm size.

Important determinants in the relation towards innovation activity appear to be productivity and population density, which make up for the most variation after acknowledging spatial effects, although population density shows a large variation itself. Delineated as minor effects are firm size (turnover of firms) in a region and research institutes as they do not seem to influence regional innovative activity to a large extent.

Considering the individual spatial effects of the covariates and in which German districts they explain more or less spatial variation of innovative activity, the maps of figures 16.1b to 16.8b allow a small-scale interpretation. For each district, the size of the estimated effect of a determinant on innovative activity is illustrated, additionally to the general curve plot of the effect. The spatial dispersion and importance of the effect are thus explicitly visualized.

These maps can further improve future work, seeing that this way the remaining spatial variation in the residuals could be reduced more precisely. For example, one can see in figure 16.5b, that population density explains a lot of variation in innovation (the dependent variable) in major cities and metropolises, where population density is very high and therefore a defining major factor for innovation in the model here. For peripheral regions this does not apply, as the effect there varies strongly.

Nevertheless, innovative activity varies not only spatially, but also temporally, as the inclusion of a time dimension can account for some regional divergences. The effect of time in the model points to a diminishing relationship towards innovative activity. This suggests an overestimation of the effects on innovation if the time dimension is omitted. The same holds for the spatial component of the model. Missing out on spatial correlation in the model severely affects the reliability and interpretability of the model, as the results of the estimation show (compare for instance the residual plot of figure 16.10).

For innovation policy, the estimated results can be implemented ambiguously, depending on the exact motivation. If regional cohesion is what is strived for, implications are to support regions in which (yet still) limited amounts of R+D funding are allocated among the firms, as this seems to have a negative effect on innovative activity.

If innovative activity shall be maximized, firms in economically prospering regions should be the focus of allocation. However, the situation in regions with highest funding sums in this sample is also to be considered with caution, as the impact on innovation appears to be negative for highest sums, which suggests aiming towards a better balancing of the funding money.

As innovation still seems prone to agglomerated districts, policies focusing stronger on peripheral districts could also be beneficial. Supporting smaller firms tends to be reasonable as well, as firm size and innovative activity are rather adversely correlated.

Furthermore, based on the estimated effects of the determinants on innovation, policies to promote innovation can select individual regions to either boost innovation or compensate for a lack thereof. If the relation of a determinant towards innovation is positive, then policy can boost innovation in regions with positive effects and compensate in regions with lower or negative effects, by strengthening the determinant.

Thus, policy cannot only fund innovation directly, but also indirectly by focusing on the effects for innovation's determinants, and increase innovation via an increase in the determinant.

18 Comprehensive Conclusion

18.1 First Part

Regional Allocations of Innovative Activity – The Case of 3D Printing

Issues

Does innovative activity in high-technologies concentrate elsewhere than innovation in general? If so, then where are hotspots and cold spots? Where are the differences? What are implications of the results?

In the first paper of the thesis, innovative activity undergoes a close investigation. Hotspots and cold spots of innovation among German zipcode areas are highlighted with the help of a KDE approach. Innovations from the high-tech field of additive manufacturing (3D printing) are shown accordingly to check for differences in innovation patterns between high-tech innovation and all innovations.

The kernel density method produces illustrative visual results and shows that high-tech innovation settles slightly more to the outer areas of the general innovation allocation. Therefore, high-tech innovation locates more distinctly and should be considered as a separate type of innovation, even if the distinctions are not major. For example, the Ruhr area and the southern German border seem to be the most distinct hotspots of high-tech. Those regions and further regions deviating from the overall innovation allocation could suffer,

I. Rhoden, *Space and Time in German Innovative Activity*,
https://doi.org/10.1007/978-3-658-28600-2_18

or at least prosper less than optimally, under a too generally targeted innovation promoting policy.

Based on the diverging allocations, innovation promoting policy can consider targeting funds more specifically. The assumption made is that the overall aim is to increase growth in innovation, which is a major positive factor for economic growth. To maximize the effects of funding, high-tech innovation (i.e. 3D printing technologies) can be promoted explicitly by designing policies to that exact cause (instead of just focusing on innovation in general). Additionally, funding can be targeted at specific administrative districts, either with the aim of boosting performance in prospering regions, or compensating lacking regions.

18.2 Second Part

Regional Determinants of Innovative Activity – Geoadditive Modeling of Diverging Allocations

Issues

Which factors can explain the spatial pattern of innovative activity in Germany, and to what extent?

In the second paper a set of innovation determining factors is added to explain variation in innovative activity. First an OLS model is specified, which is then set aside in favor of a geoadditive model. This model allows explaining innovative activity on NUTS-3 level in Germany by factors like productivity, R+D funding or firm size. The importance and need for a spatial dimension in this relationship is controlled for in the model by including an extra term for spatial autocorrelation. Additionally, determinants are either linearly or nonlinearly incorporated, which improves overall model fit.

The results of the REML estimation show not only that most determinants impact innovation favorably, but also that the incorporation of the spatial dimension is a necessary feature of the model; otherwise the effects may be not reliable. Significant and positive are the indicator for high-tech clusters, R+D funding, industry share, productivity, and market potential. Negative and significant are GRW funding, and, for the OLS model but not for the geoadditive model, firm size and population density. In addition to general function plots the estimated effects can also be traced back directly to the specific administrative district. Thus, precise leveraging points emerge, where innovation promoting policy could now directly focus its efforts, based on the NUTS-3 level.

For innovation promoting policy, as it is also apparent in the models, funding for R+D is positive for innovative activity. If the aim is maximizing the latter, then funds could be increased. The GRW funding, which is targeted to firms in structurally weak regions, does not seem to benefit innovative activity. Policies aiming for an increase in innovative activity should therefore focus on increasing means for determinants impacting the relation positively.

18.3 Third Part

Innovative Activity over Space and Time – Spatiotemporal Modeling of Innovation Promoting Factors

Issues

Where can innovative activity be explained, by which determinants, and to what extent? Where should policy promoting innovation best be applied, based on the model's results?

The third modeling approach augments the geoadditive model, which is first of all a static modeling set, by including a time dimension consisting of six extra years of data. This makes the model a spatiotemporal model, where all information available is included to explain the differing patterns of German innovative activity on NUTS-3 level.

The results show reasonable effects that follow the preceding work of the static geoadditive model of the second paper both in direction and magnitude. It is presumed that the method used adds to the models' reliability and to its interpretability. The effects estimated suggest mainly positive impacts for the covariates on innovative activity. As the necessity of the spatial effect is unquestioned here, the now attached time effect illustrates clearly that innovative activity is not only a spatial, but also a temporal process. The estimated values suggest that leaving out the time dimension leads to overstated effects. Again, the results can be directly constituted down to the exact administrative region, so that policy could specifically target innovation promoting measures.

Based on the estimated effects for the determinants, innovation promoting policy can select individual administrative districts and either boost innovation or compensate for a lack of innovation. This has to be matched to the effect of the determinant, dependent on the relation of the determinant towards innovation. If the relation of a determinant towards innovation is consistently positive, meaning that the higher the values of the determinant, the higher the innovation; then funding can boost regions with large estimated effects and compensate regions with low estimated effects.

If the relation towards innovation is negative, then funding can boost innovation in regions with low absolute values of the determinant and reinforce in regions with high absolute values of the determinant. Accordingly, this means that it could be necessary to reduce the value of a determinant to increase innovation. This is i.e. the case with the determinant *firm size*: In regions with high average firm size, the effect on innovation is negative. The lower firm size gets, the more the effect onto innovation increases. Policy could therefore reinforce innovation by strengthening regions with smaller firms and compensate in regions with larger firms by incentivizing smaller firm sizes.

18.4 Résumé

All in all, the three different approaches of this thesis open the case of regional and temporal behavior and determinacy of innovation activity in Germany for the timeframe 2000-2016. It is shown that by using techniques like KDE and by introducing geoadditive models into the innovation economics landscape, insights into the process of innovation generation can be gained. The methods used are readily available for a manifold of research fields and do not deny their usability in the context presented here.

The works of this thesis are in line with the general literature on endogenous economic growth. The exact framework is built in the separate papers. The theory generates the foundation for the determinants used in the explanation process of the models.

Compared to the selected works in chapter 2 of the prologue of this thesis, this thesis adds to the research in innovation economics in Germany because of its broad coverage of characteristics. The geographical level is as refined as data availability allows, and the inclusion of innovation determining factors is as diverse as theory permits. The models calculated are more detailed than other approaches in the field, as an explicit consideration of space and time is formulated. Estimation methods used also add to the explanatory content of the models, assisted by the usage of Bayesian prior knowledge.

The results and insights gained allow several most explicit economic and political consequences and offer possibilities for very detailed support in promoting innovation, and therefore, economic growth. The reflection of the estimated effects onto the map of German administrative districts, separately for each estimated effect, can furthermore increase understanding of the complex spatial characteristics of innovative activity.

Moreover, the results of the estimations can facilitate a new application of economic innovation policy measures. Especially with the precise visualization of the effects for each German administrative district, policy can now improve allotment of funds. For each determinant not only the effect on innovation is disclosed, but also in which region the corresponding determinant accounts for exactly how much of its estimated effect in the relation towards innovation. The varying magnitudes of the effects of each determinant in each region show that the German innovative landscape is nothing, but diverse. If innovation activity shall be increased, this has to be taken into account. A generalized policy approach not bearing this diversification in mind cannot maximize its potential towards innovation maximization.

Nevertheless, as the dataset is a complete bibliographical set of information on patents, several further options for investigation could be developed. Additionally, the methodical toolbox also provides interesting potential for further investigation possibilities, as supplementary layers of geographical and temporal units could be added in a multilevel modeling approach. This might allow modeling the innovation activity relation to its determinants even more precisely, and, being meaningful of the added complexity, could account for several supplementary factors which would make targeting innovation promoting policies still more explicit.

Bibliography

Abramovitz, M. (1986). "Catching Up, Forging Ahead, and Falling Behind". In: *The Journal of Economic History* 46.2, pp. 385–406.

Acs, Z. J., Anselin, L., and Varga, A. (2002). "Patents and innovation counts as measures of regional production of new knowledge". In: *Research Policy* 31.7, pp. 1069–1085. DOI: 10.1016/s0048-7333(01)00184-6.

Acs, Z. J., Audretsch, D. B., and Feldman, M. P. (1994). "R&D spillovers and innovative activity". In: *Managerial and Decision Economics* 15.2, pp. 131–138.

Acs, Z. J. and Varga, A. (2002). "Geography, Endogenous Growth, and Innovation". In: *International Regional Science Review* 25.1, pp. 132–148. DOI: 10.1177/016001702762039484. eprint: https://doi.org/10.1177/016001702762039484.

Additive Manufacturing: Strategic Research Agenda (2017). *AM Platform.* URL: http://www.rm-platform.com/ (visited on 01/03/2018).

Aghion, P. and Howitt, P. (1998). *Endogenous growth theory.* Cambridge, MA: MIT Press.

Ahuja, G., Lampert, C. M., and Tandon, V. (2008). "Moving Beyond Schumpeter: Management Research on the Determinants of Technological Innovation". In: *The Academy of Management Annals* 2.1, pp. 1–98. DOI: 10.1080/19416520802211446.

Alecke, B., Alsleben, C., Scharr, F., and Untiedt, G. (2006). "Are there really high-tech clusters? The geographic concentration of German manufacturing industries and its determinants". In: *The Annals of Regional Science* 40.1, pp. 19–42. DOI: 10.1007/s00168-005-0014-x.

I. Rhoden, *Space and Time in German Innovative Activity*,
https://doi.org/10.1007/978-3-658-28600-2

Almeida, P. and Kogut, B. (1997). "The Exploration of Technological Diversity and Geographic Localization in Innovation: Start-Up Firms in the Semiconductor Industry". In: *Small Business Economics* 9.1, pp. 21–31. DOI: 10.1023/A:1007995512597.

Ames, E. and Rosenberg, N. (1963). "Changing Technological Leadership and Industrial Growth". In: *The Economic Journal* 73.289, pp. 13–31.

Anderson, C. (2013). *Makers*. Random House UK Ltd. 257 pp.

Arrow, K. J. (1969). "Classificatory Notes on the Production and Transmission of Technological Knowledge". In: *American Economic Review* 59.2, pp. 29–35.

Arundel, A. (2001). "The relative effectiveness of patents and secrecy for appropriation". In: *Research Policy* 30.4, pp. 611–624. DOI: 10.1016/s0048-7333(00)00100-1.

Asheim, B. T. and Isaksen, A. (1997). "Location, agglomeration and innovation: Towards regional innovation systems in Norway?" In: *European Planning Studies* 5.3, pp. 299–330. DOI: 10.1080/09654319708720402.

ASTM International (2012). *Standard Terminology for Additive Manufacturing Technologies. Designation: F2792 -12a.* West Consho hocken, PA. URL: http://web.mit.edu/2.810/www/files/readings/AdditiveManufacturingTerminology.pdf (visited on 01/03/2018).

Audretsch, D. B. (1998). "Agglomeration and the location of innovative activity". In: *Oxford Review of Economic Policy* 14.2, pp. 18–29. DOI: 10.1093/oxrep/14.2.18.

Audretsch, D. B. (2003). "Innovation And Spatial Externalities". In: *International Regional Science Review* 26.2, pp. 167–174. DOI: 10.1177/0160017602250973.

Audretsch, D. B. and Fritsch, M. (2002). "Growth Regimes over Time and Space". In: *Regional Studies* 36.2, pp. 113–124. DOI: 10.1080/00343400220121909.

Baldwin, R. E. and Forslid, R. (2000). "The core–periphery model and endogenous growth: Stabilizing and destabilizing integration". In: *Economica* 67.267, pp. 307–324.

Basile, R., Benfratello, L., and Castellani, D. (2012). "Geoadditive Models for Regional Count Data: An Application to Industrial Location". In: *Geographical Analysis* 45.1, pp. 28–48. DOI: 10.1111/gean.12001.

Baumol, W. J. (2002). *The free-market innovation machine: Analyzing the growth miracle of capitalism.* Princeton university press.

Bayes, T. and Price, R. (1763). "An Essay Towards Solving a Problem in the Doctrine of Chances. By the late Rev. Mr. Bayes, communicated by Mr. Price, in a letter to John Canton, MA. and F.R.S." In: *Philosophical Transactions of the Royal Society of London* 53, pp. 370–418.

Beise, M., Cleff, T., Heneric, O., and Rammer, C. (2002). *Lead Markt Deutschland: Zur Position Deutschlands als führender Absatzmarkt für Innovationen. Thematische Schwerpunktstudie im Rahmen der Berichterstattung zur technologischen Leistungsfähigkeit im Auftrag des bmb+f.* Endbericht. 02-02. Zentrum für Europäische Wirtschaftsforschung (ZEW).

Belitz, C., Brezger, A., Klein, N., Kneib, T., Lang, S., and Umlauf, N. (2015). *BayesX - Software for Bayesian inference in structured additive regression models.* Version 3.0.2. URL: http://www.bayesx.org (visited on 01/05/2018).

Belitz, C., Brezger, A., Klein, N., Kneib, T., Lang, S., and Umlauf, N. (2018a). *Bayes X - Software for Bayesian Inference in Structured Additive Regression Models. Tutorials Manual.* Version 3.0.2.

Belitz, C., Brezger, A., Klein, N., Kneib, T., Lang, S., and Umlauf, N. (2018b). *Bayes X - Software for Bayesian Inference in Structured Additive Regression Models. Methodology Manual.* Version 3.0.2.

Belitz, C., Brezger, A., Klein, N., Kneib, T., Lang, S., and Umlauf, N. (2018c). *Bayes X - Software for Bayesian Inference in Structured Additive Regression Models. Reference Manual.* Version 3.0.2.

Bell, M. and Pavitt, K. (1993). "Technological Accumulation and Industrial Growth: Contrasts Between Developed and Developing Countries". In: *Industrial and Corporate Change* 2.2, pp. 157–210. DOI: 10.1093/icc/2.2.157. eprint: /oup/backfile/content_ public/journal/icc/2/2/10.1093_icc_2.2.157/3/2-2-157.pdf.

Benos, N., Karagiannis, S., and Karkalakos, S. (2015). "Proximity and growth spillovers in European regions: The role of geographical, economic and technological linkages". In: *Journal of Macroeconomics* 43, pp. 124–139. DOI: 10.1016/j.jmacro.2014.10.003.

Berger, S., Kempermann, H., Koppel, O., Orth, A. K., and Röben, E. (2017). *Innovationsatlas 2017. Die Innovationskraft deutscher Wirtschaftsräume im Vergleich.* Research rep. IW-Analysen Nr. 117. Institut der deutschen Wirtschaft Köln GmbH. 62 pp.

Bertuglia, C. S., Lombardo, S., and Nijkamp, P., eds. (1997). *Innovative Behaviour in Space and Time.* Springer Berlin Heidelberg. DOI: 10.1007/978-3-642-60720-2.

Binz, C., Truffer, B., and Coenen, L. (2014). "Why space matters in technological innovation systems - Mapping global knowledge dynamics of membrane bioreactor technology". In: *Research Policy* 43.1, pp. 138–155. DOI: 10.1016/j.respol.2013.07.002.

Bivand, R. S., Pebesma, E. J., Gomez-Rubio, V., and Pebesma, E. J. (2013). *Applied spatial data analysis with R.* Vol. 747248717. Springer.

Blanchard, P., Huiban, J.-P., Musolesi, A., and Sevestre, P. (2012). "Where there is a will, there is a way? Assessing the impact of obstacles to innovation". In: *Industrial and Corporate Change* 22.3, pp. 679–710. DOI: 10.1093/icc/dts027.

Blangiardo, M., Cameletti, M., Baio, G., and Rue, H. (2013). "Spatial and spatio-temporal models with R-INLA". In: *Spatial and Spatio-temporal Epidemiology* 4, pp. 33–49. DOI: 10.1016/j.sste.2012.12.001.

Blundell, R., Griffith, R., and Reenen, J. V. (1999). "Market Share, Market Value and Innovation in a Panel of British Manufacturing Firms". In: *The Review of Economic Studies* 66.3, pp. 529–554.

Bocci, C. (2009). "Geoadditive Models for Data with Spatial Information".

Bocci, C., Caporali, E., and Petrucci, A. (2012). "Geoadditive modeling for extreme rainfall data". In: *AStA Advances in Statistical Analysis* 97.2, pp. 181–193. DOI: 10.1007/s10182-012-0192-7.

Bos, J. W. B., Economidou, C., and Sanders, M. W. J. L. (2013). "Innovation over the industry life-cycle: Evidence from EU manufacturing". In: *Journal of Economic Behavior & Organization* 86, pp. 78–91. DOI: 10.1016/j.jebo.2012.12.025.

Boschma, R. (2005). "Proximity and Innovation: A Critical Assessment". In: *Regional Studies* 39.1, pp. 61–74. DOI: 10.1080/0034340052000320887.

Boschma, R. (2009). *Evolutionary economic geography and its implications for regional innovation policy.* Papers in Evolutionary Economic Geography (PEEG) 0912. Utrecht University, Department of Human Geography and Spatial Planning, Group Economic Geography.

Boschma, R. (2016). "Relatedness as driver of regional diversification: a research agenda". In: *Regional Studies* 51.3, pp. 351–364. DOI: 10.1080/00343404.2016.1254767.

Breidenbach, P., Budde, R., Döhrn, R., and Neumann, U. (2016). *Ländervergleich Nordrhein-Westfalen - Indikatoren der industriellen Entwicklung. Forschungsprojekt im Auftrag der FDP-Landtagsfraktion Nordrhein-Westfalen.* Research rep. RWI - Leibniz-Institut für Wirtschaftsforschung.

Breschi, S. (2000). "The Geography of Innovation: A Cross-sector Analysis". In: *Regional Studies* 34.3, pp. 213–229. DOI: 10.1080/00343400050015069.

Breschi, S. and Malerba, F. (2001). "The geography of innovation and economic clustering: some introductory notes". In: *Industrial and corporate change* 10.4, pp. 817–833.

Brezger, A., Kneib, T., and Lang, S. (2005). "BayesX: Analyzing Bayesian Structural Additive Regression Models". In: 14.

Bundesinstitut für Bau-, Stadt- und Raumforschung (2018). *Indikatoren und Karten zur Raum- und Stadtentwicklung (INKAR).* Federal Office for Building and Regional Planning, Bundesamt für Bauwesen und Raumordnung (BBR). URL: http://www.inkar.de/ (visited on 09/11/2018).

Bundesministerium für Bildung und Forschung (2015). *Deutschlands Spitzencluster - Germany's Leading-Edge Clusters.* Bundesministerium für Bildung und Forschung/Federal Ministry of Education and Research (BMBF).

Bundesministerium für Bildung und Forschung (2017). *The new High-Tech Strategy. Innovations for Germany.* Bundesministerium für Bildung und Forschung/ Federal Ministry of Education and Research (BMBF).

Bundesministerium für Bildung und Forschung (2018a). *Research Performing Organisations.* Bundesministerium für Bildung und Forschung / Federal Ministry of Education and Research (BMBF). URL: `https://www.research-in-germany.org/en/research-landscape/research-organisations.html` (visited on 09/11/2018).

Bundesministerium für Bildung und Forschung, ed. (2018b). *Research performing organisations.* URL: `https://www.research-in-germany.org/en/research-landscape/research-organisations.html`.

Bundesministerium für Wirtschaft und Energie (2017). *Jahreswirtschaftsbericht 2017. Für inklusives Wachstum in Deutschland und Europa.* Federal Ministry for Economic Affairs and Energy (Bundesministerium für Wirtschaft und Energie, BMWi).

Bundesministerium für Wirtschaft und Energie, ed. (2018). *Cluster Excellence in Germany.* URL: `https://www.clusterplattform.de/CLUSTER/Navigation/EN/Home/home.html`.

Bundesministerium für Wirtschaft und Energie (2019a). *Außenwirtschaftsförderungsrichtlinie (AWR).* Funding. Förderdatenbank. URL: `http://www.foerderdatenbank.de/Foerder-DB/Navigation/Foerderrecherche/suche.html?get=96755dd290e9fce2624fb49a81fc41fe;views;document&doc=8606` (visited on 03/22/2019).

Bundesministerium für Wirtschaft und Energie (2019b). *Beschäftigtentransfer (Förderung von Transfergesellschaften).* Funding. Förderdatenbank. URL: `http://www.foerderdatenbank.de/Foerder-DB/Navigation/Foerderrecherche/suche.html?get=96755dd290e9fce2624fb49a81fc41fe;views;document&doc=9318` (visited on 03/22/2019).

Bundesministerium für Wirtschaft und Energie (2019c). *Bildungsprä mie - Förderung von Prämiengutscheinen und Beratungsleistungen.*

Funding. Förderdatenbank. URL: http://www.foerderdatenbank.de/Foerder-DB/Navigation/Foerderrecherche/suche.html?get=96755dd290e9fce2624fb49a81fc41fe;views;document&doc=10212 (visited on 03/22/2019).

Bundesministerium für Wirtschaft und Energie (2019d). *BMWi- Innovationsgutscheine (go-Inno)*. Funding. Förderdatenbank. URL: http://www.foerderdatenbank.de/Foerder-DB/Navigation/Foerderrecherche/suche.html?get=96755dd290e9fce2624fb49a81fc41fe;views;document&doc=8558 (visited on 03/22/2019).

Bundesministerium für Wirtschaft und Energie (2019e). *BMWi-Markterschließungsprogramm*. Funding. Förderdatenbank. URL: http://www.foerderdatenbank.de/Foerder-DB/Navigation/Foerderrecherche/suche.html?get=96755dd290e9fce2624fb49a81fc41fe;views;document&doc=11658 (visited on 03/22/2019).

Bundesministerium für Wirtschaft und Energie (2019f). *Bundesprogramm Ländliche Entwicklung - LandMobil - unterwegs in ländlichen Räumen*. Funding. Förderdatenbank. URL: http://www.foerderdatenbank.de/Foerder-DB/Navigation/Foerderrecherche/suche.html?get=96755dd290e9fce2624fb49a81fc41fe;views;document&doc=14023 (visited on 03/22/2019).

Bundesministerium für Wirtschaft und Energie (2019g). *CONNECT Education-Research-Innovation (Bildung- Forschung- Innovation)*. Förderdatenbank. URL: http://www.foerderdatenbank.de/Foerder-DB/Navigation/Foerderrecherche/suche.html?get=96755dd290e9fce2624fb49a81fc41fe;views;document&doc=14031 (visited on 03/22/2019).

Bundesministerium für Wirtschaft und Energie (2019h). *EFRE-NRW - Förderwettbewerb Produktion.NRW*. Funding. Förderdatenbank. URL: http://www.foerderdatenbank.de/Foerder-DB/Navigation/Foerderrecherche/suche.html?get=96755dd290e9fce2624fb49a81fc41fe;views;document&doc=12489 (visited on 03/22/2019).

Bundesministerium für Wirtschaft und Energie (2019i). *Entwicklung digitaler Technologien - Innovationswettbewerb: Künstliche Intelligenz als Treiber für volkswirtschaftlich relevante Ökosysteme*. Funding. Förderdatenbank. URL: http://www.foerderdatenbank.de/Foerder-DB/Navigation/Foerderrecherche/suche.html?get=96755dd290e9fce2624fb49a81fc41fe;views;document&doc=7528.

Bundesministerium für Wirtschaft und Energie (2019j). *Experimenteller Wohnungs- und Städtebau (ExWoSt)*. Funding. Förderdatenbank. URL: http://www.foerderdatenbank.de/Foerder-DB/Navigation/Foerderrecherche/suche.html?get=96755dd290e9fce2624fb49a81fc41fe;views;document&doc=10797 (visited on 03/22/2019).

Bundesministerium für Wirtschaft und Energie (2019k). *Förderdatenbank*. URL: http://www.foerderdatenbank.de/.

Bundesministerium für Wirtschaft und Energie (2019l). *Förderrichtlinien Stadterneuerung 2008*. Funding. Förderdatenbank. URL: http://www.foerderdatenbank.de/Foerder-DB/Navigation/Foerderrecherche/suche.html?get=96755dd290e9fce2624fb49a81fc41fe;views;document&doc=7319 (visited on 03/22/2019).

Bundesministerium für Wirtschaft und Energie (2019m). *Förderung der Entwicklung innovativer Konzepte und Maßnahmen in der beruflichen Weiterbildung*. Funding. Förderdatenbank. URL: http://www.foerderdatenbank.de/Foerder-DB/Navigation/Foerderrecherche/suche.html?get=96755dd290e9fce2624fb49a81fc41fe;views;document&doc=13855 (visited on 03/22/2019).

Bundesministerium für Wirtschaft und Energie (2019n). *Förderung der Nachhaltigen Stadtentwicklung (RiLiSE)*. Funding. Förderdatenbank. URL: http://www.foerderdatenbank.de/Foerder-DB/Navigation/Foerderrecherche/suche.html?get=96755dd290e9fce2624fb49a81fc41fe;views;document&doc=10307 (visited on 03/22/2019).

Bundesministerium für Wirtschaft und Energie (2019o). *Förderung der regionalen Entwicklung*. Funding. Förderdatenbank. URL: http://www.foerderdatenbank.de/Foerder-DB/Navigation/Foerderrecherche/suche.html?get=96755dd290e9fce2624fb49a81fc41fe;views;document&doc=8311 (visited on 03/22/2019).

Bundesministerium für Wirtschaft und Energie (2019p). *Förderung des kommunalen Straßenbaus (RL-KSB).* Funding. Förderdatenbank. URL: http://www.foerderdatenbank.de/Foerder-DB/Navigation/Foerderrecherche/suche.html?get=96755dd290e9fce2624fb49a81fc41fe;views;document&doc=11053 (visited on 03/22/2019).

Bundesministerium für Wirtschaft und Energie (2019q). *Förderung des Neu- und Ausbaus sowie der Reaktivierung von privaten Gleisanschlüssen (Gleisanschlussförderrichtlinie).* Funding. Förderdatenbank. URL: http://www.foerderdatenbank.de/Foerder-DB/Navigation/Foerderrecherche/suche.html?get=96755dd290e9fce2624fb49a81fc41fe;views;document&doc=10580 (visited on 03/22/2019).

Bundesministerium für Wirtschaft und Energie (2019r). *Förderung von Forschung, Innovationen und Technologien (Pro FIT) - Frühphasenfinanzierung von Technologieunternehmen.* Funding. Förderdatenbank. URL: http://www.foerderdatenbank.de/Foerder-DB/Navigation/Foerderrecherche/suche.html?get=96755dd290e9fce2624fb49a81fc41fe;views;document&doc=8868 (visited on 03/22/2019).

Bundesministerium für Wirtschaft und Energie (2019s). *Förderung von Innovation durch Hochschulen und Forschungseinrichtungen.* Funding. Förderdatenbank. URL: http://www.foerderdatenbank.de/Foerder-DB/Navigation/Foerderrecherche/suche.html?get=96755dd290e9fce2624fb49a81fc41fe;views;document&doc=9698 (visited on 03/22/2019).

Bundesministerium für Wirtschaft und Energie (2019t). *Förderung von Maßnahmen des Wissens- und Technologietransfers im Saarland.* Funding. Förderdatenbank. URL: http://www.foerderdatenbank.de/Foerder-DB/Navigation/Foerderrecherche/suche.html?get=96755dd290e9fce2624fb49a81fc41fe;views;document&doc=13130 (visited on 03/22/2019).

Bundesministerium für Wirtschaft und Energie (2019u). *INVEST - Zuschuss für Wagniskapital.* Funding. Förderdatenbank. URL: http://www.foerderdatenbank.de/Foerder-DB/Navigation/Foerder

recherche/suche.html?get=96755dd290e9fce2624fb49a81fc41 fe;views;document&doc=11908 (visited on 03/22/2019).

Bundesministerium für Wirtschaft und Energie (2019v). *Messepräsentationen.* Funding. Förderdatenbank. URL: http://www.foerderdatenbank.de/Foerder-DB/Navigation/Foerderrecherche/suche.html?get=96755dd290e9fce2624fb49a81fc41fe;views;document&doc=8314 (visited on 03/22/2019).

Bundesministerium für Wirtschaft und Energie (2019w). *Programm für Internationalisierung - Förderung von Gemeinschaftsprojekten.* Funding. Förderdatenbank. URL: http://www.foerderdatenbank.de/Foerder-DB/Navigation/Foerderrecherche/suche.html?get=96755dd290e9fce2624fb49a81fc41fe;views;document&doc=9868 (visited on 03/22/2019).

Bundesministerium für Wirtschaft und Energie (2019x). *Regionales Förderprogramm des Saarlandes für kleine und mittlere Unternehmen der gewerblichen Wirtschaft.* Funding. Förderdatenbank. URL: http://www.foerderdatenbank.de/Foerder-DB/Navigation/Foerderrecherche/suche.html?get=96755dd290e9fce2624fb49a81fc41fe;views;document&doc=8943 (visited on 03/22/2019).

Bundesministerium für Wirtschaft und Energie (2019y). *Städtebauförderung - Förderung von Investitionen in nationale Projekte des Städtebaus.* Funding. Förderdatenbank. URL: http://www.foerderdatenbank.de/Foerder-DB/Navigation/Foerderrecherche/suche.html?get=96755dd290e9fce2624fb49a81fc41fe;views;document&doc=12260 (visited on 03/22/2019).

Cafarelli, B. and Castrignanò, A. (2011). "The use of geoadditive models to estimate the spatial distribution of grain weight in an agronomic field: a comparison with kriging with external drift". In: *Environmetrics* 22.6, pp. 769–780. DOI: 10.1002/env.1092.

Cai, W.-g. and Zhou, X.-l. (2014). "On the drivers of eco-innovation: empirical evidence from China". In: *Journal of Cleaner Production* 79, pp. 239–248. DOI: 10.1016/j.jclepro.2014.05.035.

Cantner, U., Graf, H., and Hinzmann, S. (2015). "The role of geographical proximity for project performance: Evidence from the

German "Leading-Edge Cluster Competition"". In: *Jena Economic Research Papers* 2015-025.

Capello, R. and Lenzi, C. (2013). "Spatial heterogeneity in knowledge, innovation, and economic growth nexus: Conceptual reflections and empirical evidence". In: *Journal of Regional Science* 54.2, pp. 186–214. DOI: 10.1111/jors.12074.

Capello, R. and Nijkamp, P. (2009). *Handbook of Regional Growth and Development Theories*. Edward Elgar Publishing. DOI: 10.4337/9781848445987.

Caragliu, A. and Nijkamp, P. (2015). "Space and knowledge spillovers in European regions: the impact of different forms of proximity on spatial knowledge diffusion". In: *Journal of Economic Geography* 16.3, pp. 749–774. DOI: 10.1093/jeg/lbv042.

Carpenter, B., Gelman, A., Hoffman, M., Lee, D., Goodrich, B., Betancourt, M., Brubaker, M., Guo, J., Li, P., and Riddell, A. (2017). "Stan: A Probabilistic Programming Language". In: *Journal of Statistical Software, Articles* 76.1, pp. 1–32. DOI: 10.18637/jss.v076.i01.

Castaldi, C. and Los, B. (2017). "Geographical patterns in US inventive activity 1977–1998: The "regional inversion" was underestimated". In: *Research Policy* 46.7, pp. 1187–1197. DOI: 10.1016/j.respol.2017.04.005.

Chandler, R. and Scott, M. (2011). *Statistical Methods for Trend Detection and Analysis in the Environmental Sciences*. Wiley.

Chen, Y.-C. (2017). "A Tutorial on Kernel Density Estimation and Recent Advances". In: *arXiv preprint arXiv:1704.03924*.

Cheshire, P. and Magrini, S. (2000). "Endogenous processes in European regional growth: convergence and policy". In: *Growth and Change* 31.4, pp. 455–479.

Coccia, M. (2015). "Spatial patterns of technology transfer and measurement of its friction in the geo-economic space". In: *Int. J. Technology Transfer and Commercialisation* 9.3, pp. 255–267.

Cohen, W. M. (2010). "Fifty Years of Empirical Studies of Innovative Activity and Performance". In: *Handbook of The Economics of Innovation, Vol. 1*. Elsevier, pp. 129–213. DOI: 10.1016/s0169-7218(10)01004-x.

Cohen, W. M. and Levinthal, D. A. (1990). "Absorptive Capacity: A New Perspective on Learning and Innovation". In: *Administrative Science Quarterly* 35.1, p. 128. DOI: 10.2307/2393553.

Conner, B. P., Manogharan, G. P., Martof, A. N., Rodomsky, L. M., Rodomsky, C. M., Jordan, D. C., and Limperos, J. W. (2014). "Making sense of 3-D printing: Creating a map of additive manufacturing products and services". In: *Additive Manufacturing* 1-4, pp. 64–76. DOI: 10.1016/j.addma.2014.08.005.

Cooke, P., Asheim, B., Boschma, R., Martin, R., Schwartz, D., and Todtling, F. (2013). *Handbook of Regional Innovation and Growth*. Edward Elgar Pub.

Cuerva, M. C., Triguero-Cano, Á., and Córcoles, D. (2014). "Drivers of green and non-green innovation: empirical evidence in Low-Tech SMEs". In: *Journal of Cleaner Production* 68, pp. 104–113. DOI: 10.1016/j.jclepro.2013.10.049.

Davelaar, E. J. and Nijkamp, P. (1997). "Spatial Dispersion of Technological Innovation: A Review". In: *Innovative Behaviour in Space and Time*. Ed. by C. S. Bertuglia, S. Lombardo, and P. Nijkamp. Berlin, Heidelberg: Springer Berlin Heidelberg, pp. 17–40. DOI: 10.1007/978-3-642-60720-2_2.

Deng, H. and Wickham, H. (2011). "Density estimation in R". In: *Electronic publication*.

Deutsches Patent- und Markenamt, ed. (2017). *Patente und Gebrauchsmuster – lieferbare Altdaten: Bibliographische Daten, XML. Patente und Gebrauchsmuster - Altdaten*. DPMAdatenabgabe.

Deutsches Patent- und Markenamt (2018). *Patent Protection- Overview*. URL: https://www.dpma.de/english/patents/patent_protection/index.html (visited on 01/04/2018).

Die Bundesregierung (1969). *Gesetz über die Gemeinschaftsaufgabe „Verbesserung der regionalen Wirtschaftsstruktur" (GRW-Gesetz - GRWG)*. Zuletzt geändert durch Art. 269 Zehnte ZuständigkeitsanpassungsVO vom 31. 8. 2015 (BGBl. I S. 1474).

Die Bundesregierung (2019). *Förderkatatog.* URL: https://foerderportal.bund.de/foekat/jsp/StartAction.do.

Divisekera, S. and Nguyen, V. K. (2018). "Determinants of innovation in tourism evidence from Australia". In: *Tourism Management* 67, pp. 157–167. DOI: 10.1016/j.tourman.2018.01.010.

Dosi, G. (1982). "Technological paradigms and technological trajectories: A suggested interpretation of the determinants and directions of technical change". In: *Research Policy* 11.3, pp. 147–162. DOI: https://doi.org/10.1016/0048-7333(82)90016-6.

Eckey, H. F. (2008). *Regionalökonomie.* Gabler Verlag. 328 pp.

Englmann, F. C. and Walz, U. (1995). "Industrial Centers and Regional Growth in the Presence of Local Inputs". In: *Journal of Regional Science* 35.1, pp. 3–27. DOI: 10.1111/j.1467-9787.1995.tb01397.x. eprint: https://onlinelibrary.wiley.com/doi/pdf/10.1111/j.1467-9787.1995.tb01397.x.

Enright, M. J. (1996). "Regional Clusters and Economic Development: A Research Agenda." In: *Business Networks : Prospects for Regional Development.* Ed. by U. H. Staber, N. V. Schaefer, and B. Scharma. Gruyter, Walter de GmbH.

Epanechnikov, V. A. (1969). "Non-parametric estimation of a multivariate probability density". In: *Theory of Probability & Its Applications* 14.1, pp. 153–158.

European Commission (2016a). *European Innovation Scoreboard 2016.* DOI: 10.2873/84537.

European Commission (2016b). *Regional Innovation Scoreboard 2016.* DOI: 10.2873/84730.

European Factories of the Future Research Association (2013). *Factories of the Future: Multi-Annual Roadmap for the Contractual PPP under Horizon 2020.* European Commission. DOI: 10.2777/29815.

Eurostat (2018). *Regional statistics by NUTS classification (reg). Regional demographic statistics (reg_dempoar).* European Commission. URL: https://ec.europa.eu/eurostat/data/database (visited on 09/11/2018).

Fagerberg, J., Mowery, D. C., and Nelson, R. R., eds. (2006). *The Oxford Handbook of Innovation.* Oxford University Press. 680 pp.

Fagerberg, J., Srholec, M., and Verspagen, B. (2010). "Innovation and Economic Development". In: *Handbook of the Economics of Innovation, Volume 2*. Elsevier, pp. 833–872. DOI: 10.1016/s0169-7218(10)02004-6.

Fahrmeir, L., Kneib, T., and Lang, S. (2009). *Regression: Modelle, Methoden und Anwendungen (Statistik und ihre Anwendungen) (German Edition)*. Springer.

Feldman, M. P. (2013). *Geography of Innovation*. Springer Netherlands.

Feldman, M. P. and Audretsch, D. B. (1996). "R&D Spillovers and the Geography of Innovation and Production". In: 86, pp. 630–640.

Feldman, M. P. and Audretsch, D. B. (1999). "Innovation in cities:" in: *European Economic Review* 43.2, pp. 409–429. DOI: 10.1016/s0014-2921(98)00047-6.

Feldman, M. P. and Kogler, D. F. (2010). "Stylized Facts in the Geography of Innovation". In: *Handbook of The Economics of Innovation, Vol. 1*. Elsevier, pp. 381–410. DOI: 10.1016/s0169-7218(10)01008-7.

Fertig, M., Görlitz, K., Peistrup, M., Schmidt, C. M., Winter, B., Grenzmann, C., Kreuels, B., Apel, H., and Engel, D. (2008). *Innovationsbericht 2008. Zur Leistungsfähigkeit des Landes Nordrhein-Westfalen in Wissenschaft, Forschung und Technologie*. Endbericht: Forschungsprojekt für das Ministerium für Innovation, Wissenschaft, Forschung und Technologie des Landes Nordrhein-Westfalen. Rheinisch-Westfälisches Institut für Wirtschaftsforschung and Stifterverband-Wissenschaftsstatistik, Essen.

Finkenstädt, B., Held, L., and Isham, V., eds. (2006). *Statistical Methods for Spatio-Temporal Systems*. CHAPMAN & HALL. 286 pp.

Fornahl, D. and Brenner, T. (2009). "Geographic concentration of innovative activities in Germany". In: *Structural Change and Economic Dynamics* 20.3, pp. 163–182. DOI: 10.1016/j.strueco.2009.05.001.

Freeman, C. (1982). "The economics of industrial innovation". In: University of Illinois at Urbana-Champaign's Academy for Entrepre neurial Leadership Historical Research Reference in Entrepreneurship.

Fujita, M., Krugman, P., and Venables, A. J. (1999). *The Spatial Economy: Cities, Regions, and International Trade*. The MIT Press.

Gartner, J., Maresch, D., and Fink, M. (2015). "The Potential of Additive Manufacturing for Technology Entrepreneurship: An Integrative Technology Assessment". In: *Creativity and Innovation Management* 24.4, pp. 585–600. DOI: 10.1111/caim.12132.

Gelman, A., Carlin, J. B., Stern, H. S., Dunson, D. B., Vehtari, A., and Rubin, D. B. (2014). *Bayesian Data Analysis, 3Rd Edn.* T&F/Crc Press.

Gerschenkron, A. (1962). *Economic Backwardness in Historical Perspective (Belknap Press S)*. Belknap Press.

Gertler, M. S. (2003). "Tacit knowledge and the economic geography of context, or The undefinable tacitness of being (there)". In: *Journal of Economic Geography* 3.1, pp. 75–99. DOI: 10.1093/jeg/3.1.75.

Gilbert, B. A. and Campbell, J. T. (2015). "The geographic origins of radical technological paradigms: A configurational study". In: *Research Policy* 44.2, pp. 311–327. DOI: 10.1016/j.respol.2014.08.006.

Gilman, E., Chaloupka, M., Merrifield, M., Malsol, N. D., and Cook, C. (2015). "Standardized catch and survival rates, and effect of a ban on shark retention, Palau pelagic longline fishery". In: *Aquatic Conservation: Marine and Freshwater Ecosystems* 26.6, pp. 1031–1062. DOI: 10.1002/aqc.2599.

Google LLC, ed. (2019). *Google Maps Geocoding API. Google Maps Platform Web Services*. URL: https://developers.google.com/maps/documentation/geocoding/start.

Gress, D. R. and Kalafsky, R. V. (2015). "Geographies of production in 3D: Theoretical and research implications stemming from additive manufacturing". In: *Geoforum* 60, pp. 43–52. DOI: 10.1016/j.geoforum.2015.01.003.

Gridlogics Technologies Pvt Ltd (2014). *3D Printing Technology Insight Report. An analysis of patenting activity around 3D-Printing from 1990-Current.* Tech. rep., p. 44.

Griliches, Z. (1990). *Patent Statistics as Economic Indicators: A Survey.* Tech. rep. DOI: 10.3386/w3301.

Griliches, Z. (1998). *R&D and Productivity.* UNIV OF CHICAGO PR. 400 pp.

Grillitsch, M. and Nilsson, M. (2015). "Innovation in peripheral regions: Do collaborations compensate for a lack of local knowledge spillovers?" In: *The Annals of Regional Science* 54.1, pp. 299–321. DOI: 10.1007/s00168-014-0655-8.

Grossenbacher, T. (2019). *Beautiful thematic maps with ggplot2 (only).* URL: https://timogrossenbacher.ch/2016/12/beautiful-thematic-maps-with-ggplot2-only/.

Guerrero, D. C. and Sero, M. A. (1997). "Spatial Distribution of Patents in Spain: Determining Factors and Consequences on Regional Development". In: *Regional Studies* 31.4, pp. 381–390. DOI: 10.1080/00343409750132982.

Hagl, R. (2015). *Das 3D-Druck-Kompendium.* DOI: 10.1007/978-3-658-07047-2.

Hajek, P., Henriques, R., and Hajkova, V. (2014). "Visualising components of regional innovation systems using self-organizing maps—Evidence from European regions". In: *Technological Forecasting and Social Change* 84, pp. 197–214. DOI: 10.1016/j.techfore.2013.07.013.

Hall, B. H., Griliches, Z., and Hausman, J. (1984). *Patents and R&D: Is There A Lag?* Tech. rep. DOI: 10.3386/w1454.

Hall, B. H. and Rosenberg, N., eds. (2010a). *Handbook of the Economics of Innovation: 2 (Handbooks in Economics).* Elsevier.

Hall, B. H. and Rosenberg, N., eds. (2010b). *Handbook of the Economics of Innovation, Volume 1.* Elsevier LTD, Oxford. 804 pp.

Harms, R., Schulz, A., Kraus, S., and Fink, M. (2009). "The conceptualisation of'opportunity'in strategic management research". In: *International Journal of Entrepreneurial Venturing* 1.1, pp. 57–71.

Harrison, B., Kelley, M. R., and Gant, J. (1996). "Innovative firm behavior and local milieu: exploring the intersection of agglomeration, firm effects, and technological change". In: *Economic geography* 72.3, pp. 233–258.

Hastie, T. J. and Tibshirani, R. J. (1990). *Generalized Additive Models (Chapman & Hall/CRC Monographs on Statistics & Applied Probability)*. Chapman and Hall/CRC.

Hastie, T. (1996). "Pseudosplines". In: *Journal of the Royal Statistical Society. Series B (Methodological)* 58.2, pp. 379–396.

Hitt, M. A., Hoskisson, R. E., and Kim, H. (1997). "International diversification: Effects on innovation and firm performance in product-diversified firms". In: *Academy of Management Journal* 40.4, pp. 767–798.

Hlavac, M. (2015). *stargazer: Well-Formatted Regression and Summary Statistics Tables*. R package version 5.2. Harvard University. Cambridge, USA.

Hodgson, G. M. (1993). "Theories of Economic Evolution: A Preliminary Taxonomy". In: *The Manchester School* 61.2, pp. 125–143. DOI: 10.1111/j.1467-9957.1993.tb00228.x.

Hoover, E. M. (1948). *The Location of Economic Activity*. New York: McGraw-Hill.

Horbach, J. (2008). "Determinants of environmental innovation—New evidence from German panel data sources". In: *Research Policy* 37.1, pp. 163–173. DOI: 10.1016/j.respol.2007.08.006.

Institut der deutschen Wirtschaft Köln Consult GmbH (2018). *Patentradar. Patentradar Auswertungsbeispiele: 3D-Druck*. Technologie analysen. URL: https://www.iwconsult.de/patentradar/de/technologie.php (visited on 11/12/2018).

Isaksen, A. and Karlsen, J. (2012). "What Is Regional in Regional Clusters? The Case of the Globally Oriented Oil and Gas Cluster in Agder, Norway". In: *Industry & Innovation* 19.3, pp. 249–263. DOI: 10.1080/13662716.2012.669616.

Jacobs, J. (1969). *The Economy of Cities*. New York: Vintage.

Jaffe, A., Trajtenberg, M., and Henderson, R. (1993). "Geographic Localization of Knowledge Spillovers As Evidenced By Patent Citations". In: 108, pp. 577–98.

Janger, J., Schubert, T., Andries, P., Rammer, C., and Hoskens, M. (2017). "The EU 2020 innovation indicator: A step forward in measuring innovation outputs and outcomes?" In: *Research Policy* 46.1, pp. 30–42. DOI: 10.1016/j.respol.2016.10.001.

Kammann, E. E. and Wand, M. P. (2003). "Geoadditive models". In: *Journal of the Royal Statistical Society: Series C (Applied Statistics)* 52.1, pp. 1–18. DOI: 10.1111/1467-9876.00385.

Keller, D., Niebuhr, A., and Stiller, S. (2004). "Die deutsche For schungslandschaft: Starke regionale Disparitäten". In: *Wirtschaftsdienst* 84 (2), pp. 121–125.

Ketels, C. and Protsiv, S. (2016). *European Cluster Panorama 2016. European Cluster Observatory.* Center for Strategy and Competitiveness, Stockholm School of Economics, European Commission.

Kim, J., Kim, Y., and Flacher, D. (2012). "R&D investment of electricity-generating firms following industry restructuring". In: *Energy Policy* 48.C, pp. 103–117. DOI: 10.1016/j.enpol.2012.04.0.

Kline, S. J. and Rosenberg, N. (1986). "An overview of innovation". In: *The Positive Sum Strategy: Harnessing Technology for Economic Growth.* Ed. by R. Landau and N. Rosenberg. National Academy of Sciences, pp. 275–306.

Kneib, T. and Fahrmeir, L. (2007). "A Mixed Model Approach for Geoadditive Hazard Regression". In: *Scandinavian Journal of Statistics* 34.1, pp. 207–228. DOI: 10.1111/j.1467-9469.2006.00524.x.

Kneib, T. and Fahrmeir, L. (2011). "A space-time study on forest health". In: Chandler, R. and Scott, M. *Statistical Methods for Trend Detection and Analysis in the Environmental Sciences*, pp. 333-358.

Knorr-Held, L. (2000). "Bayesian modelling of inseparable space-time variation in disease risk". In: *Statistics in medicine* 19.17-18, pp.2555 -2567.

Krugman, P. (1990). *Increasing Returns and Economic Geography.* Tech. rep. 3275. DOI: 10.3386/w3275.

Krugman, P. (1991). *Geography and Trade*. Cambridge, MA: MIT Press.

Kruschke, J. K. (2015). *Doing Bayesian Data Analysis*. Elsevier LTD, Oxford.

Kruth, J. P. (1991). "Material Incress Manufacturing by Rapid Prototyping Techniques". In: *CIRP Annals* 40.2, pp. 603–614. DOI: 10.1016/s0007-8506(07)61136-6.

Kürtössy, J. (2004). "Innovation indicators derived from patent data". In: *Periodica Polytechnica. Social and Management Sciences* 12.1, p. 91.

Lachmayer, R., Lippert, R. B., and Fahlbusch, T., eds. (2016). *3D-Druck beleuchtet*. Springer Berlin Heidelberg. DOI: 10.1007/978-3-662-49056-3.

Lall, S. (1992). "Technological capabilities and industrialization". In: *World Development* 20.2, pp. 165–186.

Landau, R. and Rosenberg, N. (1986). *The Positive Sum Strategy: Harnessing Technology for Economic Growth*. National Academies Press.

Lang, D. T. and CRAN Team, the (2018). *XML: Tools for Parsing and Generating XML Within R and S-Plus*. R package version 3.98-1.16.

Löfqvist, L. (2012). "Motivation for innovation in small enterprises". In: *International Journal of Technology Management* 60.3/4, p. 242. DOI: 10.1504/ijtm.2012.049441.

Lucas, R. E. (1988). "On the mechanics of economic development". In: *Journal of monetary economics* 22.1, pp. 3–42.

Lundvall, B.-A. (1992). *National Systems of Innovation: Towards a Theory of Innovation and Interactive Learning*. London: Pinter Publrs.

Malerba, F. and Orsenigo, L. (1993). "Technological Regimes and Firm Behavior". In: *Industrial and Corporate Change* 2.1, pp. 45–71. DOI: 10.1093/icc/2.1.45.

Malerba, F. and Orsenigo, L. (1997). "Technological Regimes and Sectoral Patterns of Innovative Activities". In: *Industrial and Corporate Change* 6.1, pp. 83–118. DOI: 10.1093/icc/6.1.83.

Marshall, A. (1890). *Principles of Economics.* Palgrave Macmillan.
Martin, P. and Ottaviano, G. I. P. (2001). "Growth and Agglomeration". In: *International Economic Review* 42.4, pp. 947–968. DOI: 10.1111/1468-2354.00141.
Maskell, P., Eskelinen, H., Hannibalsson, I., Malmberg, A., and Vatne, E. (1997). *Competitiveness, Localised Learning and Regional Development: Specialization and Prosperity in Small Open Economies.* ROUTLEDGE CHAPMAN HALL. 272 pp.
Maskell, P. and Malmberg, A. (1999). "Localised learning and industrial competitiveness". In: *Cambridge Journal of Economics* 23.2, pp. 167–185. DOI: 10.1093/cje/23.2.167.
McCann, P. and Oort, F. van (2009). *Theories of Agglomeration and Regional Economic Growth: A Historical Review.* DOI: 10.4337/9781848445987.00007.
McCann, P. and Ortega-Argiles, R. (2016). "Regional innovation, R&D and knowledge spillovers: the role played by geographical and non-geographical factors". In: *Handbook on the Geographies of Innovation.* Edward Elgar Publishing. Chap. 1, pp. 22–44.
Ministerium für Wirtschaft, Innovation, Digitalisierung und Energie des Landes Nordrhein-Westfalen (2014). *Innovationsstrategie des Landes Nordrhein-Westfalen im Rahmen der EU-Strukturfonds 2014-2020.* Land Nordrhein-Westfalen.
Mohnen, P., Mairesse, J., and Dagenais, M. (2006). "Innovativity: A comparison across seven European countries". In: *Economics of Innovation and New Technology* 15.4-5, pp. 391–413. DOI: 10.1080/10438590500512950. eprint: https://doi.org/10.1080/10438590500512950.
Moran, P. A. P. (1950). "Notes on Continuous Stochastic Phenomena". In: *Biometrika* 37.1/2, p. 17. DOI: 10.2307/2332142.
Morgan, K. (2004). "The exaggerated death of geography: learning, proximity and territorial innovation systems". In: *Journal of Economic Geography* 4.1, pp. 3–21. DOI: 10.1093/jeg/4.1.3.
Nelson, R. R. and Winter, S. G. (1982). *An Evolutionary Theory of Economic Change.* Cambridge, MA: Harvard University Press.

Nelson, R. R. (1993). *National Innovation Systems: A Comparative Analysis*. Oxford University Press.

Nijkamp, P., Poot, H. J., and Rouwendal, J. (1991). "A non-linear dynamic model of spatial economic development and R&D policy". In: *The Annals of Regional Science* 25.4, pp. 287–302. DOI: 10.1007/bf01581854.

OECD (2005). *The Measurement of Scientific and Technological Activities Oslo Manual: Guidelines for Collecting and Interpreting Innovation Data, 3rd Edition*. OECD. 166 pp.

OECD (2009). *OECD Patent Statistics Manual*. OECD Paris. 161 pp.

Oinas, P. and Malecki, E. J. (2002). "The Evolution of Technologies in Time and Space: From National and Regional to Spatial Innovation Systems". In: *International Regional Science Review* 25.1, pp. 102–131. DOI: 10.1177/016001702762039402.

Ospina, R., Larangeiras, A. M., and Frery, A. C. (2014). "Visualization of Skewed Data". In: *Revista Colombiana de Estadística* 37.2Spe, pp. 399–417. DOI: 10.15446/rce.v37n2spe.47945.

Paci, L., Gelfand, A. E., and Holland, D. M. (2013). "Spatio-temporal modeling for real-time ozone forecasting". In: *Spatial Statistics* 4, pp. 79–93. DOI: 10.1016/j.spasta.2013.04.003.

Pakes, A. and Griliches, Z. (1980). "Patents and R&D at the firm level: A first report". In: *Economics Letters* 5.4, pp. 377–381. DOI: 10.1016/0165-1765(80)90136-6.

Pantano, E. (2014). "Innovation drivers in retail industry". In: *International Journal of Information Management* 34.3, pp. 344–350. DOI: 10.1016/j.ijinfomgt.2014.03.002.

Patent Act (1936). *Patentgesetz*. Patent Act as published on 16 December 1980 (Federal Law Gazette 1981 I p. 1), as last amended by Article 2 of the Act of 4 April 2016 (Federal Law Gazette I p. 558). Patentgesetz in der Fassung der Bekanntmachung vom 16. Dezember 1980 (BGBl. 1981 I S. 1), das zuletzt durch Artikel 9 des Gesetzes vom 17. Juli 2017 (BGBl. I S. 2541) geändert worden ist.

Patrick, J. D., Harvill, J. L., and Hansen, C. W. (2016). "A semiparametric spatio-temporal model for solar irradiance data". In: *Renewable Energy* 87, pp. 15–30. DOI: 10.1016/j.renene.2015.10.001.

Polenske, K. R., ed. (2007). *The Economic Geography of Innovation.* Cambridge Univ Pr. 349 pp.

Polt, W., Berger, M., Boekholt, P., Cremers, K., Egeln, J., Gassler, H., Hofer, R., and Rammer, C. (2010). *Das deutsche Forschungs- und Innovationssystem. Ein internationaler Systemvergleich zur Rolle von Wissenschaft, Interaktionen und Governance für die technologische Leistungsfähigkeit.* Studien zum deutschen Innovationssystem. 11-2010. Joanneum Research Forschungsgesellschaft mbH, Technopolis Group, and Zentrum für Europäische Wirtschaftsforschung (ZEW).

Porter, M. E. (2000). "Location, Competition and Economic Development: Local Clusters in a Global Economy". In: *Economic Development Quarterly* 14.1, pp. 15–34.

Prognos AG (2015). *Digitalisierung als Rahmenbedingung für Wachstum - Update. vbw-Studie.* München: vbw Vereinigung der Bayerischen Wirtschaft e.V.

Prognos AG (2016). *Prognos Zukunftsatlas 2016. Das Ranking für Deutschlands Regionen.* Research rep.

R Core Team (2019). *R: A Language and Environment for Statistical Computing.* R Foundation for Statistical Computing. Vienna, Austria.

Ratanawaraha, A. and Polenske, K. R. (2007). "Measuring the geography of innovation: a literature review". In: *The Economic Geography of Innovation.* Ed. by K. R. Polenske. CAMBRIDGE UNIV PR.

Ratinho, T., Harms, R., and Walsh, S. (2015). "Structuring the Technology Entrepreneurship publication landscape: Making sense out of chaos". In: *Technological forecasting and social change* 100, pp. 168–175.

Rehfeld, D. (2015). *3D-Drucken: Anmerkungen zum momentanen Hype.* ger. Forschung Aktuell, Institut Arbeit und Technik (IAT), Gelsenkirchen 9/2015. urn:nbn:de:0176-201509016. Gelsenkirchen.

Romer, P. (1986). "Increasing Returns and Long-run Growth". In: *Journal of Political Economy* 94.5, pp. 1002–37.

Romer, P. (1990). "Endogenous Technological Change". In: *Journal of Political Economy* 98.5, S71–S102.

Romer, P. (1994). "The Origins of Endogenous Growth". In: *The Journal of Economic Perspectives* 8.1, pp. 3–22.

Sanyal, P. and Cohen, L. R. (2009). "Powering Progress: Restructuring, Competition, and R&D in the U.S. Electric Utility Industry". In: *The Energy Journal* 30.2, pp. 41–79.

Scherer, F. M. (1965). "Firm Size, Market Structure, Opportunity, and the Output of Patent Inventions". In: *The American Economic Review* 55.5 (1). Ed. by A. E. Association, pp. 1097–1125.

Scherer, F. M. (1986). *Innovation and Growth: Schumpeterian Perspectives.* MIT PR. 297 pp.

Schumpeter, J. A. (1934). *The Theory of Economic Development: An Inquiry into Profits, Capital, Credit, Interest, and the Business Cycle.* Harvard University Press. Harvard University Press, Cambridge, MA.

Schumpeter, J. A. (1939). *Business cycles I, II.* Vol. 1. McGraw-Hill New York.

Scott, A. (1988). "Flexible production systems and regional development: the rise of new industrial spaces in North America and western Europe". In: *International Journal of Urban and Regional Research* 12.2, pp. 171–186. DOI: `10.1111/j.1468-2427.1988.tb00448.x`. eprint: `https://onlinelibrary.wiley.com/doi/pdf/10.1111/j.1468-2427.1988.tb00448.x`.

Scott, D. W. (2015). *Multivariate Density Estimation: Theory, Practice, and Visualization.* JOHN WILEY & SONS INC. 384 pp.

Shearmur, R., Carrincazeaux, C., and Doloreux, D., eds. (2016). *Handbook on the Geographies of Innovation.* Edward Elgar Publishing. 512 pp.

Silverman, B. W. (1986). *Density Estimation for Statistics and Data Analysis.* Taylor & Francis Ltd. 176 pp.

Smith, K. (2005). "Measuring innovation". In: Oxford University Press.

Smith, K. (1992). "Technological innovation indicators: experience and prospects". In: *Science and Public Policy*. DOI: 10.1093/spp/19.6.383.

Solow, R. M. (1956). "A contribution to the theory of economic growth". In: *The quarterly journal of economics* 70.1, pp. 65–94.

Staber, U. H., Schaefer, N. V., and Scharma, B. (1996). *Business Networks*. Gruyter, Walter de GmbH.

Statistisches Bundesamt (2018a). *Inlandsproduktberechnung. Volkswirtschaftliche Gesamtrechnungen, Inlandsprodukt.* Version 23. 11. 2017. URL: https://www.destatis.de/DE/ZahlenFakten/GesamtwirtschaftUmwelt/VGR/Inlandsprodukt/Tabellen/Gesamtwirtschaft.html.

Statistisches Bundesamt (2018b). *Regional Database Germany*. URL: https://www.regionalstatistik.de/genesis/online/ (visited on 09/11/2018).

Storper, M. (1997). *The Regional World: Territorial Development in a Global Economy*. GUILFORD PUBN. 338 pp.

Swan, T. W. (1956). "Economic growth and capital accumulation". In: *Economic Record* 32.2, pp. 334–361. DOI: 10.1111/j.1475-4932.1956.tb00434.x.

Tavassoli, S. (2015). "Innovation determinants over industry life cycle". In: *Technological Forecasting and Social Change* 91, pp. 18–32. DOI: 10.1016/j.techfore.2013.12.027.

Terrell, G. R. and Scott, D. W. (1992). "Variable Kernel Density Estimation". In: *The Annals of Statistics* 20.3, pp. 1236–1265.

Trajtenberg, M. (1990). "A penny for your quotes: patent citations and the value of innovations". In: *The Rand Journal of Economics*, pp. 172–187.

Umlauf, N., Adler, D., Kneib, T., Lang, S., and Zeileis, A. (2015). "Structured Additive Regression Models: AnRInterface toBayesX". In: *Journal of Statistical Software* 63.21. DOI: 10.18637/jss.v063.i21.

Untiedt, G., Karl, H., Rosche, J., Kersting, M., and Alecke, B. (2016). *Aufgaben, Struktur und mögliche Ausgestaltung eines gesamtdeutschen Systems zur Förderung von strukturschwachen Regionen ab*

2020. Endbericht zum Dienstleistungsprojekt Nr. 13/14 des Bundesministeriums für Wirtschaft und Energie zum 31. März 2016. Ruhr forschungsinstitut für Innovations- und Strukturpolitik e.V.

van Buuren, S. and Groothuis-Oudshoorn, K. (2011). "mice: Multivariate Imputation by Chained Equations in R". In: *Journal of Statistical Software* 45.3, pp. 1–67.

Van der Veeken, S. (2010). "Robust and nonparametric methods for skewed data."

Vernon, R. (1966). "International Investment and International Trade in the Product Cycle". In: *The Quarterly Journal of Economics* 80.2, pp. 190–207. DOI: 10.2307/1880689.

Volkswirtschaftliche Gesamtrechnung der Länder (2016). *Bruttoinlandsprodukt, Bruttowertschöpfung in den Ländern der Bundesrepublik Deutschland 1991 bis 2015.* Vol. Reihe 1 Ländderergebnisse Band 1.

Walz, U. (1997). "Growth and Deeper Regional Integration in a Three-Country Model". In: *Review of International Economics* 5.4, pp. 492–507.

Weinberg, M. (2010). "It will be Awesome if They don't Screw it up: 3D Printing, Intellectual Property, and the Fight Over the Next Great Disruptive Technology". In: Institute For Emerging Innovation, Public Knowledge.

Weller, C., Kleer, R., and Piller, F. T. (2015). "Economic implications of 3D printing: Market structure models in light of additive manufacturing revisited". In: *International Journal of Production Economics* 164, pp. 43–56. DOI: 10.1016/j.ijpe.2015.02.020.

Wickham, H. (2016). *ggplot2: Elegant Graphics for Data Analysis.* Springer-Verlag New York.

Wickham, H., François, R., Henry, L., and Müller, K. (2018). *dplyr: A Grammar of Data Manipulation.* R package version 0.7.7.

Wickham, H. and Henry, L. (2018). *tidyr: Easily Tidy Data with 'spread()' and 'gather()' Functions.* R package version 0.8.1.

Wolfe, D. and Vatne, E. (2011). "Neo-Schumpeterian Perspectives on Innovation and Growth". In: *Handbook of Regional Innovation and*

Growth. Ed. by P. Cooke, B. Asheim, R. Boschma, R. Martin, D. Schwartz, and F. Todtling. Edward Elgar Publishing. Chap. 3.

Wood, S. N. (2003). "Thin-plate regression splines". In: *Journal of the Royal Statistical Society (B)* 65.1, pp. 95–114.

Wood, S. N. (2004). "Stable and Efficient Multiple Smoothing Parameter Estimation for Generalized Additive Models". In: *Journal of the American Statistical Association* 99.467, pp. 673–686. DOI: 10.1198/016214504000000980. eprint: https://doi.org/10.1198/016214504000000980.

Wood, S. N. (2017). *Generalized Additive Models: An Introduction with R, Second Edition (Chapman & Hall/CRC Texts in Statistical Science)*. Chapman and Hall/CRC.

Zuur, A. F. and Camphuysen, C. (2012). "Generalised additive models applied on northern gannets". In: Zuur, A. F. *A Beginner's Guide to Generalized Additive Models with R*, pp. 145–168.

Zuur, A. F. (2012). *A Beginner's Guide to Generalized Additive Models with R*. Highland Statistics Ltd.

Appendix

Table A.1: IPC codes for additive manufacturing technologies. Classification on four-digit level to identify technologies related to additive manufacturing for the analyses of this work. (IW 2018; Gridlogics Technologies Pvt Ltd 2014).

International Patent Classification (IPC)	
Code	Description
A61B	DIAGNOSIS; SURGERY; IDENTIFICATION (analysing biological material G01N, e.g. G01N 33/48)
A61C	DENTISTRY; APPARATUS OR METHODS FOR ORAL OR DENTAL HYGIENE (non-driven toothbrushes A46B; preparations for dentistry A61K 6/00; preparations for cleaning the teeth or mouth A61K 8/00, A61Q 11/00)
A61D	VETERINARY INSTRUMENTS, IMPLEMENTS, TOOLS, OR METHODS

Table A.1 – *Continued on the next page*

I. Rhoden, *Space and Time in German Innovative Activity*,
https://doi.org/10.1007/978-3-658-28600-2

International Patent Classification (IPC) Code	Description
A61F	FILTERS IMPLANTABLE INTO BLOOD VESSELS; PROSTHESES; DEVICES PROVIDING PATENCY TO, OR PREVENTING COLLAPSING OF, TUBULAR STRUCTURES OF THE BODY, E.G. STENTS; ORTHOPAEDIC, NURSING OR CONTRACEPTIVE DEVICES; FOMENTATION; TREATMENT OR PROTECTION OF EYES OR EARS; BANDAGES, DRESSINGS OR ABSORBENT PADS; FIRST-AID KITS (dental prosthetics A61C) [2006.01]
A61G	TRANSPORT, PERSONAL CONVEYANCES, OR ACCOMMODATION SPECIALLY ADAPTED FOR PATIENTS OR DISABLED PERSONS (appliances for aiding patients or disabled persons to walk A61H 3/00); OPERATING TABLES OR CHAIRS; CHAIRS FOR DENTISTRY; FUNERAL DEVICES (embalming corpses A01N 1/00)
A61H	PHYSICAL THERAPY APPARATUS, e.g. DEVICES FOR LOCATING OR STIMULATING REFLEX POINTS IN THE BODY; ARTIFICIAL RESPIRATION; MASSAGE; BATHING DEVICES FOR SPECIAL THERAPEUTIC OR HYGIENIC PURPOSES OR SPECIFIC PARTS OF THE BODY (electrotherapy, magnetotherapy, radiation therapy, ultrasound therapy A61N)

Table A.1 – *Continued on the next page*

International Patent Classification (IPC) Code	Description
A61J	CONTAINERS SPECIALLY ADAPTED FOR MEDICAL OR PHARMACEUTICAL PURPOSES; DEVICES OR METHODS SPECIALLY ADAPTED FOR BRINGING PHARMACEUTICAL PRODUCTS INTO PARTICULAR PHYSICAL OR ADMINISTERING FORMS; DEVICES FOR ADMINISTERING FOOD OR MEDICINES ORALLY; BABY COMFORTERS; DEVICES FOR RECEIVING SPITTLE
A61K	PREPARATIONS FOR MEDICAL, DENTAL, OR TOILET PURPOSES (devices or methods specially adapted for bringing pharmaceutical products into particular physical or administering forms A61J 3/00; chemical aspects of, or use of materials for deodorisation of air, for disinfection or sterilisation, or for bandages, dressings, absorbent pads or surgical articles A61L; soap compositions C11D)
A61L	METHODS OR APPARATUS FOR STERILISING MATERIALS OR OBJECTS IN GENERAL; DISINFECTION, STERILISATION, OR DEODORISATION OF AIR; CHEMICAL ASPECTS OF BANDAGES, DRESSINGS, ABSORBENT PADS, OR SURGICAL ARTICLES; MATERIALS FOR BANDAGES, DRESSINGS, ABSORBENT PADS, OR SURGICAL ARTICLES (preservation of bodies or disinfecting characterised by the agent employed A01N; preserving, e.g. sterilising, food or foodstuffs A23; preparations for medical, dental or toilet purposes A61K) [4]

Table A.1 – *Continued on the next page*

International Patent Classification (IPC) Code	Description
A61M	DEVICES FOR INTRODUCING MEDIA INTO, OR ONTO, THE BODY (introducing media into or onto the bodies of animals A61D 7/00; means for inserting tampons A61F 13/26; devices for administering food or medicines orally A61J; containers for collecting, storing or administering blood or medical fluids A61J 1/05); DEVICES FOR TRANSDUCING BODY MEDIA OR FOR TAKING MEDIA FROM THE BODY (surgery A61B; chemical aspects of surgical articles A61L; magnetotherapy using magnetic elements placed within the body A61N 2/10); DEVICES FOR PRODUCING OR ENDING SLEEP OR STUPOR [5]
A61N	ELECTROTHERAPY; MAGNETOTHERAPY; RADIATION THERAPY; ULTRASOUND THERAPY (measurement of bioelectric currents A61B; surgical instruments, devices or methods for transferring non-mechanical forms of energy to or from the body A61B 18/00; anaesthetic apparatus in general A61M; incandescent lamps H01K; infra-red radiators for heating H05B) [6]
A61P	SPECIFIC THERAPEUTIC ACTIVITY OF CHEMICAL COMPOUNDS OR MEDICINAL PREPARATIONS [7]
A61Q	SPECIFIC USE OF COSMETICS OR SIMILAR TOILET PREPARATIONS [2006.01]
B05B	SPRAYING APPARATUS; ATOMISING APPARATUS; NOZZLES (spray-mixers with nozzles B01F 5/20; processes for applying liquids or other fluent materials to surfaces by spraying B05D)

Table A.1 – *Continued on the next page*

International Patent Classification (IPC) Code	Description
B05C	APPARATUS FOR APPLYING LIQUIDS OR OTHER FLUENT MATERIALS TO SURFACES, IN GENERAL (spraying apparatus, atomising apparatus, nozzles B05B; plant for applying liquids or other fluent materials to objects by electrostatic spraying B05B 5/08)
B05D	PROCESSES FOR APPLYING LIQUIDS OR OTHER FLUENT MATERIALS TO SURFACES, IN GENERAL (conveying articles or workpieces through baths of liquid B65G, e.g. B65G 49/02)
B22C	FOUNDRY MOULDING (moulding refractory materials in general B28B)
B22D	CASTING OF METALS; CASTING OF OTHER SUBSTANCES BY THE SAME PROCESSES OR DEVICES (shaping of plastics or substances in a plastic state B29C; metallurgical processing, selection of substances to be added to metal C21, C22)
B22F	Working Metallic Powder; Manufacture Of Articles From Metallic Powder; Making Metallic Powder
B23B	TURNING; BORING (using an electrode which takes the place of a tool B23H, e.g. making holes B23H 9/14; working by laser beam B23K 26/00; arrangements for copying or controlling B23Q)
B23C	MILLING (broaching B23D; broach-milling in making gears B23F; arrangements for copying or controlling B23Q)

Table A.1 – *Continued on the next page*

International Patent Classification (IPC)	
Code	Description
B23D	PLANING; SLOTTING; SHEARING; BROACHING; SAWING; FILING; SCRAPING; LIKE OPERATIONS FOR WORKING METAL BY REMOVING MATERIAL, NOT OTHERWISE PROVIDED FOR (making toothed gears or the like B23F; cutting metal by applying heat locally B23K; arrangements for copying or controlling B23Q)
B23F	MAKING GEARS OR TOOTHED RACKS (by stamping B21D; by rolling B21H; by forging or pressing B21K; by casting B22; arrangements for copying or controlling B23Q; machines or devices for grinding or polishing, in general B24B)
B23G	THREAD CUTTING; WORKING OF SCREWS, BOLT HEADS OR NUTS, IN CONJUNCTION THEREWITH (thread-forming by corrugating tubes B21D 15/04; by rolling B21H 3/02; by forging, pressing or hammering B21K 1/56; making helical grooves by turning B23B 5/48; by milling B23C 3/32; by grinding B24B 19/02; arrangements for copying or controlling B23Q)

Table A.1 – *Continued on the next page*

International Patent Classification (IPC)	
Code	Description
B23H	WORKING OF METAL BY THE ACTION OF A HIGH CONCENTRATION OF ELECTRIC CURRENT ON A WORKPIECE USING AN ELECTRODE WHICH TAKES THE PLACE OF A TOOL; SUCH WORKING COMBINED WITH OTHER FORMS OF WORKING OF METAL (processes for the electrolytic or electrophoretic production of coatings, electroforming, or apparatus therefor C25D; processes for the electrolytic removal of material from objects C25F; manufacturing printed circuits using precipitation techniques to apply the conductive material to form the desired conductive pattern H05K 3/18) [4]
B23K	SOLDERING OR UNSOLDERING; WELDING; CLADDING OR PLATING BY SOLDERING OR WELDING; CUTTING BY APPLYING HEAT LOCALLY, e.g. FLAME CUTTING; WORKING BY LASER BEAM (making metal-coated products by extruding metal B21C 23/22; building up linings or coverings by casting B22D 19/08; casting by dipping B22D 23/04; manufacture of composite layers by sintering metal powder B22F 7/00; arrangements on machine tools for copying or controlling B23Q; covering metals or covering materials with metals, not otherwise provided for C23C; burners F23D)
B23P	OTHER WORKING OF METAL; COMBINED OPERATIONS; UNIVERSAL MACHINE TOOLS (arrangements for copying or controlling B23Q)

Table A.1 – *Continued on the next page*

International Patent Classification (IPC) Code	Description
B23Q	DETAILS, COMPONENTS, OR ACCESSORIES FOR MACHINE TOOLS, e.g. ARRANGEMENTS FOR COPYING OR CONTROLLING (tools of the kind used in lathes or boring machines B23B 27/00); MACHINE TOOLS IN GENERAL, CHARACTERISED BY THE CONSTRUCTION OF PARTICULAR DETAILS OR COMPONENTS; COMBINATIONS OR ASSOCIATIONS OF METAL-WORKING MACHINES, NOT DIRECTED TO A PARTICULAR RESULT
B29B	PREPARATION OR PRETREATMENT OF THE MATERIAL TO BE SHAPED; MAKING GRANULES OR PREFORMS; RECOVERY OF PLASTICS OR OTHER CONSTITUENTS OF WASTE MATERIAL CONTAINING PLASTICS [4]
B29C	Shaping or joining of plastics; shaping of substances in a plastic state, in general; after-treatment of the shaped products, e.g. Repairing
B29D	PRODUCING PARTICULAR ARTICLES FROM PLASTICS OR FROM SUBSTANCES IN A PLASTIC STATE (making granules B29B 9/00; making preforms B29B 11/00) [4]
B29K	INDEXING SCHEME ASSOCIATED WITH SUBCLASSES B29B, B29C OR B29D, RELATING TO MOULDING MATERIALS OR TO MATERIALS FOR REINFORCEMENTS, FILLERS OR PREFORMED PARTS, e.g. INSERTS [4]
B29L	INDEXING SCHEME ASSOCIATED WITH SUBCLASS B29C, RELATING TO PARTICULAR ARTICLES

Table A.1 – *Continued on the next page*

International Patent Classification (IPC) Code	Description
B32B	Layered products, i.e. Products built-up of strata of flat or non-flat, e.g. Cellular or honeycomb, form
B41J	Typewriters; selective printing mechanisms, i.e. Mechanisms printing otherwise than from a forme; correction of typographical errors
B41M	Printing, Duplicating, Marking, Or Copying Processes; Colour Printing
B44C	Producing Decorative Effects
C04B	Lime; Magnesia; Slag; Cements; Compositions Thereof
C08B	POLYSACCHARIDES; DERIVATIVES THEREOF (polysaccharides containing less than six saccharide radicals attached to each other by glycosidic linkages C07H; fermentation or enzyme-using processes C12P 19/00; production of cellulose D21) [4]
C08C	TREATMENT OR CHEMICAL MODIFICATION OF RUBBERS
C08F	MACROMOLECULAR COMPOUNDS OBTAINED BY REACTIONS ONLY INVOLVING CARBON-TO-CARBON UNSATURATED BONDS (production of liquid hydrocarbon mixtures from lower carbon number hydrocarbons, e.g. by oligomerisation, C10G 50/00; fermentation or enzyme-using processes to synthesise a desired chemical compound or composition or to separate optical isomers from a racemic mixture C12P; graft polymerisation of monomers containing carbon-to-carbon unsaturated bonds on to fibres, threads, yarns, fabrics or fibrous goods made from such materials D06M 14/00) [2]

Table A.1 – *Continued on the next page*

International Patent Classification (IPC)	
Code	Description
C08G	MACROMOLECULAR COMPOUNDS OBTAINED OTHERWISE THAN BY REACTIONS ONLY INVOLVING CARBON-TO-CARBON UNSATURATED BONDS (fermentation or enzyme-using processes to synthesise a desired chemical compound or composition or to separate optical isomers from a racemic mixture C12P) [2]
C08H	DERIVATIVES OF NATURAL MACROMOLECULAR COMPOUNDS (polysaccharides C08B; natural rubber C08C; natural resins or their derivatives C09F; working up pitch, asphalt or bitumen C10C 3/00)
C08J	WORKING-UP; GENERAL PROCESSES OF COMPOUNDING; AFTER-TREATMENT NOT COVERED BY SUBCLASSES C08B, C08C, C08F, C08G or C08H (working, e.g. shaping, of plastics B29) [2]
C08K	USE OF INORGANIC OR NON-MACROMOLECULAR ORGANIC SUBSTANCES AS COMPOUNDING INGREDIENTS (paints, inks, varnishes, dyes, polishes, adhesives C09) [2]
C08L	COMPOSITIONS OF MACROMOLECULAR COMPOUNDS (compositions based on polymerisable monomers C08F, C08G; artificial filaments or fibres D01F; textile treating compositions D06)
C22B	PRODUCTION OR REFINING OF METALS (making metallic powder or suspensions thereof B22F 9/00; production of metals by electrolysis or electrophoresis C25); PRETREATMENT OF RAW MATERIALS

Table A.1 – *Continued on the next page*

International Patent Classification (IPC)	
Code	Description
C22C	ALLOYS (treatment of alloys C21D, C22F)
C22F	CHANGING THE PHYSICAL STRUCTURE OF NON-FERROUS METALS OR NON-FERROUS ALLOYS (processes specific to heat treatment of ferrous alloys or steels and devices for heat treatment of metals or alloys C21D)
G01C	Photogrammetry
G02B	Optical Elements, Systems, Or Apparatus
G03B	Stereoscopic Photography
G03F	Photomechanical production of textured or patterned surfaces, e.g. For printing, for processing of semiconductor devices; materials therefore
G05B	Control Or Regulating Systems In General; Functional Elements Of Such Systems; Monitoring Or Testing Arrangements For Such Systems Or Elements
G06F	Electric Digital Data Processing
G06T	Image Data Processing Or Generation, In General
H01B	CABLES; CONDUCTORS; INSULATORS; SELECTION OF MATERIALS FOR THEIR CONDUCTIVE, INSULATING OR DIELECTRIC PROPERTIES (selection for magnetic properties H01F 1/00; waveguides H01P)
H01C	RESISTORS
H01F	MAGNETS; INDUCTANCES; TRANSFORMERS; SELECTION OF MATERIALS FOR THEIR MAGNETIC PROPERTIES

Table A.1 – *Continued on the next page*

International Patent Classification (IPC) Code	Description
H01G	CAPACITORS; CAPACITORS, RECTIFIERS, DETECTORS, SWITCHING DEVICES, LIGHT-SENSITIVE OR TEMPERATURE-SENSITIVE DEVICES OF THE ELECTROLYTIC TYPE (selection of specified materials as dielectric H01B 3/00; capacitors with potential-jump or surface barrier H01L 29/00)
H01H	ELECTRIC SWITCHES; RELAYS; SELECTORS; EMERGENCY PROTECTIVE DEVICES (contact cables H01B 7/10; electrolytic self-interrupters H01G 9/18; emergency protective circuit arrangements H02H; switching by electronic means without contact-making H03K 17/00)
H01J	ELECTRIC DISCHARGE TUBES OR DISCHARGE LAMPS (spark-gaps H01T; arc lamps with consumable electrodes H05B; particle accelerators H05H)

Table A.1 – *Continued on the next page*

International Patent Classification (IPC)	
Code	Description
H01K	SEMICONDUCTOR DEVICES; ELECTRIC SOLID STATE DEVICES NOT OTHERWISE PROVIDED FOR (use of semiconductor devices for measuring G01; resistors in general H01C; magnets, inductors, transformers H01F; capacitors in general H01G; electrolytic devices H01G 9/00; batteries, accumulators H01M; waveguides, resonators, or lines of the waveguide type H01P; line connectors, current collectors H01R; stimulated-emission devices H01S; electromechanical resonators H03H; loudspeakers, microphones, gramophone pick-ups or like acoustic electromechanical transducers H04R; electric light sources in general H05B; printed circuits, hybrid circuits, casings or constructional details of electrical apparatus, manufacture of assemblages of electrical components H05K; use of semiconductor devices in circuits having a particular application, see the subclass for the application)
H01L	Semiconductor Devices; Electric Solid State Devices Not Otherwise Provided For
H01M	PROCESSES OR MEANS, e.g. BATTERIES, FOR THE DIRECT CONVERSION OF CHEMICAL ENERGY INTO ELECTRICAL ENERGY
H01P	WAVEGUIDES; RESONATORS, LINES OR OTHER DEVICES OF THE WAVEGUIDE TYPE (operating at optical frequencies G02B)
H01Q	AERIALS (radiators or aerials for microwave heating H05B 6/72)

Table A.1 – *Continued on the next page*

International Patent Classification (IPC)	
Code	Description
H01R	ELECTRICALLY-CONDUCTIVE CONNECTIONS; STRUCTURAL ASSOCIATIONS OF A PLURALITY OF MUTUALLY-INSULATED ELECTRICAL CONNECTING ELEMENTS; COUPLING DEVICES; CURRENT COLLECTORS (switches, fuses H01H; coupling devices of the waveguide type H01P 5/00; switching arrangements for the supply or distribution of electric power H02B; installations of electric cables or lines, or of combined optical and electric cables or lines, or of auxiliary apparatus H02G; printed means for providing electric connections to or between printed circuits H05K)
H01S	DEVICES USING STIMULATED EMISSION
H01T	SPARK GAPS; OVERVOLTAGE ARRESTERS USING SPARK GAPS; SPARKING PLUGS; CORONA DEVICES; GENERATING IONS TO BE INTRODUCED INTO NON-ENCLOSED GASES (overvoltage protection circuits H02H)
H04L	Transmission of digital information, e.g. Telegraphic communication
H04N	Pictorial Communication
H05K	Printed Circuits; Casings Or Constructional Details Of Electric Apparatus; Manufacture Of Assemblages Of Electrical Components

Table A.2: Selection of relevant regional policies. (BMWi 2019k).

Program name
State level policies
CONNECT Education-Research-Innovation (Bildung-Forschung-Innovation), (BMWi 2019g)
Development of digital technologies (Entwicklung digitaler Technologien - Innovationswettbewerb: Künstliche Intelligenz als Treiber für volkswirtschaftlich relevante Ökosysteme), (BMWi 2019i)
Education bonus (Bildungsprämie - Förderung von Prämiengutscheinen und Beratungsleistungen), (BMWi 2019c)
Experimental urban development (Experimenteller Wohnungs- und Städtebau (ExWoSt)), (BMWi 2019j)
Funding for private railway siding (Förderung des Neu- und Ausbaus sowie der Reaktivierung von privaten Gleisanschlüssen (Gleisanschlussförderrichtlinie)), (BMWi 2019q)
go-Inno (BMWi-Innovationsgutscheine (go-Inno)), (BMWi 2019d)
INVEST - Funding for venture capital (INVEST - Zuschuss für Wagniskapital), (BMWi 2019u)
Market development program (BMWi-Markterschließungsprogramm), (BMWi 2019e)
State program for rural development (Bundesprogramm Ländliche Entwicklung - LandMobil - unterwegs in ländlichen Räumen), (BMWi 2019f)
Urban development funding (Städtebauförderung - Förderung von Investitionen in nationale Projekte des Städtebaus), (BMWi 2019y)

Table A.2 – *Continued on the next page*

Program name
Federal state level policies
EFRE NRW - production funding (EFRE-NRW - Förderwettbewerb Produktion.NRW) (North-Rhine Westphalia), (BMWi 2019h)
Foreign trade funding (Außenwirtschafts-förderungsrichtlinie (AWR)) (Schleswig Holstein), (BMWi 2019a)
Funding for innovation by universities and R+D institutes (Förderung von Innovation durch Hochschulen und Forschungseinrichtungen) (Lower Saxony), (BMWi 2019s)
Funding for innovative professional education (Förderung der Entwicklung innovativer Konzepte und Maßnahmen in der beruflichen Weiterbildung) (Baden-Württemberg), (BMWi 2019m)
Funding for municipal roadmaking (Förderung des kommunalen Straßenbaus (RL-KSB)) (Thuringia), (BMWi 2019p)
Funding for regional development (Förderung der regionalen Entwicklung) (Hessen), (BMWi 2019o)
Funding for research, innovation and technology (Förderung von Forschung, Innovationen und Technologien (Pro FIT) - Frühphasenfinanzierung von Technologieunternehmen) (Berlin), (BMWi 2019r)
Funding for sustainable urban development (Förderung der Nachhaltigen Stadtentwicklung (RiLiSE)) (Hessen), (BMWi 2019n)
Knowledge transfer funding (Förderung von Maßnahmen des Wissens- und Technologietransfers im Saarland) (Saarland), (BMWi 2019t)

Table A.2 – *Continued on the next page*

Program name
Personnel transfer (Beschäftigtentransfer (Förderung von Transfergesellschaften)) (North-Rhine Westphalia), (BMWi 2019b)
Program for Internationalization (Programm für Internationalisierung - Förderung von Gemeinschaftsprojekten) (Berlin), (BMWi 2019w)
Regional funding program of the Saarland (Regionales Förderprogramm des Saarlandes für kleine und mittlere Unternehmen der gewerblichen Wirtschaft) (Saarland), (BMWi 2019x)
Trade fair presentations (Messepräsentationen) (Lower Saxony), (BMWi 2019v)
Urban renewal funding (Förderrichtlinien Stadterneuerung 2008) (North-Rhine Westphalia), (BMWi 2019l)

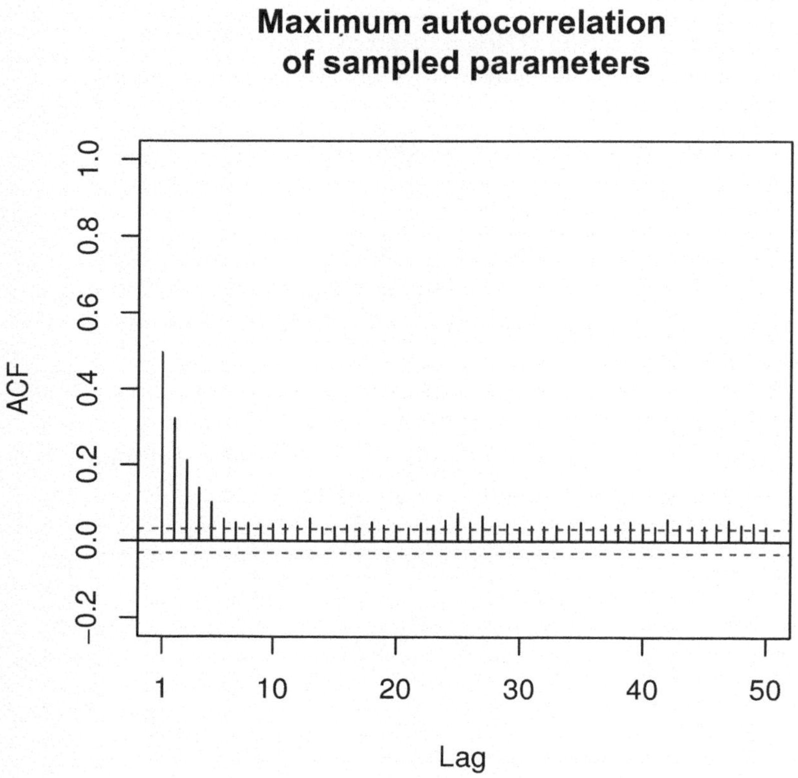

Figure A.1: Model autocorrelation.

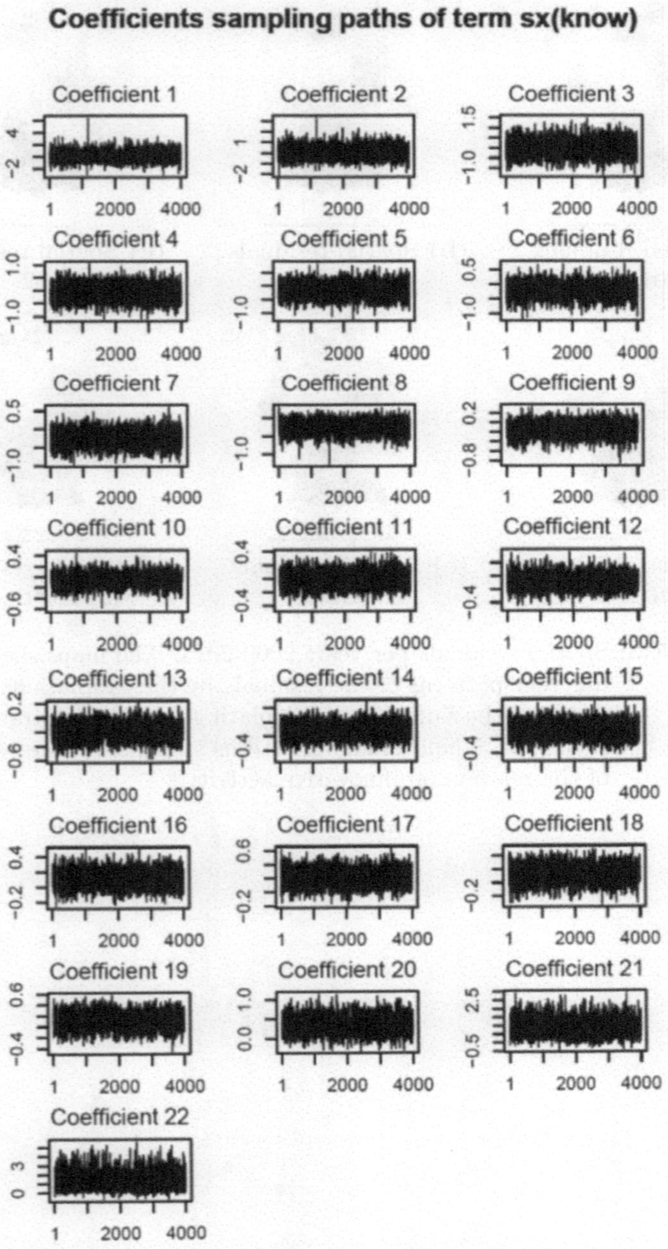

Figure A.2: Traceplots, example for knowledge intensity.

(a) Spatial residuals for 2014.

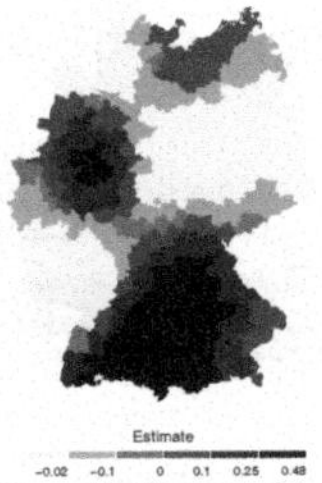

(b) Spatial residuals for 2013.

(c) Spatial residuals for 2012.

(d) Spatial residuals for 2011.

(e) Spatial residuals for 2010.

(f) Spatial residuals for 2009.

Figure A.3: Spatial residuals per year: 2009-2014. The maps show the different patterns of the residuals by the estimations when isolating the sample and calculating a model separately for each year. The change in patterns suggests a time-variance of the relation on innovative activity.

The manufacturer's authorised representative in the EU is Springer
Nature Customer Service Centre GmbH, Europaplatz 3, 69115 Heidelberg,
Germany. If you have any concerns regarding our products, please
contact ProductSafety@springernature.com

Printed and bound by CPI Group (UK) Ltd, Croydon, CR0 4YY
30/09/2026
02225434-0002